WORD DIVISION & SPELLING MANUAL

D0211496

25,000+ WORDS

DR. DEVERN J. PERRY

Brigham Young University
Department of Management
Communication

a
b
c
d
e
f
g
h
i
j
k
l
m
n
o
p
q
r
s
t
u
v
w
x
y
z

South-Western Publishing Co.

4TH EDITION

Executive Editor:	Carol Lynne Ruhl
Acquisitions Editor:	Randy Sims
Production Editors:	Vince Patton and Timothy Bailey
Coordinating Editor:	Angela C. McDonald
Editorial Production:	Cinda Johnston
Senior Designer:	Jim DeSollar
Production Artist:	Steven McMahon
Marketing Manager:	Colleen Thomas

Cover Photo: © H.D. THOREAU/WESTLIGHT
PHOTONICA/© MASAAKI KAZAMA

Copyright © 1994

by SOUTH-WESTERN PUBLISHING CO.

Cincinnati, Ohio

ISBN: 0-538-61995-3 (KF16DA)
0-538-62750-6 (KF16DA1)

3 4 5 6 7 8 9   K 01 00 99 98 97 96 95

Printed in the United States of America

FOREWORD

The English language is constantly changing. As new technologies are incorporated, new avenues opened, and new products marketed, new words are coined. In a very short time, these words become part of our everyday writing and speaking vocabularies.

Perhaps no invention in history has had the effect on the English language as has the computer. Many words used frequently today were not used prior to the late 1980s. Some words are added and meanings change so often that dictionaries have a difficult time keeping up with the language.

However, the computer is not the only invention to have a major impact on the words used in the English language. Many events and happenings in the space-age world and modern office technology have also contributed to our expanding vocabulary.

WORD DIVISION AND SPELLING MANUAL, Fourth Edition has been published to help the users spell and divide these new and older, frequently used words correctly. This edition contains over 25,000 words, approximately 5,000 more than the Third Edition.

The Fourth Edition contains most of the words incorporated in the Third Edition, plus many commonly used words from the vocabularies of the computer, the space-age, and office technology. In addition, this edition has been expanded to contain many additional words not previously included. Commonly used derivatives of root words contained in the Third Edition have also been added to provide more help to the user.

The Fourth Edition of **WORD DIVISION AND SPELLING MANUAL** has also been enhanced to include spelling rules that provide several examples of each rule. For example, when does a word form its plural by adding *s* or by adding *es*? The rules in this manual explain when to add *s* and when to add *es*. When is the silent *e* dropped or when is it retained on the addition of a suffix? The words in the manual provide numerous examples of these rules.

The Guidelines for Word Division, at the beginning of the manual, provide principles for when a word may or may not be correctly divided. The Guidelines for Spelling, following the word list, help the user correctly spell difficult words and derivatives of root words.

The word divisions contained in this manual were made according to the guidelines and the points of syllabication as indicated in **WEBSTER'S NINTH NEW COLLEGIATE DICTIONARY**, published by Merriam-Webster, Inc.

As in previous editions, word division is indicated by both a hyphen and a dot. Preferred word division locations, according to the Guidelines for Word Division, are indicated by a hyphen. Acceptable, but not preferred, points of word division are indicated by a dot. For example, the word *demonstrator* appears as *dem-on-stra•tor* in this manual. While the word may be correctly divided at any one of the three points, the two preferred divisions are indicated by the hyphen. A shorter word, however, such as *inform*, may be divided at the dot and appears as *in•form*, although the preferred method is to avoid dividing this word.

A double hyphen is used to indicate a compound word. According to the Guidelines for Word Division, these words should be divided only at the hyphen: *self--confidence*.

The compactness of this book makes it practical and easy to use. As a result, the same size has been retained in the Fourth Edition. Keeping the spiral binding allows the user to open the manual and keep it open to a desired page.

If you have additional comments on how this manual may be improved in future editions, please direct them to your South-Western marketing representative.

Symbols Used in WORD DIVISION AND SPELLING MANUAL

- • point of acceptable, but not preferred, word division
- - point of preferred word division
- -- hyphenated compound word. Word division should occur only at the hyphen.

GUIDELINES FOR WORD DIVISION

The following guidelines were used in the preparation of **WORD DIVISION AND SPELLING MANUAL**, Fourth Edition.

Although the most acceptable point for dividing a word is sometimes a matter of opinion, enough of the word should appear on the first line to give the reader the concept of the entire word and enough of the word should be carried to the next line to have two significantly sized parts. Word pronunciation is also an important factor in determining the best division point.

When determining the points at which to end a line, remember that how a line ends has considerable influence on the degree of ease with which the reader can follow the thought of the written expression. Therefore, the division of words should be logical, with as little attention called to the word division as possible.

1. Divide words only between syllables. Words written or pronounced as one syllable, such as *clutched*, *health*, and *judged*, must not be divided.

2. Ascertain the first part of the word contains at least two letters (*in-cite*, not *i-deals*); and the last part of the word contains at least three letters (*read-ing,* not *read-er*). Preferably, divide the word into two approximately equal parts, each one conveying the concept of the entire word.

   Although acceptable, avoid dividing two letters at the beginning of a word. These acceptable, but not preferred, divisions are indicated by a dot rather than a hyphen in this book; for example, *di•rec-tion*.

3. Avoid dividing words of five or fewer letters, regardless of the number of syllables, such as *abide* and *canal*. If possible, avoid dividing words of six letters. For example, *facade* is better understood than is *fa•cade*.

4. Divide words between two consonants when a double consonant occurs in a word because of suffixes (*sit-ting,* not *sitt-ing*). However, when a root word is spelled with a

double consonant, divide between the root word and the suffix (*sell-ing,* not *sel-ling*).

5. Divide compound words written without the hyphen between the elements of the compound (*butter-fly,* not *but-terfly*). Compound words written with a hyphen should be divided only at the point of the existing hyphen (*self--confidence*).

6. Write a single vowel functioning as a syllable with the first part of the word (*tabu-late,* not *tab-ulate*).

Exceptions to this general rule:

Join a single-vowel syllable to the last part of the word if the word ends in a two-letter syllable (*hast-ily,* not *hasti-ly*).

Join single-vowel syllables *a, i,* and *u* to the final syllables *ble, bly, cle,* or *cal* (*reli-able, insol-ubly, chron-icle,* and *hyster-ical*). This exception is violated in several words in this book because one rule takes precedence over another (*ar•ti-cle*).

7. Divide between two one-vowel syllables occurring together within a word: *evalu-ation.*

8. Divide dates, names, and addresses at the most logical point for readability. Divide between the day of the month and the year (*January 1, - 19xx,* not *January - 1, 19xx*). Divide between a person's first and last names (*Tracy - Johnson,* not *Tracy John-son*), (*Lynn - Randolph, M.D.,* not *Lynn Randolph - M.D.*). Divide the address between the city and the state (*Cincinnati, - Ohio 45227-1342*), not between the state and the ZIP Code (*Cincinnati, Ohio - 45227-1342*).

9. Avoid dividing figures, abbreviations, and signs representing words or abbreviations (*$1,000,000,* not *$1,- 000,000; OPEC,* not *OP-EC; #590485,* not *#59-90485*).

10. Minimize the division of words as much as possible. Avoid dividing the last word of a paragraph or the last word on a page. Although computer word processing packages may do otherwise, avoid dividing the last word of more than two consecutive lines, if possible.

aba•cus
aban-don
aban-doned
aban-don•ing
aban-don-ment

abate
abated
abate-ment
abat-ing
abbey

abbeys
ab•bre-vi-ate
ab•bre-vi-ated
ab•bre-vi-at•ing
ab•bre-via-tion

ab•di-cate
ab•di-cated
ab•di-cat•ing
ab•di-ca-tion
ab•di-ca•tor

ab•do-men
ab•domi-nal
ab•domi-nally
ab•duct
ab•duc-ted

ab•duc-ting
ab•duc-tion
ab•duc-tor
ab•er-rance
ab•er-ra-tion

abet-ment
abet-ted
abey-ance
abhor
ab•horred

ab•hor-rent
ab•hor-ring
abide
abid-ing
abili-ties

abil-ity
ablaze
able
able--bodied
ab•nor-mal

ab•nor-mali-ties
ab•nor-mal•ity
ab•nor-mally
aboard
abode

abol-ish
abol-ished
abol-ish•ing
abol-ish-ment
abo-li-tion

abo-li-tion•ary
abo-li-tion•ist
abomi-na•ble
abomi-na•bly
abomi-nate

abomi-na-tion
ab•orig-ine
abort
aborted
abort-ing

abor-tion
abor-tion•ist
abor-tive
abound
about

above
above-board
above-ground
above--mentioned
abra-sion

abra-sive
abreast
abridge
abridged
abridg-ing

abridg-ment
abroad
ab•ro-gate
ab•ro-gated
ab•ro-gat•ing

ab•ro-ga-tion
abrupt
abruptly
abrupt-ness
ab•scess

ab•scessed
ab•scound
ab•scound-ing
ab•sence
ab•sent

ab•sen-tee
ab•sently
ab•so-lute
ab•so-lutely
ab•so-lu-tion

ab•solve	aca-de-mi-cian	ac•cli-mate
ab•solv-ing	acade-mies	ac•cli-mat•ing
ab•sorb	acad-emy	ac•cli-ma-tize
ab•sorb-able	a cap-pella	ac•co-lade
ab•sorb-ance	ac•cede	ac•com-mo-date
ab•sorbed	ac•ceded	ac•com-mo-dated
ab•sor-bency	ac•ced-ing	ac•com-mo-da-tion
ab•sor-bent	ac•cel-er•ate	ac•com-pa-nied
ab•sorb-ing	ac•cel-er-ated	ac•com-pa-nies
ab•sorp-tion	ac•cel-er-at•ing	ac•com-pa-ni-ment
ab•stain	ac•cel-era-tion	ac•com-pa-nist
ab•stain-ing	ac•cel-era•tor	ac•com-pany
ab•sti-nence	ac•cel-er-ome•ter	ac•com-pa-ny•ing
ab•sti-nent	ac•cent	ac•com-plice
ab•stract	ac•cent-ing	ac•com-plish
ab•stracted	ac•cen-tu•ate	ac•com-plished
ab•stract-ing	ac•cen-tu-at•ing	ac•com-plishes
ab•strac-tion	ac•cen-tua-tion	ac•com-plish•ing
ab•stract-ness	ac•cept	ac•com-plish-ment
ab•surd	ac•cept-able	ac•cord
ab•sur-dity	ac•cep-tance	ac•cor-dance
abun-dance	ac•cepted	ac•corded
abun-dant	ac•cept-ing	ac•cord-ing
abun-dantly	ac•cess	ac•cord-ingly
abuse	ac•ces-si-bil•ity	ac•cor-dion
abuses	ac•ces-si•ble	ac•costed
abus-ing	ac•cess-ing	ac•cost-ing
abu-sive	ac•ces-so-rial	ac•count
abut-ment	ac•ces-so-ries	ac•count-abil•ity
abys-mal	ac•ces-sory	ac•count-able
abys-mally	ac•ci-dent	ac•coun-tancy
abyss	ac•ci-den•tal	ac•coun-tant
aca-de•mia	ac•ci-den-tally	ac•counted
aca-demic	ac•claim	ac•count-ing
aca-demi-cally	ac•cla-ma-tion	ac•credit

2

ac•credi-ta-tion
ac•cred-ited
ac•cred-it•ing
ac•cru-able
ac•crual

ac•crue
ac•cru-ing
ac•cu-mu-late
ac•cu-mu-lated
ac•cu-mu-lat•ing

ac•cu-mu-la-tion
ac•cu-mu-la-tive
ac•cu-mu-la•tor
ac•cu-racy
ac•cu-rate

ac•cu-rately
ac•cu-sa-tion
ac•cu-sa-tive
ac•cu-sa-tory
ac•cuse

ac•cuser
ac•cus-ing
ac•cus-tom
ac•cus-tomed
ace-tate

achiev-able
achieve
achieve-ment
achiever
achiev•ers

achiev-ing
ach•ing
acid
acid-ity
ac•knowl-edge

ac•knowl-edged
ac•knowl-edges
ac•knowl-edg•ing
acne
acous-ti•cal

acous-ti-cally
acous-tics
ac•quaint
ac•quain-tance
ac•quain-tances

ac•quainted
ac•quaint-ing
ac•qui-esce
ac•qui-esc•ing
ac•quire

ac•quired
ac•quire-ment
ac•quir-ing
ac•qui-si-tion
ac•quit

ac•quit-tal
ac•quit-tance
ac•quit-ted
ac•quit-ting
acre

acre-age
Ac•ri-lan
ac•ri-mo-ni•ous
ac•ri-mony
ac•ro-bat

ac•ro-batic
ac•ro-nym
across
acrylic
acted

act•ing
ac•tion
ac•ti-vate
ac•ti-vated
ac•ti-vat•ing

ac•ti-va-tion
ac•tive
ac•tively
ac•tiv-ist
ac•tivi-ties

ac•tiv-ity
ac•tual
ac•tu-al•ity
ac•tu-ally
ac•tu-ar•ial

ac•tu-ary
ac•tu-ate
ac•tu-ated
ac•tu-at•ing
ac•tua-tor

acu•ity
acu-punc-ture
acute
acutely
acute-ness

adage
ada•gio
ada-mant
adapt
adapt-able

ad•ap-ta-tion
adapted
adapter
adapt-ing
adap-tion

adap-tive
ad•denda
ad•den-dum
ad•dict
ad•dicted

ad•dic-ting
ad•dic-tion
ad•dic-tive
add•ing
ad•di-tion

ad•di-tional
ad•di-tive
add--on
ad•dress
ad•dress-abil•ity

ad•dress-able
ad•dressed
ad•dresses
ad•dress-ing
ad•duc-ible

ad•duc-ing
ade-noi•dal
ade-noids
adept
adept-ness

ade-qua-cies
ade-quacy
ade-quate
ade-quately
ad•here

ad•hered
ad•her-ence
ad•her-ent
ad•her-ing
ad•he-sion

ad•he-sive
ad•he-sive-ness
ad•ja-cent
ad•jec-tive
ad•join

ad•join-ing
ad•journ
ad•journed
ad•journ-ing
ad•journ-ment

ad•ju-di-cate
ad•ju-di-cated
ad•ju-di-cat•ing
ad•ju-di-ca-tion
ad•ju-di-ca•tor

ad•ju-di-ca-tory
ad•junct
ad•just
ad•just-able
ad•justed

ad•juster
ad•just-ing
ad•just-ment
ad•ju-tant
ad•min-is•ter

ad•min-is-tered
ad•min-is-ter•ing
ad•min-is-trate
ad•min-is-trat•ing
ad•min-is-tra-tion

ad•min-is-tra-tive
ad•min-is-tra•tor
ad•mi-ra•ble
ad•mi-ra•bly
ad•mi-ral

ad•mi-ra-tion
ad•mire
ad•mirer
ad•mir-ing
ad•mis-si•ble

ad•mis-sion
ad•mis-sive
admit
ad•mit-tance
ad•mit-ted

ad•mit-tedly
ad•mit-ting
ad•mon-ish
ad•mon-ish•ing
ad•mon-ish-ment

ad•mo-ni-tion
adobe
ado-les-cence
ado-les-cent
adopt

adopted
adopt-ing
adop-tion
adop-tive
ador-able

ado-ra-tion
adore
ador-ing
adorn
adorn-ment

adrena-line
adrift
ad•sorb
ad•sorb-able
ad•sor-bent

ad•sorb-ing
ad•sorp-tion
ad•sorp-tive
adult
adul-ter•ous

adul-tery
adult-hood
ad•vance
ad•vance-ment
ad•vances

ad•vanc-ing
ad•van-tage
ad•van-ta-geous
ad•van-tages
ad•ven-ture

ad•ven-turer
ad•ven-ture-some
ad•ven-tur•ing
ad•ven-tur•ous
ad•verb

ad•ver-bial
ad•ver-sar•ies
ad•ver-sary
ad•verse
ad•versely

ad•ver-sity
ad•ver-tise
ad•ver-tised
ad•ver-tise-ment
ad•ver-tiser

ad•ver-tis•ers
ad•ver-tis•ing
ad•vice
ad•vis-able
ad•vis-ably

ad•vise
ad•vised
ad•vis-edly
ad•vise-ment
ad•viser

ad•vises
ad•vis-ing
ad•vi-sory
ad•vo-cacy
ad•vo-cate

ad•vo-cated
ad•vo-cat•ing
aer•ate
aer-ated
aer-at•ing

aera-tion
ae•rial *(adj.)*
aer•ial *(n.)*
aero-bal-lis-tics
aero-bic

aero-com-mander
aero-dy-namic
aero-dy-nam•ics
aero-nau•tic
aero-nau-ti•cal

aero-nau-tics
aer-on•omy
aero-pause
aero-sol
aero-space

aes-theti-cally
aes-thet•ics
af•fa-ble
af•fa-bly
af•fair

af•fect
af•fected
af•fect-ing
af•fec-tion
af•fec-tion•ate

af•fi-ance
af•fi-ant
af•fi-da•vit
af•fili-ate
af•fili-ated

af•fili-at•ing
af•fili-ation
af•fin-ity
af•firm
af•fir-ma-tion

af•fir-ma-tive
affix
af•fixed
af•fixes
af•fix-ing

af•flict
af•flicted
af•flict-ing
af•flic-tion
af•flu-ence

af•flu-ent
af•ford
af•ford-able
af•forded
af•ford-ing

af•for-es-ta-tion
af•front
Af•ghan
afire
afloat

5

afraid
Af•ri•can
Afro--American
after
after-birth

after-body
after-burner
after-glow
after-noon
after-taste

after-thought
after-wards
again
against
ag•ates

aged
age-less
agen-cies
agency
agenda

agen-dum
agent
ag•glom-er-ate
ag•glom-era-tion
ag•gra-vate

ag•gra-va-ting
ag•gra-va-tion
ag•gre-gate
ag•gre-ga-tion
ag•gres-sion

ag•gres-sive
ag•gres-sively
ag•gres-sor
agile
aging

agi-tate
agi-tated
agi-ta-ting
agi-ta-tion
agi-ta•tor

ag•nos-tic
ag•nos-ti-cism
ago-nies
ago-nize
ago-niz•ing

agony
agrar-ian
agree
agree-able
agree-ably

agreed
agree-ing
agree-ment
ag•ri-busi-ness
ag•ri-cul-tural

ag•ri-cul-tur-ally
ag•ri-cul-ture
agrono-mist
agron-omy
ahead

aid
aide
aided
aid•ing
ai•le-ron

ail•ing
ail-ment
aimed
aim•ing
aim-less

aim-lessly
air-borne
air-brush
air--condition
air--conditioned

air-craft
aired
air-fare
air-field
air-freight

air•ing
air-lift
air-line
air-liner
air-lock

air-mail
air-mailing
air-plane
air-port
air-sick

air-space
air-speed
air-stream
air-strip
air-tight

air-wave
air•way
air-worthy
aisle
Ala-bama

Ala-bamian
ala-bas•ter
a la carte
alac-rity
a la mode

alarm
alarmed
alarm-ing
alarm-ingly
alarm-ist

Alaska
Alas-kan
al•bino
album
al•bums

al•che-mist
al•chemy
al•co-hol
al•co-holic
al•co-hol•ism

al•cove
alert
alerted
alert-ing
alertly

al•falfa
algae
al•ge-bra
al•ge-braic
al•go-rithm

alias
aliases
alibi
alien
alien-ate

alien-at•ing
alien-ation
align
aligned
align-ment

ali-mony
alive
al•kali
al•ka-line
al•le-ga-tion

al•lege
al•leged
al•leg-edly
al•leges
al•le-giance

al•leg-ing
al•le-gor-ical
al•le-gory
al•le-gro
al•ler-gen

al•ler-gic
al•ler-gies
al•ler-gist
al•lergy
al•le-vi•ate

al•le-vi-ated
al•le-via-tion
al•le-vi-at•ing
al•li-ance
al•lied

al•lies
al•li-ga•tor
al•lo-cate
al•lo-cated
al•lo-cat•ing

al•lo-ca-tion
al•lo-cu-tion
allot
al•lot-ment
al•lot-ted

al•lot-ting
allow
al•low-able
al•low-ance
al•lowed

al•low-ing
al•lows
alloy
al•loys
al•lude

al•luded
al•lud-ing
al•lu-sion
al•lu-sive
al•ma-nac

al•mond
al•most
alone
along
aloof

aloof-ness
aloud
al•pha-bet
al•pha-betic
al•pha-bet-ical

al•pha-beti-cally
al•pha-bet•ize
al•pha-bet-iz•ing
al•pha-nu-meric
al•pha-nu-mer-ical

al•pine
al•ready
altar
alter
al•ter-ation

al•ter-ca-tion
al•tered
al•ter-ing
al•ter-nate
al•ter-nately

al•ter-nat•ing
al•ter-na-tion
al•ter-na-tive
al•ter-na•tor
al•ters

al•though
al•time-ter
al•ti-tude
al•ti-tu-di•nal
al•to-gether

al•tru-ism
al•tru-is•tic
alu-mi-num
alumna
alumni

alum-nus
al•ways
ama-teur
ama-teur•ish
ama-teur•ism

amazed
amaze-ment
amaz-ing
amaz-ingly
ama•zon

am•bas-sa•dor
am•bi-dex-trous
am•bi-ence
am•bi-ent
am•bi-gu•ity

am•bigu-ous
am•bi-tion
am•bi-tious
am•biva-lence
am•biva-lent

am•bu-lance
am•bu-la-tory
am•bush
ame-lio-rate
ame-lio-ra-tion

amend
amen-da-tory
amended
amend-ing
amend-ment

ame-ni-ties
ame-nity
Amer-ica
Ameri-can
Ameri-can•ize

ami-able
ami-ca-bil•ity
ami-ca•ble
ami-ca•bly
amity

am•mo-nia
am•mu-ni-tion
am•ne-sia
am•nesty
amoeba

amoe•bas
among
amoral
amor-ally
amo-rous

am•or-ti-za-tion
am•or-tize
am•or-tized
am•or-tiz•ing
amount

amounted
amount-ing
am•per-age
am•pere
am•per-sand

am•phib-ian
am•phibi-ous
am•phi-the•ater
am•pi-cil•lin
am•pli-fi-ca-tion

am•pli-fied
am•pli-fier
am•plify
am•pli-fy•ing
am•pu-tate

am•pu-tated
am•pu-tat•ing
am•pu-ta-tion
am•pu-tee
amuse

amuse-ment
amus-ing
ana-gram
an•al-ge•sia
an•al-ge•sic

ana•log
ana-log-ical
analo-gies
analo-gous
anal-ogy

analy-ses
analy-sis
ana-lyst
ana-lytic
ana-lyt-ical

ana-lyze
ana-lyzed
ana-lyzer
ana-lyz•ing
an•ar-chy

ana-tom-ical
anat-omy
an•ces-tor
an•ces-tral
an•ces-try

an•chor
an•chored
an•chor-ing
an•chovy
an•cient

an•ciently
an•cil-lary
an•droid
an•ec-dotal
an•ec-dote

ane•mia
ane•mic
ane-mome•ter
an•es-the•sia
an•es-the-si-ology

an•es-thetic
anes-the-tist
anes-the-tize
an•eu-rysm
angel

an•gelic
an•gel-ical
an•gels
anger
an•gered

an•gina
angle
an•gler
an•gles
an•gli-cize

an•gling
an•grily
angry
an•guish
an•guish-ing

an•gu-lar
an•hy-drous
ani•mal
ani-mate
ani-mated

ani-ma-tion
ani-ma•tor
ani-mos•ity
ankle
an•klet

an•nal-ist
an•nals
annex
an•nex-ation
an•nexed

an•nexes
an•nex-ing
an•ni-hi-late
an•ni-hi-lated
an•ni-hi-lat•ing

an•ni-hi-la-tion
an•ni-ver-sa-ries
an•ni-ver-sary
an•no-tate
an•no-tated

an•no-tat•ing
an•no-ta-tion
an•nounce
an•nounced
an•nounce-ment

an•nouncer
an•nounces
an•nounc-ing
annoy
an•noy-ance

an•noyed
an•noy-ing
an•nual
an•nu-ally
an•nu-itant

an•nu-ities
an•nu-ity
annul
an•nu-lar
an•nulled

an•nul-ling
an•nul-ment
anoint
anoint-ing
anoma-lies

anom-aly
ano-nym•ity
anony-mous
an•other
an•swer

an•swered
an•swer-ing
ant-acid
an•tago-nism
an•tago-nist

an•tago-nis•tic
an•tago-nize
an•tago-niz•ing
Ant-arc•tica
an•te-ced•ent

an•te-date
an•te-lope
an•te-na•tal
an•tenna
an•te-rior

an•them
an•tholo-gist
an•thol-ogy
an•thro-pol•ogy
an•ti-abor-tion

an•ti-abor-tion•ist
an•ti-air-craft
an•ti-al-ler-genic
an•ti-bac-te-rial
an•ti-bi-otic

an•ti-body
an•ti-car-cino•gen
an•tici-pate
an•tici-pated
an•tici-pat•ing

an•tici-pa-tion
an•tici-pa-tory
an•ti-cli-mactic
an•ti-cli•max
an•ti-co-agu-lant

an•ti-cor-ro-sive
an•ti-de-pres-sant
an•ti-dotal
an•ti-dote
an•ti-freeze

an•ti-gen
an•ti-grav•ity
an•ti-his-ta-mine
an•ti-knock
an•ti-mag-netic

an•ti-mis-sile
an•ti-oxi-dant
an•tipa-thy
an•ti-per-spi-rant
an•ti-pol-lu-tion

an•ti-pov-erty
an•ti-quate
an•tique
an•tiq-uity
an•ti-sat-el-lite

an•ti-sep•tic
an•ti-so•cial
an•tithe-sis
an•ti-toxic
an•ti-toxin

an•ti-trust
ant-onym
anxi-eties
anxi-ety
anx-ious

anx-iously
any-body
any•how
any-more
any•one

any-place
any-thing
any-time
any•way
any-where

apart
apart-heid
apart-ment
apa-thetic
apa•thy

ap•er-ture
aph-elion
api•ary
apoca-lypse
apoca-lyp•tic

apoca-lyp-ti•cal
apoc-ry•pha
apo•gee
apolo-getic
apolo-gies

apolo-gist
apolo-gize
apolo-giz•ing
apol-ogy
apo-plexy

apos-tasy
apos-tate
apos-ta-tize
apos-ta-tiz•ing
apos-tle

apos-tro•phe
apos-tro-phrize
ap•pall
ap•palled
ap•pall-ing

ap•pa-ra•tus
ap•parel
ap•par-ent
ap•par-ently
ap•pa-ri-tion

ap•peal
ap•pealed
ap•peal-ing
ap•peal-ingly
ap•pear

ap•pear-ance
ap•peared
ap•pear-ing
ap•pease
ap•pease-ment

ap•peas-ing
ap•pel-lant
ap•pel-late
ap•pend
ap•pend-age

ap•pen-dec-tomy
ap•pended
ap•pen-di-cies
ap•pen-di-ci•tis
ap•pend-ing

ap•pen-dix
ap•pe-tite
ap•pe-tizer
ap•pe-tiz•ing
ap•plaud

ap•plauded
ap•plaud-ing
ap•plause
apple
ap•ples

ap•pli-ance
ap•pli-ca•ble
ap•pli-cant
ap•pli-ca-tion
ap•pli-ca•tor

ap•plied
ap•plies
ap•pli-qué
apply
ap•ply-ing

ap•point
ap•pointed
ap•point-ing
ap•point-ment
ap•por-tion

ap•por-tioned
ap•por-tion•ing
ap•por-tion-ment
ap•po-si-tion
ap•posi-tive

ap•praisal
ap•praise
ap•praise-ment
ap•praiser
ap•prais-ing

ap•pre-cia•ble
ap•pre-cia•bly
ap•pre-ci•ate
ap•pre-ci-ated
ap•pre-ci-at•ing

ap•pre-cia-tion
ap•pre-cia-tive
ap•pre-hend
ap•pre-hended
ap•pre-hend•ing

ap•pre-hen-si•ble
ap•pre-hen-sion
ap•pre-hen-sive
ap•pren-tice
ap•pren-tice-ship

ap•prise
ap•prised
ap•pris-ing
ap•proach
ap•proach-able

ap•proached
ap•proaches
ap•proach-ing
ap•pro-ba-tion
ap•pro-pri•ate

ap•pro-pri-ately
ap•pro-pri-ates
ap•pro-pri-at•ing
ap•pro-pria-tion
ap•proval

ap•prove
ap•prov-ing
ap•proxi-mate
ap•proxi-mated
ap•proxi-mately

ap•proxi-mat•ing
ap•proxi-ma-tion
apri-cot
April
apron

ap•ro-pos
ap•ti-tude
aqua-ma•rine
aqua-plane
aquar-ium

aquatic
aq•ue-duct
Ara-bian
Ara•bic
ar•bi-tra•ble

ar•bi-trarily
ar•bi-trary
ar•bi-trate
ar•bi-tra-tion
ar•bi-tra•tor

ar•bo-re•tum
ar•cade
ar•chaeo-log-ical
ar•chae-olo-gist
ar•chae-ol•ogy

ar•chaic
ar•cha-ism
arch-enemy
ar•cher
ar•chery

arches
ar•chi-tect
ar•chi-tec-tural
ar•chi-tec-tur-ally
ar•chi-tec-ture

ar•chi-val
ar•chive
ar•chived
ar•chiv-ing
ar•chiv-ist

arc•tic
ar•du-ous
area
arena
are•nas

Ar•gen-tina
ar•gu-able
ar•gu-ably
argue
ar•gued

ar•gu-ing
ar•gu-ment
ar•gu-men-ta-tive
ar•gyle
arise

arisen
arises
aris-ing
ar•is-toc-racy
aris-to-crat

aris-to-cratic
arith-me•tic
Ari-zona
Ari-zonan
Ar•kan-san

Ar•kan-sas
ar•ma-ment
arm-chair
Ar•me-nia
arm•ful

armies
ar•mi-stice
arm-load
armor
ar•mored

ar•mory
army
aroma
aro-matic
arose

around
arouse
arouses
arous-ing
ar•raign

ar•raigned
ar•raign-ing
ar•raign-ment
ar•range
ar•ranged

ar•range-ment
ar•ranges
ar•rang-ing
array
ar•ray-ing

ar•rear
ar•rear-age
ar•rest
ar•rested
ar•rest-ing

ar•rival
ar•rive
ar•rived
ar•riv-ing
ar•ro-gance

ar•ro-gant
arrow
arrow-head
ar•rows
ar•se-nal

ar•se-nic
arson
ar•son-ist
ar•te-rial
ar•ter-ies

ar•tery
ar•thritic
ar•thri-tis
ar•ti-cle
ar•ticu-late

ar•ticu-lated
ar•ticu-lat•ing
ar•ticu-la-tion
ar•ti-facts
ar•ti-fi-cial

ar•ti-fi-cially
ar•til-ler•ies
ar•til-lery
art•ist
ar•tis-tic

art-istry
as•bes-tos
as•cend
as•cen-dancy
as•cended

as•cend-ing
as•cen-sion
as•cer-tain
as•cer-tained
as•cer-tain•ing

as•cer-tain-ment
as•cribe
as•crib-ing
ashamed
Asia

Asian
asi-nine
asked
ask•ing
asleep

as•para-gus
as•pect
as•phalt
as•phyxi-ate
as•phyxi-at•ing

as•phyxi-ation
as•pi-rant
as•pi-rate
as•pi-rat•ing
as•pi-ra-tion

as•pi-ra•tor
as•pire
as•pi-rin
as•pir-ing
as•sail-ant

as•sail-ing
as•sas-sin
as•sas-si-nate
as•sas-si-na-tion
as•sault

as•saulted
as•sault-ing
as•sayed
as•say-ing
as•sem-ble

as•sem-bled
as•sem-bler
as•sem-blies
as•sem-bling
as•sem-bly

as•sent
as•sented
as•sent-ing
as•sert
as•serted

as•ser-tion
as•ser-tive
as•sess
as•sessed
as•sesses

as•sess-ing
as•sess-ment
as•ses-sor
asset
as•sets

as•si-du•ity
as•sid-uous
as•sign
as•sign-able
as•signed

as•signer
as•sign-ing
as•sign-ment
as•simi-late
as•simi-lated

as•simi-lat•ing
as•simi-la-tion
as•simi-la-tive
as•simi-la•tor
as•sist

as•sis-tance
as•sis-tant
as•sis-tant-ship
as•sisted
as•sist-ing

as•so-ci•ate
as•so-ci-ated
as•so-ci-at•ing
as•so-cia-tion
as•so-cia-tive

as•sort
as•sorted
as•sort-ment
as•sume
as•sumed

as•sum-ing
as•sump-tion
as•sur-ance
as•sure
as•suredly

as•sur-ing
as•ter-isk
as•ter-oid
asthma
asth-matic

astig-ma-tism
as•ton-ish
as•ton-ish•ing
as•ton-ish-ment
as•tound

as•tound-ing
as•tro-dome
as•trolo-ger
as•tro-log-ical
as•trol-ogy

as•tro-naut
as•tro-nau-ti•cal
as•tro-nau-tics
as•trono-mer
as•tron-omy

as•tro-phys•ics
as•tute
as•tutely
as•tute-ness
asy•lum

asym-met•ric
asym-me•try
asyn-chro-nous
athe-ist
ath-lete

ath-letic
ath-leti-cally
ath-let•ics
At•lan-tic
at•mo-sphere

at•mo-spheric
atomic
atrium
atro-cious
atroc-ity

at•ro-phy
at•tach
at•ta-ché
at•tached
at•taches

at•tach-ing
at•tach-ment
at•tack
at•tacked
at•tacker

at•tack-ing
at•tain
at•tain-able
at•tained
at•tain-ing

at•tain-ment
at•tempt
at•tempted
at•tempt-ing
at•tend

at•ten-dance
at•ten-dant
at•tended
at•tender
at•tend-ing

at•ten-tion
at•ten-tive
at•ten-tively
at•test
at•tested

at•test-ing
at•tire
at•tir-ing
at•ti-tude
at•ti-tu-di•nal

at•tor-ney
at•tract
at•tracted
at•tract-ing
at•trac-tion

at•trac-tive
at•trac-tively
at•trac-tive-ness
at•trib-ut-able
at•tri-bute *(n.)*

at•trib-ute *(v.)*
at•trib-uted
at•trib-ut•ing
at•tribu-tive
at•tri-tion

atyp-ical
auc-tion
auc-tion•eer
auc-tion•ing
au•dac-ity

a

au•di-ble
au•di-ence
au•di-ences
audio
au•dio-cas-sette

au•di-ol•ogy
au•dio-tape
au•dio-vi•sual
audit
au•dited

au•dit-ing
au•di-tion
au•di-tor
au•di-to-rium
au•di-tory

au•dits
aug-ment
aug-men-ta-tion
aug-mented
Au•gust

aus-pices
aus-pi-cious
aus-pi-ciously
aus-tere
aus-ter•ity

Aus-tra•lia
Aus-tra-lian
au•then-tic
au•then-ti-cate
au•then-ti-cat•ing

au•then-ti-ca•tion
au•then-tic•ity
au•thor
au•thored
au•thori-tarian

au•thori-ta-tive
au•thori-ties
au•thor-ity
au•tho-ri-za-tion
au•tho-rize

au•tho-riz•ing
au•tism
au•tis-tic
au•to-baud
au•to-clave

au•to-code
au•toc-racy
au•to-crat
au•to-cratic
au•to-dial

au•to-dial•ing
au•to-ex-port
au•to-fax•ing
au•to-graph
au•to-im-mune

au•to-load
au•to-mat
au•to-mate
au•to-mated
au•to-matic

au•to-mati-cally
au•to-ma-tion
au•to-ma-tize
au•toma-ton
au•to-mo-bile

au•to-mo-tive
au•tono-mous
au•ton-omy
au•to-pi•lot
au•to-print

au•top-sies
au•topsy
au•to-rout•ing
au•to-save
au•tumn

aux-il-ia-ries
aux-il-iary
avail-abil•ity
avail-able
ava-lanche

avenge
aveng-ing
ave•nue
av•er-age
av•er-aged

av•er-ag•ing
averse
aver-sion
averted
avert-ing

avi•ary
avia-tion
avia-tor
av•idly
avi-on•ics

avo-cado
avo-ca-tion
avoid
avoid-able
avoid-ance

avoided
avoid-ing
await
await-ing
awake

awaken	ba•by-ish	back-yard
awak-ened	bac-ca-lau-re•ate	bacon
awak-en•ing	bache-lor	bac-te•ria
award	bache-lor-hood	bac-te-rial
awarded	back-ache	bac-te-ri-cide
award-ing	back-bite	bac-te-ri-olo-gist
aware	back-biting	bac-te-ri-ol•ogy
aware-ness	back-bone	bad•ger
awe-some	back-break•ing	badges
awful	back-drop	badly
awk-ward	backer	bad-min•ton
awk-wardly	back•ers	baf•fle
awk-ward-ness	back-fire	baf-fled
aw•ning	back-fir•ing	baf-fling
awoke	back-ground	bagel
awry	back-hoe	ba•gels
axial	back-ing	bag•ful
axiom	back-lash	bag-gage
axi-om-atic	back-log	bagged
axis	back-out	bag-gi-ness
axle	back-pack	bag-ging
azi-muth	back-packer	bag-pipe
	back-packing	bai-liff
	back-rest	bail-ing
	back-side	baili-wick
	back-slide	bailor
	back-space	bail-out
	back-spacing	bait-ing
	back-stage	baked
	back-stop	baker
	back-stroke	bak-er•ies
bab•ble	back-track	bak•ers
bab-bling	back-tracking	bak•ery
ba•bied	backup	bak•ing
ba•bies	back-wards	bal-ance
ba•by-ing		

bal-anced	ban•ish	barely
bal-ances	ban-ishes	bar-gain
bal-anc•ing	ban-ish•ing	bar-gain•ing
bal-co-nies	ban-ish-ment	barge
bal-cony	ban-is•ter	barges
bald-ness	banjo	bar•ing
balked	ban•jos	bari-tone
balk•ing	bank-book	bark-ing
bal•lad	bank-card	bar•ley
bal-last	banked	bar-na•cle
bal-le-rina	banker	barn-storm
bal-lis-tics	bank-ers	barn-stormer
bal-loon	bank-ing	ba•rome-ter
bal•lot	bank-rupt	baro-met•ric
bal-lot•ing	bank-rupt-cies	ba•roque
ball-park	bank-ruptcy	bar-racks
ball-point	bank-rupt•ing	bar-ra-cuda
ball-room	banned	bar-rage
balmy	ban•ner	barred
ba•lo-ney	ban-ning	bar•rel
Bal•tic	ban-quet	bar-rels
bam•boo	ban•ter	bar•ren
bam-boo•zle	ban-ter•ing	bar-ri-cade
banal	bap-tism	bar-ri-caded
ba•nal-ity	bap-tize	bar-rier
ba•nana	bar-bar•ian	bar-ring
ban-dage	bar-baric	bar-ris•ter
ban-dag•ing	bar-be•cue	bar•ter
ban-danna	bar-be-cu•ing	bary-cen-tric
banded	bar-bell	basal
band-ing	bar•ber	base-ball
ban•dit	bar-ber•ing	base-band
band-wagon	barber-shop	base-board
band-width	bar-bi-tu-rate	base-line
bang-ing	bare-foot	base-ment

17

bases	battle-ground	beck-oned
bash-ful	battle-ship	beck-on•ing
BASIC	bau•ble	be•come
basic	baud	be•com-ing
ba•si-cally	bawled	bed-ding
ba•sics	bawl-ing	bed-fast
basil	bayo-net	bed•lam
ba•silica	bayou	bed-post
basin	ba•zaar	bed-rid•den
basis	ba•zooka	bed-rock
bas•ket	beaches	bed-roll
basket-ball	bea•con	bed-room
bask-ing	bear-able	bed-side
bas•set	bearded	bed-sores
bas-si•net	bearer	bed-spread
bas-soon	bear-ing	bed-time
bas-soon•ist	beastly	beef-eater
batches	beat-able	beef-steak
bated	beaten	bee-hive
bath-ing	beat-ing	bee-keeper
bath-robe	beat-nik	bee-line
bath-room	beau-te•ous	beeper
bath-tub	beau-ti-cian	beep-ing
baton	beau-ties	bees-wax
bat-tal•ion	beau-ti-fi-ca-tion	bee-tles
bat•ted	beau-ti-fied	be•fall
bat•ter	beau-ti•ful	be•fallen
bat-tered	beau-ti-fully	be•fell
bat-ter•ies	beau-tify	be•fit-ting
bat-tery	beau-ti-fy•ing	be•fore
bat-ting	beauty	be•fore-hand
bat•tle	bea•ver	be•friend
bat-tled	be•came	be•fud-dle
battle-field	be•cause	began
battle-front	beckon	beg•gar

beg-garly
begged
begin
be•gin-ner
be•gin-ning

be•got-ten
be•guile
begun
be•half
be•have

be•hav-ing
be•hav-ior
be•hav-ioral
be•held
be•hind

be•hold
be•hold-ing
beige
being
be•la-bor

be•la-bor•ing
be•lated
be•lat-edly
Bel-gium
be•lief

be•liev-able
be•lieve
be•liever
be•liev-ing
be•lit-tle

be•lit-tling
bel•lig-er-ence
bel•lig-er•ent
belly-ach•ing
be•long

be•long-ing
below
belt-way
benches
bench-mark

bench--top
bend-able
bend-ing
be•neath
bene-dic-tion

bene-dic-tory
bene-fac•tor
bene-fi-cial
bene-fi-cia-ries
bene-fi-ciary

bene-fit
bene-fited
bene-fit•ing
be•nevo-lence
be•nevo-lent

be•nign
be•queath
be•rate
be•reave
be•reave-ment

ber-ries
berry
ber-serk
be•side
be•sides

be•siege
be•stow
be•stowal
beta
be•tray

be•trayal
be•trayed
be•tray-ing
bet•ter
bet•ter-ing

bet•ter-ment
bet-ting
bet•tor
be•tween
bevel

bev-eled
bev-el•ing
bev-er•age
bev-er-ages
be•ware

be•wil-der
be•wil-dered
be•wil-der-ment
be•witch
be•yond

bi•an-nual
bi•an-nu-ally
bias
bi•ased
bible

bi•bles
bib-li•cal
bib•li-og-ra•pher
bib•lio-graphic
bib•lio-graph-ical

bib•li-og-ra•phy
bib•lio-phile
bi•cam-eral
bi•car-bon•ate
bi•cen-ten-nial

bi•ceps
bicker
bick-er•ing
bi•con-di-tional
bi•cus-pid

bi•cy-cle
bi•cy-cling
bi•cy-clist
bid•der
bid-ding

bi•di-rec-tional
bi•di-rec-tion-ally
bi•en-nial
bi•en-ni-ally
bi•en-nium

bi•fo-cals
biga-mist
bigamy
big•ger
big-gest

big-hearted
bigot
big-oted
big-otry
bik•ing

bi•kini
bi•lat-eral
bi•lat-er-ally
bi--level
bi•lin-ear

bi•lin-gual
bill-board
billed
bil•let
bill-fold

bil-liards
bill-ing
bil-lion
bil-lion-aire
bi•monthly

bi•nary
bi•na-tional
binder
bind-ers
bind-ery

bind-ing
bin-ocu•lar
bin-ocu-lars
bi•no-mial
bio-chem-ical

bio-chem•ist
bio-chem-is•try
bio-de•grad-able
bio•feed-back
bi•og-ra-pher

bio-graphic
bio-graph-ical
bi•og-ra•phy
bio-logic
bio-log-ical

bi•olo-gist
bi•ol-ogy
bio-medi-cine
bi•onic
bi•on-ics

bio•pak
bi•opsy
bio-rhythm
bio-sci-ence
bio-syn-thetic

bi•par-ti•san
bi•plane
bi•po-lar
bi•pro-pel-lant
bird-house

birth-day
birth-mark
birth-right
birth-stone
bis-cuit

bi•sect
bi•sec-tion
bi•sexual
bison
bi•syn-chro-nous

bit
bit•ing
bit•map
bit•map-ping
bit•ter

bit-terly
bit-ter-ness
bitter-sweet
bi•tu-mi-nous
biv-ouac

biv-ouacked
bi•weekly
bi•zarre
black-ball
black-board

blacken
black-ened
black-en•ing
black-list
black-mail

black-out
black-top
blad-der
blam-able
blame

blame-less
blam-ing
blan-ket
blan-ket•ing
blar-ing

blasé
blas-phe-mous
blas-phemy
blasted
blaster

blast-ing
blast--off
bla-tancy
bla-tant
bla-tantly

blazer
blaz-ing
bleacher
bleach-ing
bleak-est

bleary
bled
bleed
bleed-ing
blem-ish

blem-ishes
blem-ish•ing
blended
blender
blend-ing

blessed
bless-ing
blight
blimp
blinder

blind-fold
blind-ing
blindly
blind-ness
blinker

blink-ing
bliss-ful
bliss-fully
blis-ter
blis-tered

blithe
blitz
blitz-ing
bliz-zard
bloc

block
block-ade
block-age
block-buster
blocker

block-ing
blond-ish
blood-curdling
blood-hound
blood-ied

blood-iest
bloodi-ness
blood-less
blood-letting
blood-shed

blood-shot
blood-stain
blood-thirsty
bloody
bloom-ing

blooper
blos-som
blos-som•ing
blot-ted
blot-ter

blot-ting
blouse
blouses
blow-down
blower

blow-ers
blow-ing
blow-out
blow-torch
blub-ber

blud-geon
blue-berry
blue-bird
blue--collar
blue-grass

blue--green
blue-print
bluff-ing
blu-ish
blun-der

bluntly
blunt-ness
blurred
blur-ring
blurry

blus-ter•ous
blus-tery
boarded
boarder
board-ing

board-walk
boast-ful
boast-fully
boast-ing
boater

boat-ing
bobbed
bob•bin
bob-bing
bob-cat

bob-sled
bod•ice
bod•ied
bod•ies
bodily

body
body-guard
body-suit
bogged
bog•gle

bogus
boiled
boiler
boiler-plate
boil-ers

boil-ing
bois-ter•ous
bolded
bolder
bold-face

boldly
bold-ness
bo•lero
bo•lo-gna
bol-ster

bom-bard
bom-bar-dier
bom-bard•ing
bom-bard-ment
bom-bast

bom-bas•tic
bomber
bomb-ing
bomb-proof
bomb-shell

bo•nanza
bond-age
bonded
bond-holder
bond-ing

bone-less
bon-fire
bon•net
bon•sai
bonus

bo•nuses
book-binder
book-binding
book-case
book-dealer

booked
book-end
book-ing
book-ish
book-keeper

book-keeping
book-let
book-lore
book-maker
book-making

book-mark
book-mobile
book-seller
book-shelf
book-store

book-worm
Bool-ean
boo-mer•ang
boom-ing
boon

boon-dog•gle
boor-ish
boost
booster
boost-ing

boot
booted
booth
boot-leg
boot-leg•ger

boot-strap
boot-strap-ping
boot--up
bor•der
bor-dered

bor-der•ing
border-line
bore-dom
bor•ing
born

borne
bor-ough
bor•row
bor-rowed
bor-rower

bor-row•ers
bor-row•ing
bosses
bossy
bo•tan-ical

bota-nist
bot•any
bother
both-ered
both-er•ing

both•er-some
bot•tle
bottle-neck
bot-tling
bot•tom

bot-tomed
bot-tom•ing
bot•tom-less
botu-lism
bouil-lon

boul-der
bou-le-vard
bounc-ing
bound-aries
bound-ary

bounded
bound-ing
bound-less
boun-te•ous
boun-ti•ful

bounty
bou-quet
bou-tique
bou-ton-niere
bow•ery

bowler
bowl-ing
boxed
boxer
boxes

box•ing
boy-cott
boy-cotted
boy•sen-berry
brace-let

brac-ing
bracket
brack-eted
brack-et•ing
brack-ets

brack-ish
brag-gart
bragged
brag-ging
braille

brain
brain-child
brain-less
brain-power
brain-storm

brain-storming
brain-teaser
brain-wash
brain-washing
brake

branch
branches
branch-ing
brand
branded

brand-ing
brandy
brav-ery
brav-est
bravo

brawl
brawler
brawl-ing
brawn
brawni-ness

brawny
bra.zen
Bra•zil
Bra-zil•ian
braz-ing

breach
breaches
breach-ing
bread-stuff
breadth

bread-winner
break-able
break-age
break-away
break-down

breaker
break-ers
break--even
break-fast
break--in *(n.)*

break-ing
break-out *(n.)*
break-through *(n.)*
breast-bone
breast-stroke

breath
breathe
breath-ing
breath-less
breath-lessly

breath-taking
bred
breed
breed-ing
breeze

breeze-way
breezy
brev-ity
brewer
brew-er•ies

brew-ery
brew-ing
brib-ery
brib-ing
brick-bat

brick-layer
bridal
bride-groom
brides-maid
bridges

bridge-ware
bridge-work
bridg-ing
bri•dle
brief

brief-case
briefed
brief-est
brief-ing
briefly

bri-gade
briga-dier
brighten
brighter
bright-est

brightly
bright-ness
bril-liance
bril-liant
bril-liantly

bring-ing
bri-quette
briskly
bris-tle
Brit-ain

Brit-ish
brit-tle
broached
broad-band
broad-cast

broad-caster
broad-cast•ing
broaden
broad-ened
broad-en•ing

broader
broad-est
broad-loom
broadly
broad--minded

broad-side
Broad-way
broc-coli
bro-chure
broil

broiled
broiler
broil-ing
bro•ken
bro•ker

bro•ker-age
bro-kered
bron-chial
bron-chi•tis
bronco

brood-ing
broom-stick
brother
broth•er-hood
broth-erly

broth-ers
brought
brow-beat
browned
brownie

brown-ish
brown-nose
brown-out
browse
browser

brows-ing
bruise
bruises
bruis-ing
brunch

bru-nette
brushed
brushes
brush-ing
brusque

bru•tal
bru-tal•ity
bru-tal•ize
bru-tally
brut-ish

bub•ble
bub-bled
bub•bly
bu•bonic
buc-ca-neer

bucka-roo
buck-board
bucket
buck•et-ful
buckle

buck-led
buck-shot
buck-skin
buck-wheat
bud-dies

bud-ding
buddy
bud•get
bud-get•ary
bud-geted

bud-get•ing
budg-ing
buf-falo
buffer
buff-er•ing

buff-ers
buf•fet
buff-ing
buggy
bugle

bu•gling
builder
build-ers
build-ing
buildup

built--in
bul-bous
Bul-garia
Bul-garian
bulg-ing

bulk-head
bulky
bull-dog
bull-dozer
bul•let

bul-le•tin
bul•let-proof
bull-headed
bul-lion
bull-ish

bully
bul•ly-ing
bul-wark
bumble-bee
bumped

bumper
bump-ing
bumpy
bunches
bun•dle

bun-dled
bun-dling
bun-ga•low
bun•gee
bun•gle

bun-gling
bun•ion
bunk-ing
bun-ting
buoy

buoy-ancy
buoy-ant
bur•den
bur-dened
bur-den-some

bu•reau
bu•reau-cracy
bu•reau-crat
bu•reau-cratic
bur-geoned

bur-geon•ing
bur-glar
bur-glar•ies
bur-glar•ize
burglar-proof

bur-glary
bur-gundy
burial
bur•ied
bur•ies

bur•lap
bur-lesque
burly
Bur-mese
burned

burner	butter-fly	ca•bled
burn-ing	butter-milk	ca•ble-gram
burn-out	butter-scotch	ca•bles
bur•row	but-tery	cable-text
bur-row•ing	but•ton	ca•bling
bur•sar	but-toned	ca•boose
bur-si•tis	button-hole	cac-cia-tore
burst-ing	but-ton•ing	cache
bury	but-tress	ca•chet
bury-ing	buyer	cach-ing
bushed	buy•ers	cackle
bushel	buy•ing	cacti
bushes	buz-zard	cac•tus
bush-whack	buzzer	ca•daver
bus•ied	buzz-word	ca•dav-er•ous
busier	bylaw	cad•die
busi-est	by•laws	ca•dence
busily	by•line	ca•denza
busi-ness	by•pass	cadet
busi-nesses	by•pass-ing	cafe-te•ria
business-like	by--product	cafe-to-rium
business-plan	by•stander	caf-feine
bus•ses	byte	ca•jole
bus-sing		Cajun
busted		cake-walk
bus•tle		ca•lami-ties
bus-tling		ca•lami-tous
busy-body		ca•lam-ity
busy-work		cal-cify
bu•tane		cal-cium
butcher	caba-ret	cal-cu-la•ble
butch-ery	cab-bage	cal-cu-late
but•ter	cabin	cal-cu-lat•ing
but-tered	cabi-net	cal-cu-la-tion
butter-fat	cable	cal-cu-la•tor

cal-culi
cal-cu•lus
cal-en•dar
calf-skin
cali-ber

cali-brate
cali-bra-tion
calico
Cali-for•nia
Cali-for-nian

cali-pers
cal-is-then•ics
calk-ing
call-back
called

caller
call-ers
cal-lig-ra-pher
cal-lig-ra•phy
call-ing

cal-li•ope
cal-lous
cal-lous-ness
calmly
calm-ness

calo-rie
calo-ries
ca-lum-ni•ous
cal-vary
calves

ca•lypso
ca•ma-ra-de•rie
Cam-bo•dia
Cam-bo-dian
cameo

cam•era
cam-ou-flage
cam-ou-flag•ing
cam-paign
cam-paigner

cam-paign•ing
camper
camp-fire
camp-ground
camp-ing

camp-site
cam•pus
cam-puses
Can•ada
Ca•na-dian

canal
ca•nals
ca•nary
can•cel
can-celed

can-cel•ing
can-cel-la-tion
can•cer
can-cer•ous
can•did

can-di-dacy
can-di-date
can-didly
can-did-ness
can-died

can-dies
can•dle
candle-power
candle-stick
can•dor

candy
ca•nine
can-is•ter
can•ker
can-nery

can-ni•bal
can-ni-bal•ism
can-ning
can•non
can•not

canoe
ca•noe-ing
ca•noes
canon
can-on•ize

can•opy
can-ta-loupe
can-tan-ker•ous
can-teen
Can-ton•ese

can•vas
can-vass
can-vassed
can-vass•ing
can•yon

ca•pa-bili-ties
ca•pa-bil•ity
ca•pa-ble
ca•pa-bly
ca•paci-tate

ca•paci-ties
ca•paci-tor
ca•pac-ity
cap-il-lary
capi-tal

capi-tal•ism
capi-tal•ist
capi-tal-is•tic
capi-tal•ize
capi-tal-ized

capi-tol
ca•pitu-late
ca•pitu-la-tion
ca•pri-cious
cap-size

cap-siz•ing
cap-stone
cap-sule
cap-tain
cap-tion

cap-tion•ing
cap-ti-vate
cap-ti-vat•ing
cap-ti-va-tion
cap-tive

cap-tiv•ity
cap•tor
cap-ture
cap-tur•ing
cara-mel

carat
cara-van
car•bon
car-bon•ate
car-bon-ized

car-bon-iz•ing
car-bu-re•tor
car-cass
car-casses
car-cino•gen

card-board
car-diac
car-di•gan
car-di•nal
car-di-nal•ity

car-dio-gram
car-di-olo-gist
car-di-ology
car-dio-vas-cu•lar
ca•reen

ca•reer
care-free
care-ful
care-fully
care-less

care-lessly
care-less-ness
ca•ress
ca•ress-ing
care-taker

cargo
car-goes
Ca•rib-bean
cari-bou
cari-ca-ture

car-il•lon
car•ing
car-nage
car•nal
car-nal•ity

car-na-tion
car-ni•val
car-nivo-rous
carob
ca•rouse

car-ou•sel
ca•rous-ing
car-pen•ter
car-pen•try
car•pet

car-peted
car-pet•ing
car-pool
car-pooling
car-port

car•rel
car-riage
car-ried
car-rier
car-ries

car•rot
carry
carry-all
car-ry•ing
carry--on *(adj.)*

car•tel
Car-te-sian
car-ti-lage
car-tog-ra•phy
car•ton

car-toon
car-toon•ist
car-tridge
carv-ing
cas-cade

case-book
case-load
cases
case-worker
cashed

cashes
ca•shew
cash-ier
cash-ier•ing
cash-ing

cash-mere
cas•ing
ca•sino
cas•ket
cas-se-role

cas-sette
caste
caster
cas-ti-gate
cas-ti-gat•ing

cas-ti-ga-tion
cast-ing
cas•tle
cast--off *(adj.)*
cas•tor

ca•sual
ca•su-ally
ca•su-alty
cata-clysm
cata-log

cata-loged
cata-log•ing
cata-lyst
cata-lytic
cata-ma•ran

cata-pult
cata-ract
cata-strophic
catch-all
catcher

catches
catch-ing
cate-gor-ical
cate-gori-cally
cate-go-ries

cate-go-rize
cate-go-riz•ing
cate-gory
cater
ca•tered

ca•terer
ca•ter-ing
cat•er-pil•lar
cat•gut
ca•the-dral

cathe-ter
cathe-ter•ize
cath-ode
cat•nap
cat•sup

cat•tle
cat-walk
Cau-ca-sian
cau•cus
cau-cuses

cau-cus•ing
cau-li-flower
caulk-ing
causal
caused

causes
cause-way
caus-ing
caus-tic
cau-tion

cau-tion•ary
cau-tioned
cau-tious
cau-tiously
cav-al-cade

cava-lier
cav-alry
cav•ern
cav-ern•ous
cav•iar

cavi-ties
cav•ity
CD--ROM
ceased
ceases

cede
ceded
ced•ing
ceil-ing
cele-brant

cele-brate
cele-brated
cele-brat•ing
cele-bra-tion
ce•leb-ri•ties

ce•leb-rity
cel•ery
ce•les-tial
cel•lar
cel-lo-phane

cel-lu•lar
Cel-sius
ce•ment
ce•mented
ce•ment-ing

ceme-tery	cere-mo-nies	cha-me-leon
ceme-ter•ies	cere-mo-ni•ous	cham-pagne
cen•sor	cere-mony	cham-pion
cen-sored	cer-tain	cham-pion-ship
cen-sor•ing	cer-tainly	chan-cel-lery
cen-sor-ship	cer-tainty	chan-cel•lor
cen-sure	cer-tifi-cate	chances
cen-sur•ing	cer-ti-fi-ca-tion	chan-de-lier
cen•sus	cer-ti-fied	change-able
cen-te-nary	cer-ti-fies	changed
cen-ten-nial	cer-tify	change-less
cen•ter	cer-ti-fy•ing	change-over
cen-tered	cer-vi•cal	changes
center-fold	ces-sion	chang-ing
cen-ter•ing	chafe	chan-nel
center-piece	chaff	chan-neled
cen-ti-grade	chaf-ing	chan-nel•ing
cen-ti-meter	cha-grin	chant-ing
cen-tral	cha-grin•ing	chaos
cen-tral-iza-tion	chain-ing	cha-otic
cen-tral•ize	chaired	cha-oti-cally
cen-tral-izes	chair-ing	chap-ar•ral
cen-tral-iz•ing	chair-man	cha•pel
cen-trally	chair-person	cha-pels
cen-trifu•gal	chair-woman	chap-eron
cen-tri-fuge	chaise	chap-lain
cen-tu-ries	cha•let	chap-ter
cen-tu-rion	chal-ice	char-ac•ter
cen-tury	chalk-board	char-ac-ter-is•tic
ce•ramic	chalky	char-ac-ter-is-tics
ce•ram-ics	chal-lenge	char-ac-ter-ized
ce•real	chal-lenger	char-ac-ter-iz•ing
ce•re-bral	chal-lenges	cha-rade
cere-mo-nial	chal-leng•ing	char-broiled
cere-mo-ni-ally	cham-ber	char-coal

charge-able	cheapen	cher-ish
charge-back	cheap-ened	cher-ries
charged	cheap-en•ing	cherry
charger	cheaply	cherub
charges	cheap-skate	che-ru•bic
charg-ing	cheated	chest-nut
char-iot	cheater	chew-able
cha-risma	cheat-ing	chew-ing
chari-ta•ble	check-book	chi-ca-nery
chari-ties	checked	chicken
char-ity	checker	chick-ens
char-la•tan	check-ered	chided
charmed	check-ing	chiefly
charm-ing	check-less	chif-fon
charted	check-list	child-bearing
char-ter	check-mate	child-birth
char-tered	check-out (n.)	child-hood
char-ter•ing	check-point	child-ish
chart-ing	checkup (n.)	child-less
char-treuse	cheek-bone	child-like
chased	cheered	child-proof
chases	cheer-ful	chil-dren
chas-ing	cheer-fully	Chile
chasm	cheer-ing	Chil-ean
chas-sis	cheer-leader	chili
chaste	cheer-less	chilled
chas-tise	cheery	chill-ing
chas-tity	cheese-burger	chilly
cha-teau	cheese-cake	chim-ing
chat-tel	chem-ical	chim-ney
chat-ter	chemi-cally	chim-neys
chat-ting	chem-ist	chim-pan•zee
chauf-feur	chem-is•try	china
chau-vin•ist	che-mo-sphere	china-ware
chau-vin-is•tic	che-mo-ther•apy	Chi-nese

Chi-nook
chintz
chip-munk
chipped
chip-per

chip-ping
chi-ropo-dist
chi-ro-prac•tic
chi-ro-prac•tor
chisel

chis-eled
chis-eler
chis-el•ing
chiv-al-rous
chiv-alry

chlo-ric
chlo-ride
chlo-ri-nate
chlo-ri-na-tion
chlo-rine

chlo-ro-form
chlo-ro-phyll
choco-late
choices
choir

choked
chok-ing
chol-era
cho-les-terol
choose

chooses
choos-ing
chopped
chop-per
chop-ping

choppy
chop-sticks
cho•ral
cho-rale
chord

cho-reo-graph
cho-re-og-ra-pher
cho-reo-graph•ing
cho-re-og-ra•phy
cho-ris•ter

cho•rus
chose
cho•sen
chow-der
Chris-tian

Chris-tian•ity
Christ-mas
chrome
chro-mo-some
chronic

chroni-cally
chron-icle
chro-no-log-ical
chro-no-logi-cally
chro-nol•ogy

chuck-hole
chuckle
chuck-ling
chummy
churches

churn-ing
ciga-rette
ci•gars
cinch-ing
cin•der

cin•ema
cine-matic
cin-na•mon
ci•pher
ci•pher-ing

cir•cle
cir-cled
cir-cles
cir-cling
cir-cuit

cir-cu-itous
cir-cuitry
cir-cu•lar
cir-cu-lar•ize
cir-cu-lar-ized

cir-cu-lar-iz•ing
cir-cu-late
cir-cu-lat•ing
cir-cu-la-tion
cir-cu-la-tive

cir-cu-la-tory
cir-cum-fer-ence
cir-cum-fer-en-tial
cir-cum-flex
cir-cum-lu•nar

cir-cum-navi-gate
cir-cum-plane-tary
cir-cum-scribe
cir-cum-scrip-tion
cir-cum-spect

cir-cum-spec-tion
cir-cum-stance
cir-cum-stances
cir-cum-stan-tial
cir-cum-vent

cir-cum-vented
cir-cum-ven-tion
cir•cus
cir-cuses
cir-rho•sis

cis-lu•nar
cita-del
ci•ta-tion
cite
cited

cit•ies
cit•ing
citi-zen
citi-zenry
citi-zen-ship

cit•ric
cit•rus
civic
civ•ics
ci•vil-ian

ci•vil-ity
civi-li-za-tion
civi-lize
civi-lized
claim-ant

claimed
claim-ing
clair-voy-ance
clair-voy•ant
clam-ored

clam-or•ing
clamp-ing
clam-shell
clan-des-tine
clap-ping

clari-fi-ca-tion
clari-fied
clari-fies
clar-ify
clari-fy•ing

clari-net
clar-ity
clasp-ing
classes
clas-sic

clas-si•cal
clas-si-fi-able
clas-si-fi-ca-tion
clas-si-fied
clas-sify

clas-si-fy•ing
class-mate
class-room
class-work
clause

clauses
claus-tro-pho•bia
claus-tro-pho•bic
clav-icle
cleaned

cleaner
clean-ers
clean-ing
clean-li-ness
cleanly

cleanse
cleanser
cleans-ing
cleanup
clear-ance

clear-ances
cleared
clearer
clear-headed
clear-ing

clearly
cleav-age
cleaver
cleav-ing
clem-ency

clergy
cleric
cler-ical
clerk-ing
clever

cli•ché
click-ing
cli•ent
cli-en-tele
cli-mac•tic

cli-mate
cli-ma-to-log-ical
cli-ma-tolo-gist
cli•max
climber

climb-ing
clinched
clinch-ing
cling-ing
clinic

clin-ical
clini-cally
cli-ni-cian
clin-ics
clip-board

clipped	cloudi-ness	coat-ing
clip-per	cloud-less	co•au-thor
clip-ping	cloudy	co•ax-ial
clique	clo•ver	coax-ing
cloak-room	clover-leaf	co•balt
clob-ber	clown-ing	cob-bler
clob-ber•ing	clown-ish	cobble-stone
clock-ing	club-house	COBOL
clock-wise	clum-sily	cobra
clock-work	clum-si-ness	cob•web
clogged	clumsy	cob-webs
clog-ging	clus-ter	co•caine
clois-ter	clutched	cock-ney
clone	clutches	cock-pit
cloned	clut-ter	cock-roach
clon-ing	clut-tered	cock-tail
closed	clut-ter•ing	co•co-nut
closely	coached	co•coon
close-out (n.)	coaches	cod•dle
closer	coach-ing	cod-dling
closes	co•ad-justor	code
clos-est	co•agu-lant	coded
closet	co•agu-late	co•de-fen-dant
clos-ets	co•agu-la-tion	co•deine
clos-ing	co•alesce	codi-cil
clo-sure	co•ales-cence	codi-fied
cloth	co•ales-cent	codify
clothe	co•ali-tion	cod•ing
clothes	coarse	co•edi-tor
cloth-ier	coarsely	co•ef-fi-cient
cloth-ing	coastal	co•erce
clot-ted	coaster	co•er-cion
clot-ting	coast-ing	co•er-cive
cloud-burst	coast-line	co•ex-ist
clouded	coated	cof•fee

coffee-pot
cof•fer
cof•fin
co--founder
co•gent

cogi-tate
cogi-ta-tion
cog-ni-tive
cog-ni-zance
cog-ni-zant

co-habi-ta-tion
co•her-ence
co•her-ent
co•he-sion
co•he-sive

co•hort
co•host
coiled
coin-age
co•in-cide

co•in-ci-dence
co•in-ci-dent
co•in-ci-den•tal
co•in-ci-den-tally
co•in-cid•ing

co•in-sur-ance
col-an•der
colder
cold-est
cole-slaw

colic
coli-seum
co•li-tis
col-labo-rate
col-labo-rat•ing

col-labo-ra-tion
col-labo-ra-tive
col-labo-ra-tively
col-labo-ra•tor
col-lage

col-lapse
col-laps-ible
col-laps•ing
col•lar
collar-bone

col-late
col-lat-eral
col-lat•ing
col-la-tion
col-la•tor

col-league
col-lect
col-lect-ible
col-lect•ing
col-lec-tion

col-lec-tive
col-lec-tively
col-lege
col-le-gial
col-le-gi-al•ity

col-le-gian
col-le-giate
col-le-gium
col-lide
col-li-sion

col-lo-quial
col•lo-qui-al•ism
col-lo-quium
col-lu-sion
col-lu-sive

co•logne
Co•lom-bia
Co•lom-bian
colon
colo-nel

co•lo-nial
colo-nies
colo-nist
colo-ni-za-tion
colo-nize

col•ony
color
Colo-ra-dan
Colo-rado
col-ored

color-fast
col•or-ful
col•or-ing
col•or-less
col•ors

co•los-sal
col-os-seum
co•los-tomy
col•umn
co•lum-nar

col-um-nist
coma
co•ma-tose
com•bat
com-bat•ant

com-bat•ing
com-bat•ive
com-bi-na-tion
com-bine
comb-ing

com-bin•ing
com-bus-ti•ble
com-bus-tion
com-bus-tive
co•me-dian

come-dies
com•edy
comet
com-fort
com-fort-able

com-fort•ing
comic
com-ical
com•ing
comma

com-mand
com-mander
com-mand•ing
com-mand-ment
com-memo-rate

com-memo-rated
com-memo-rates
com-memo-ra-tion
com-memo-ra-tive
com-mence

com-mence-ment
com-mences
com-menc•ing
com-mend
com-mend-able

com-men-da-tion
com-men-da-tory
com-mended
com-mend•ing
com-men-su-rate

com-ment
com-men-tar•ies
com-men-tary
com-men-ta•tor
com-mented

com-ment•ing
com-merce
com-mer-cial
com-mer-cial•ism
com-mer-cial•ize

com-mer-cially
com-mer-cials
com-mis-er•ate
com-mis-er-at•ing
com-mis-era-tion

com-mis-sary
com-mis-sion
com-mis-sioned
com-mis-sioner
com-mis-sion•ing

com•mit
com-mit-ment
com-mit•tal
com-mit•ted
com-mit•tee

com-mit-ting
com-modi-ties
com-mod•ity
com•mon
com-mon-alty

com-monly
common-place
common-wealth
com-mo-tion
com-mu•nal

com-mune
com-mu-ni-ca•ble
com-mu-ni-cate
com-mu-ni-cat•ing
com-mu-ni-ca-tion

com-mu-ni-ca-tive
com-mu-ni-ca•tor
com-mu-ni•que
com-mu-nism
com-mu-nist

com-mu-nis•tic
com-mu-ni-ties
com-mu-nity
com-mute
com-muter

com-mut•ing
com-pact
com-pact•ing
com-pact-ness
com-pac•tor

com-pa-nies
com-pan•ion
com-pan•ion-ship
com-pany
com-pa-ra•ble

com-para-tive
com-pare
com-par•ing
com-pari•son
com-part-ment

com-part-men•tal
com-pass
com-pas-sion
com-pas-sion•ate
com-pati-bil•ity

com-pat-ible
com-pa-triot
com•pel
com-pelled
com-pel-ling

com-pen-dium
com-pen-sate
com-pen-sated
com-pen-sat•ing
com-pen-sa-tion

com-pen-sa-tory
com-pete
com-peted
com-pe-tence
com-pe-ten-cies

com-pe-tency
com-pe-tent
com-pet•ing
com-pe-ti-tion
com-peti-tive

com-peti-tive-ness
com-peti•tor
com-pi-la-tion
com-pile
com-piler

com-pil•ing
com-pla-cency
com-pla-cent
com-plain
com-plainer

com-plain•ing
com-plaint
com-plai-sance
com-plai-sant
com-ple-ment

com-ple-men-tary
com-ple-mented
com-ple-ment•ing
com-plete
com-pletely

com-plet•ing
com-ple-tion
com-plex
com-plex•ion
com-plexi-ties

com-plex•ity
com-pli-ance
com-pli•ant
com-pli-cate
com-pli-cat•ing

com-pli-ca-tion
com-plied
com-plies
com-pli-ment
com-pli-men-tary

com•ply
com-ply•ing
com-po-nent
com-pose
com-poser

com-pos•ing
com-pos•ite
com-po-si-tion
com-posi•tor
com-post

com-po-sure
com-pound
com-pound•ing
com-pre-hend
com-pre-hend•ing

com-pre-hen-sion
com-pre-hen-sive
com-press
com-press-ible
com-press•ing

com-pres-sion
com-pres•sor
com-prise
com-prises
com-pro-mise

com-pro-mis•ing
comp-trol•ler
com-pul-sion
com-pul-sive
com-pul-sory

com-pu-ta-tion
com-pu-ta-tional
com-pute
com-puted
com-puter

com-put-er•ize
com-put-er-ized
com-put-er-iz•ing
com-rade
con-cate-nate

con-cate-nat•ing
con-cate-na-tion
con-cave
con-ceal
con-ceal•ing

con-cede
con-ceded
con-ced•ing
con-ceit
con-ceited

37

con-ceiv-able
con-ceive
con-ceiv•ing
con-cen-trate
con-cen-trated

con-cen-trat•ing
con-cen-tra-tion
con-cept
con-cep-tion
con-cep-tual

con-cep-tu-al•ize
con-cep-tu-ally
con-cern
con-cern•ing
con-cert

con-certed
con-cer-tino
con-ces-sion
con-cierge
con-cili•ate

con-cili-ation
con-cil-ia-tory
con-cise
con-cisely
con-clave

con-clude
con-cluded
con-clud•ing
con-clu-sion
con-clu-sive

con-clu-sively
con-coct
con-cocted
con-coct•ing
con-coc-tion

con-cord
con-cor-dance
con-course
con-crete
con•cur

con-cur-rence
con-cur-rency
con-cur-rent
con-cur-rently
con-cur-ring

con-cus-sion
con-demn
con-dem-na-tion
con-demn•ing
con-den-sa-tion

con-dense
con-dens•ing
con-de-scend
con-de-scend•ing
con-de-scen-sion

con-di-ment
con-di-tion
con-di-tional
con-di-tion-ally
con-di-tioner

con-di-tion•ing
con-dole
con-do-lence
con-do-min•ium
con-done

con-du-cive
con-duct
con-duct-ible
con-duct•ing
con-duc-tion

con-duc-tive
con-duc•tor
con-duit
con-fec-tion
con-fec-tion•ery

con-fed-er•acy
con-fed-er•ate
con-fed-era-tion
con•fer
con-fer-ence

con-fer-enc•ing
con-ferred
con-fer-ring
con-fess
con-fess•ing

con-fes-sion
con-fes•sor
con-fetti
con-fide
con-fi-dence

con-fi-dent
con-fi-den-tial
con-fi-den-ti-al•ity
con-fi-den-tially
con-fi-dently

con-fid•ing
con-fig-ur-able
con-figu-ra-tion
con-fig•ure
con-fine

con-fine-ment
con-fin•ing
con-firm
con-fir-ma-tion
con-firm•ing

con-fis-cate
con-fis-cat•ing
con-fis-ca-tion
con-flict
con-flict•ing

con-flic-tion
con-flu•ent
con-form
con-for-ma-tion
con-form•ing

con-form•ist
con-for-mity
con-found
con-founded
con-front

con-fron-ta-tion
con-fronted
con-front•ing
con-fuse
con-fuses

con-fus•ing
con-fu-sion
con-ge-nial•ity
con-geni•tal
con-gest

con-gested
con-gest•ing
con-ges-tion
con-ges-tive
con-glom-er•ate

con-glom-era-tion
con-gratu-late
con-gratu-lat•ing
con-gratu-la-tions
con-gratu-la-tory

con-gre-gate
con-gre-gated
con-gre-gat•ing
con-gre-ga-tion
con-gre-ga-tional

con-gress
con-gres-sio•nal
con-gru-ence
con-gru•ent
con-gru•ity

con-gru•ous
con-jec-tural
con-jec-ture
con-ju-gate
con-ju-ga-tion

con-junc-tion
con-junc-tive
con-nect
con-nected
Con-necti•cut

con-nect•ing
con-nec-tion
con-nec-tive
con-nec-tiv•ity
con-nec•tor

con-nive
con-nois-seur
con-no-ta-tion
con-no-ta-tive
con-note

con-quer
con-quer•ing
con-queror
con-quest
con-sci-en-tious

con-sci-en-tiously
con-scious
con-scious-ness
con-se-crate
con-se-cra-tion

con-secu-tive
con-secu-tively
con-sen•sus
con-sent
con-sent•ing

con-se-quence
con-se-quent
con-se-quen-tial
con-se-quently
con-ser-va-tion

con-ser-va-tion•ist
con-ser-va-tism
con-ser-va-tive
con-ser-va-tively
con-ser-va-tory

con-serve
con-serv•ing
con-sider
con-sid-er-able
con-sid-er•ate

con-sid-er-ation
con-sid-ered
con-sid-er•ing
con-sid•ers
con-sign

con-sign•ing
con-sign-ment
con-sist
con-sisted
con-sis-tency

con-sis-tent
con-sis-tently
con-sist•ing
con-so-la-tion
con-sole

con-soli-date
con-soli-dated
con-soli-dat•ing
con-soli-da-tion
con-so-nant

con-sort•ing
con-sor-tium
con-spicu•ous
con-spicu-ously
con-spir•acy

con-spira•tor
con-spire
con-sta•ble
con-stancy
con-stant

con-stantly
con-stel-la-tion
con-ster-na-tion
con-sti-pate
con-sti-pa-tion

con-stitu-ency
con-stitu•ent
con-sti-tute
con-sti-tut•ing
con-sti-tu-tion

con-sti-tu-tional
con-strain
con-strain•ing
con-straint
con-strict

con-stricted
con-strict•ing
con-stric-tion
con-struct
con-struct•ing

con-struc-tion
con-struc-tive
con-struc-tively
con-struc•tor
con-strue

con-stru•ing
con•sul
con-sular
con-sul•ate
con-sult

con-sul-tant
con-sul-ta-tion
con-sult•ing
con-sum-able
con-sume

con-sumer
con-sum-er•ism
con-sum•ers
com-sum•ing
con-sum-mate

con-sum-ma-tion
con-sump-tion
con-tact
con-tact•ing
con-ta-gious

con-tain
con-tainer
con-tain•ers
con-tain•ing
con-tain-ment

con-tami-nant
con-tami-nate
con-tami-nat•ing
con-tami-na-tion
con-tem-plate

con-tem-plated
con-tem-plat•ing
con-tem-pla-tion
con-tem-pla-tive
con-tem-po-rar•ies

con-tem-po-rary
con-tempt
con-tempt-ible
con-temp-tu•ous
con-tend

con-tender
con-tend•ing
con-tent
con-ten-tion
con-ten-tious

con-tent-ment
con-test
con-tes-tant
con-test•ing
con-text

con-tex-tual
con-tex-ture
con-ti-gu•ity
con-tigu•ous
con-ti-nent

con-ti-nen•tal
con-tin-gen-cies
con-tin-gency
con-tin-gent
con-tin•ual

con-tin-ually
con-tinu-ance
con-tinu-ation
con-tinue
con-tin•ued

con-tin•ues
con-tinu•ing
con-ti-nu•ity
con-tinu•ous
con-tinu-ously

con-tinuum
con-tort
con-tor-tion
con-tor-tion•ist
con-tour

con-tra-band
con-tra-cep-tive
con-tract
con-tracted
con-tract•ing

con-trac-tion
con-trac•tor
con-trac-tual
con-tra-dict
con-tra-dict•ing

con-tra-dic-tion
con-tra-dic-tory
con-tra-or•bit
con-tra-or-bital
con-trap-tion

con-trary
con-trast
con-trast•ing
con-tra-vene
con-tra-ven-tion

con-trib•ute
con-tri-but•ing
con-tri-bu-tion
con-tribu•tor
con-tribu-tors

con-tribu-tory
con-trite
con-tri-tion
con-trive
con-trol

con-trol-la•ble
con-trol•ler
con-trol-ling
con-tro-ver-sial
con-tro-versy

con-tu-sion
con-va-les-cence
con-va-les-cent
con-va-lesc•ing
con-vene

con-ve-nience
con-ve-nient
con-ve-niently
con-ven•ing
con-ven-tion

con-ven-tional
con-verge
con-ver-gence
con-ver-gent
con-ver-sant

con-ver-sa-tion
con-ver-sa-tional
con-verse
con-versely
con-vers•ing

con-ver-sion
con-vert
con-verter
con-vert-ible
con-vert•ing

con•vex
con-vex•ity
con•vey
con-vey-ance
con-vey•ing

con-veyor
con-vict
con-vict•ing
con-vic-tion
con-vince

con-vinces
con-vinc•ing
con-vinc-ingly
con-vo-ca-tion
con•voy

con-vul-sion
con-vul-sive
cooked
cook-ery
cook-ies

cook-ing
cook-out
cook-ware
cool-ant
cooled

cooler
cool-ing
co•op-er•ate
co•op-er-at•ing
co•op-era-tion

C

co•op-era-tive
co•or-di-nate
co•or-di-nat•ing
co•or-di-na-tion
co•or-di-na•tor

co•pay-ment
cop•ied
copier
cop•ies
co•pi-lot

cop•ing
co•pi-ous
cop•per
co•pro-ces•sor
copy

copy-holder
copy-ing
copy-right
copy-writer
coral

cor-dial
cor-dial•ity
cor-dially
cord-less
cor•don

cor-doned
cor-du•roy
cork-screw
cor•nea
cor•ner

cor-nered
cor-ner•ing
corner-stone
cor•net
cor-nice

corn-meal
corn-starch
cor-nu-co•pia
cor-ol-lary
co•rona

coro-nar•ies
coro-nary
coro-na-tion
coro-ner
co•rou-tine

cor-po•ral
cor-po-rate
cor-po-ra-tion
cor-po-ra-tive
corps

corpse
cor-pu-lence
cor-pu-lent
cor•pus
cor-pus•cle

cor•ral
cor-rect
cor-rect-able
cor-rect•ing
cor-rec-tion

cor-rec-tional
cor-rec-tive
cor-rectly
cor-re-late
cor-re-lat•ing

cor-re-la-tion
cor-re-spond
cor-re-spon-dence
cor-re-spon-dent
cor-re-spond•ing

cor-re-spond-ingly
cor-ri•dor
cor-ri-gi•ble
cor-robo-rate
cor-robo-rat•ing

cor-robo-ra-tion
cor-robo-ra-tive
cor-rode
cor-rod-ible
cor-rod•ing

cor-ro-sion
cor-ro-sive
cor-ru-gate
cor-ru-gated
cor-ru-ga-tion

cor-rupt
cor-rupt-ible
cor-rupt•ing
cor-rup-tion
cor-sage

cor-tege
cor-ti-sone
co•signer
co•sine
cos-metic

cos-met•ics
cos-me-tolo-gist
cos-me-tol•ogy
cos•mic
cos-mology

cos-mo-naut
cos-mo-poli•tan
cos•mos
co•spon-sor
co•spon-sored

cost-ing	count-ing	cov•ers
costly	count-less	co•vert
cos-tume	coun-tries	co•vertly
cot-tage	coun-try	cover--up
cot•ton	county	covet
couch-ing	cou•ple	cov-eted
cou•gar	cou-pled	cov-et•ous
cough-ing	cou-ples	cow•ard
coun-cil	cou-pling	cow-ard•ice
coun-cilor	cou•pon	co•worker
coun-sel	cour-age	coy•ote
coun-seled	cou-ra-geous	co•zily
coun-sel•ing	cou-rier	co•zi-ness
coun-selor	coursed	cozy
coun-sel•ors	courses	crab-bing
count-down	course-ware	crab-grass
counted	course-work	crack-down (n.)
coun-te-nance	cour-te•ous	cracked
counter	cour-te-ously	cracker
coun-ter•act	cour-te-sies	crack-ing
coun-ter-bal-anced	cour-tesy	crackle
coun-ter-charge	court-house	cra•dle
coun-ter-claim	court-ing	craft-ily
coun-tered	court--martial	crafti-ness
coun-ter-feit	court-room	crafts-man-ship
coun-ter-feit•ing	court-ship	crammed
coun-ter•ing	cousin	cram-ming
coun-ter-mine	cous-ins	cramped
coun-ter-part	co•vari-ance	cran-ber-ries
coun-ter-plea	cove-nant	cran-berry
coun-ter-sign	cove-nanted	cra-nial
coun-ter-spy	cover	cra-ni-ome•try
coun-ter-sued	cov-er•age	cra-nium
counter-top	cov-ered	crank-case
coun-ties	cov-er•ing	cranki-ness

crank-shaft
cranky
crashed
crashes
crash-ing

crash-worthy
crated
cra•ter
crat-ing
cra•vat

crav-ing
crawler
crawl-ing
crayon
cray•ons

cra-zily
cra-zi-ness
crazy
creamer
cream-ery

creamy
crease
cre•ate
cre-ated
cre-at•ing

cre-ation
cre-ative
cre-atively
cre-ative-ness
cre-ativ•ity

cre-ator
crea-ture
cre-dence
cre-den-tial
cre-denza

credi-bil•ity
cred-ible
credit
cred-it-able
cred-ited

cred-it•ing
credi-tor
credu-lous
creepi-ness
creep-ing

creepy
cre-mate
cre-mated
cre-ma-tion
cre-ma-to-rium

Cre•ole
creo-sote
creo-soted
crepe
cre-scendo

cres-cent
cre-vasse
crev-ice
cricket
cried

cries
crimi-nal
crimi-nal•ity
crimi-nally
crimi-nol•ogy

crim-son
cring-ing
crin-kle
crip-ple
crip-pled

crip-pling
cri•ses
cri•sis
cri-te•ria
cri-te-rion

critic
crit-ical
criti-cally
criti-cism
criti-cize

criti-cized
criti-ciz•ing
crit-ics
cri-tique
crock-ery

croco-dile
cro•cus
crooked
crook-ed-ness
crop-per

crop-ping
cross-bar
cross-connect
cross--country
crossed

cross--examine
crosses
cross-ing
cross-over
cross-road

cross-talk
cross-walk
crou•ton
crow-bar
crowded

crowd-ing
crowned
crown-ing
cru-cial
cru-ci•ble

cru-ci•fix
cru-ci-fix•ion
cru-cify
cru-elly
cru-elty

cruise
cruiser
cruises
crum-ble
crum-bling

cru-sade
cru-sader
cru-sad•ing
crushed
crusher

crush-ing
crush-proof
crus-ta-ceous
crutches
cry•ing

cryo-genic
cryo-gen•ics
crypt
cryp-tic
cryp-to-gram

cryp-tog-ra•phy
cryp-to-logic
crys-tal
crys-tal-li-za-tion
crys-tal-lize

crys-tal-liz•ing
cub•age
cubic
cu•bi-cal
cu•bi-cle

cuckoo
cu•cum-ber
cud•dle
cud-dle-some
cue

cui-sine
cul--de--sac
cu•li-nary
cul-mi-nate
cul-mi-nated

cul-mi-nat•ing
cul-mi-na-tion
cul-prit
cult-ist
cul-ti-vate

cul-ti-vat•ing
cul-ti-va-tion
cul-ti-va•tor
cul-tural
cul-tur-ally

cul-ture
cum-ber-some
cu•mu-la-tive
cu•mu-lus
cun-ning

cun-ningly
cup-board
cup-cake
cup•ful
cur-able

cu•rate
cu•ra-tor
curbed
curb-ing
curb-side

cur•dle
cured
cur•few
cur•ing
curio

cu•ri-os•ity
cu•ri-ous
curled
curler
cur-rant

cur-ren-cies
cur-rency
cur-rent
cur-rently
cur-ric•ula

cur-ricu•lar
cur-ricu•lum
cur-sive
cur•sor
cur-so-rily

cur-sors
cur-sory
cur-tail
cur-tail•ing
cur-tail-ment

cur-tain
curtsy
cur-va-ture
curved
cush-ion

cush-ioned
cush-ion•ing
cus-tard
cus-to-dial
cus-to-dian

cus-tody
cus•tom
cus-tom-arily
cus-tom•ary
cus-tomer

cus-tom•ers
cus-tom•ize
cus-tom-izes
cus-tom-iz•ing
cut-back *(n.)*

cu•ti-cle
cut-lery
cut•off *(n.)*
cut-offs
cut•out

cut-outs
cut•ter
cut-throat
cut-ting
cy•ber-net•ics

cycle
cy•cled
cy•cli-cal
cy•cling
cy•clone

cy•clo-rama
cyl-in•der
cym•bal
cynic
cyn-ical

cyni-cism
cy•press
cyst
Czecho-slo-va•kia

dab•ble
dab-bled
daf-fo•dil
dag•ger
dag-gers

dahlia
dai-lies
daily
dain-tily
dain-ti-ness

dainty
dair-ies
dairy
dai-sies
daisy

daisy-chain
daisy-wheel
dam•age
dam-aged
dam-ages

dam-ag•ing
dampen
damp-ened
damper
damp-ness

dancer
dances
danc-ing
dan-de-lion
dan•der

dan-druff
dandy
dan•ger
dan-ger•ous
dan-ger-ously

dan•gle
dan-gles
dan-gling
Dan•ish
dap•per

dare-devil
dar•ing
darken
darker
dark-ness

dark-room
dar-ling
dash-board
dashed
dash-ing

das-tardly
data
data-bank
data-base
data-center

data-flow
data-gram
data-link
data-logging
dated

date-line	dearly	de•canter
dat•ing	dearth	de•capi-tate
datum	death-bed	de•capi-tat•ing
daugh-ter	death-blow	de•capi-ta-tion
daunted	deathly	de•cath-lon
daw-dled	de•ba-cle	decay
daw-dling	de•base	de•cayed
dawned	de•base-ment	de•cay-ing
dawn-ing	de•bat-able	de•cease
day-break	de•bate	de•ce-dent
day-care	de•bater	de•ceit
day-dream	de•bat-ing	de•ceit-ful
day-light	de•bauch-ery	de•ceive
day-time	de•ben-ture	de•ceiv-ing
daz•zle	de•bili-tate	de•cel-er•ate
daz-zled	de•bili-tat•ing	de•cel-er-at•ing
daz-zling	de•bili-ta-tion	de•cel-era-tion
de•ac-ti-vate	debit	de•cel-era•tor
de•ac-ti-vated	deb-ited	De•cem-ber
de•ac-ti-vat•ing	deb-it•ing	de•cency
dead-beat	deb•its	de•cent
deaden	debo-nair	de•cently
dead-en•ing	de•brief	de•cen-tral•ize
dead-li•est	de•brief-ing	de•cen-tral-iz•ing
dead-line	de•bris	de•cep-tion
dead-lock	debtor	de•cep-tive
deadly	debt-ors	de•cep-tively
deafen	debug	deci-bel
deaf-en•ing	de•bug-ging	de•cide
deaf-ness	debut	de•cid-edly
dealer	de•cade	de•cid-ing
deal-ers	deca-dence	de•cidu-ous
deal-er-ship	deca-dent	deci-mal
deal-ing	de•caf-fein-ated	deci-mate
dealt	decal	deci-mat•ing

de•ci-pher
de•ci-pher•ing
de•ci-sion
de•ci-sive
de•ci-sively

dec-la-ma-tion
dec-la-ra-tion
de•clara-tive
de•clara-tory
de•clare

de•clar-ing
de•clas-sify
dec-li-na-tion
de•cline
de•clin-ing

de•code
de•coder
de•cod-ing
de•col-lator
de•com-piler

de•com-pose
de•com-pos•ing
de•com-po-si-tion
de•com-press
de•con-gest

de•con-ges-tant
de•con-gested
de•con-tami-nate
de•con-trol
decor

deco-rate
deco-rat•ing
deco-ra-tion
deco-ra-tive
deco-ra•tor

de•co-rum
de•cou-page
decoy
de•coyed
de•coy-ing

de•coys
de•crease
de•creases
de•creas-ing
de•creas-ingly

de•cree
de•cree-ing
de•crepit
de•cried
de•crimi-nal•ize

decry
de•cryp-tion
dedi-cate
dedi-cat•ing
dedi-ca-tion

dedi-ca-tory
de•duce
de•duc-ible
de•duc-ing
de•duct

de•duct-ible
de•duct-ing
de•duc-tion
de•duc-tive
deeded

deed-ing
deemed
deepen
deep-en•ing
deeper

deep-est
deeply
de•face
de•face-ment
de•fac-ing

defa-ma-tion
de•fama-tory
de•fame
de•fam-ing
de•fault

de•fault-ing
de•feat
de•feat-ist
de•fect
de•fect-ing

de•fec-tion
de•fec-tive
de•fec-tor
de•fend
de•fen-dant

de•fender
de•fend-ing
de•fense
de•fenses
de•fen-si•ble

de•fen-sive
de•fen-sively
defer
def-er-ence
de•fer-ral

de•ferred
de•fer-ring
de•fi-ance
de•fi-ant
de•fi-ciency

de•fi-cient
defi-cit
de•fied
de•fies
de•fin-able

de•fine
de•fin-ing
defi-nite
defi-nitely
defi-ni-tion

de•fini-tive
de•fini-tively
de•flate
de•flat-ing
de•fla-tion

de•fla-tion•ary
de•flect
de•flec-tion
de•flec-tor
de•form

de•form-ing
de•for-mity
de•fraud
de•fraud-ing
de•fray

de•frayal
de•frost
de•frosted
de•froster
de•frost-ing

de•funct
de•fuse
de•fus-ing
defy
de•fy-ing

de•gen-eracy
de•gen-er•ate
de•gen-er-at•ing
de•gen-era-tion
de•grad-able

deg-ra-da-tion
de•grade
de•grad-ing
de•greaser
de•greas-ing

de•gree
de•hu-man•ize
de•hu-man-iz•ing
de•hu-midify
de•hy-drate

de•hy-drat•ing
de•hy-dra-tion
deify
deity
de•ject

de•jec-tion
Dela-ware
Dela-war•ean
delay
de•lay-ing

de•lec-ta•ble
dele-gate
dele-gat•ing
dele-ga-tion
dele-ga-tory

de•lete
dele-te-ri•ous
de•let-ing
de•le-tion
de•lib-er•ate

de•lib-er-ately
de•lib-er-at•ing
de•lib-era-tion
de•lib-era-tive
deli-ca-cies

deli-cacy
deli-cate
deli-ca-tes•sen
de•li-cious
de•light

de•light-ful
de•light-fully
de•limit
de•limi-ta-tion
de•lim-iter

de•lin-eate
de•lin-eat•ing
de•lin-ea-tion
de•lin-quency
de•lin-quent

de•liri-ous
de•lir-ium
de•liver
de•liv-er-ance
de•liv-ered

de•liv-er•ies
de•liv-er•ing
de•liv-ery
de•lude
de•lud-ing

del•uge
de•lu-sion
de•luxe
delv-ing
de•mag-ne-tize

dema-gogue
de•mand
de•mand-ing
de•mar-cate
de•mar-ca-tion

de•mean
de•meanor
de•mented
de•men-tia
de•merit

de•mise
de•mo-bi-lize
de•mo-bi-liz•ing
de•moc-ra-cies
de•moc-racy

demo-crat
demo-cratic
de•modu-late
de•modu-la-tion
de•modu-la•tor

de•mog-ra-pher
de•mo-graphic
de•mog-ra•phy
de•mol-ish
de•mol-ish•ing

de•mo-li-tion
de•mon-stra•ble
dem-on-strate
dem-on-strat•ing
dem-on-stra-tion

de•mon-stra-tive
dem-on-stra•tor
de•mor-al•ize
de•mote
de•mot-ing

de•mo-tion
de•mount
demure
de•mur-rage
de•mur-ring

de•nial
de•nied
de•nies
denim
de•nomi-na-tion

de•nomi-na-tional
de•nomi-na•tor
de•no-ta-tion
de•no-ta-tive
de•note

de•not-ing
de•nounce
de•nounce-ment
dense-ness
den-sity

den•tal
dented
den-ti-frice
den-tist
den-tistry

den-ture
de•nun-cia-tion
deny
de•ny-ing
de•odor-ant

de•odor-ize
de•odor-izer
de•odor-iz•ing
de•part
de•part-ing

de•part-ment
de•part-men•tal
de•part-men-tally
de•par-ture
de•pend

de•pend-abil•ity
de•pend-able
de•pended
de•pen-dence
de•pen-dency

de•pen-dent
de•pend-ing
de•per-son-al•ize
de•pict
de•pict-ing

de•pic-tion
de•plane
de•plete
de•ple-tion
de•plor-able

de•plore
de•ploy
de•ploy-ing
de•ploy-ment
de•port

de•por-ta-tion
de•port-ing
de•port-ment
de•pose
de•poses

de•posit
de•pos-ited
de•pos-it•ing
de•po-si-tion
de•posi-tor

de•posi-to-ries	de•rive	de•sir-able
de•posi-tory	de•riv-ing	de•sire
depot	der-ma-tolo-gist	de•sir-ing
de•prave	der-ma-tol•ogy	de•sir-ous
de•prav-ity	de•scend	de•sist
de•pre-cia•ble	de•scen-dant	de•sist-ing
de•pre-ci•ate	de•scend-ing	desk-ing
de•pre-ci-ated	de•scent	desk-top
de•pre-ci-at•ing	de•scrib-able	deso-late
de•pre-cia-tion	de•scribe	deso-la-tion
de•press	de•scrib-ing	de•spair
de•pres-sant	de•scrip-tion	de•spair-ing
de•press-ing	de•scrip-tive	des-per•ate
de•pres-sion	de•scrip-tor	des-per-ately
de•pres-sor	dese-crate	des-pera-tion
de•pri-va-tion	dese-crat•ing	de•spi-ca•ble
de•prive	dese-cra-tion	de•spise
de•priv-ing	de•seg-re-gate	de•spis-ing
de•pro-gram	de•seg-re-ga-tion	de•spite
de•pro-gram•mer	de•sen-si-tize	de•spite-ful
depu-ties	de•sert *(v.)*	de•spite-fully
depu-tize	des•ert *(n.)*	de•spoil
dep•uty	de•serted	de•spon-dence
de•rail	de•sert-ing	de•spon-dent
de•rail-ment	de•ser-tion	des•pot
de•range	de•serve	des-sert
de•range-ment	de•servedly	des-ti-na-tion
de•regu-late	de•serv-ing	des-tined
de•regu-lat•ing	de•sign	des-tiny
de•regu-la-tion	des-ig-nate	des-ti-tute
dere-lict	des-ig-nat•ing	de•stroy
de•ride	des-ig-na-tion	de•stroyer
de•ri-sion	de•signer	de•stroy-ing
de•ri-sive	de•sign-ers	de•struct
de•riva-tive	de•sign-ing	de•struc-ti•ble

de•struc-tion
de•struc-tive
de•struc-tor
de•tach
de•tach-able

de•tail
de•tail-ing
de•tain
de•tain-ing
de•tain-ment

de•tect
de•tect-able
de•tect-ing
de•tec-tion
de•tec-tive

de•tec-tor
de•tente
de•ten-tion
deter
de•ter-gent

de•te-rio-rate
de•te-rio-rat•ing
de•te-rio-ra-tion
de•ter-mi-nant
de•ter-mi-na-tion

de•ter-mine
de•ter-min•ing
de•terred
de•ter-rence
de•ter-rent

de•ter-ring
de•test
de•test-able
de•test-ing
deto-nate

deto-nat•ing
deto-na-tion
deto-na•tor
de•tour
de•tour-ing

de•toxi-cant
de•toxi-cat•ing
de•toxi-ca-tion
de•toxi-fied
de•toxify

de•tract
de•tract-ing
de•trac-tion
de•trac-tor
det-ri-ment

det-ri-men•tal
de•valu-ate
de•valu-ation
de•value
dev-as-tate

dev-as-tat•ing
dev-as-ta-tion
de•velop
de•vel-oped
de•vel-oper

de•vel-op•ing
de•vel-op-ment
de•vi-ate
de•vi-at•ing
de•via-tion

de•vice
de•vi-ous
de•vise
de•vis-ing
de•void

de•volve
de•vote
de•vot-ing
de•vo-tion
de•vo-tional

de•vour
de•vout
dex-ter•ity
dex-ter•ous
dex-trose

dia-be•tes
dia-betic
dia-bolic
dia-bol-ical
di•ag-nose

di•ag-no•ses
di•ag-no•sis
di•ag-nos•tic
di•ag-nos-ti-cian
di•ago-nal

di•ago-nally
dia-gram
dia-gram-ming
dia-lect
dia-lec•tic

di•aled
di•aler
di•al-ing
dia-logue
dial--up *(adj.)*

di•aly-sis
di•ame-ter
dia-met•ric
dia-met-ri•cal
dia-mond

dia•per
dia-phragm
dia-ries
di•ar-rhea
diary

di•chotomy
dic-tate
dic-tat•ing
dic-ta-tion
dic-ta•tor

dic-ta-to-rial
dic-ta-tor-ship
dic-tion
dic-tio-nar•ies
dic-tio-nary

di•dac-tic
died
die•sel
diet
di•etary

di•eter
di•etet-ics
di•et-ing
di•eti-tian
dif•fer

dif-fer-ence
dif-fer•ent
dif-fer-en-tial
dif-fer-en-ti•ate
dif-fer-en-tia-tion

dif-fer-ently
dif-fer•ing
dif-fi-cult
dif-fi-cul-ties
dif-fi-culty

dif-fuse
dif-fus•ing
dif-fu-sion
di•gest
di•gest-ible

di•gest-ing
di•ges-tion
di•ges-tive
dig-ging
digit

digi-tal
digi-ti-za-tion
digi-tize
digi-tizer
digi-tiz•ing

dig-ni-fied
dig-nify
dig-ni-tar•ies
dig-ni-tary
dig-nity

di•gress
di•gress-ing
di•gres-sion
di•lapi-date
di•lapi-da-tion

di•late
di•la-tion
di•lemma
dili-gence
dili-gent

dili-gently
di•lute
di•lut-ing
di•lu-tion
di•men-sion

di•men-sional
di•min-ish
di•min-ish•ing
dimi-nu-tion
di•minu-tive

dim•mer
dim•ple
diner
di•ners
di•nette

din•ghy
dingy
din•ing
din•ner
din-ner-ware

di•no-saur
di•oce-san
dio-cese
diode
di•orama

di•ox-ide
diph-the•ria
diph-thong
di•ploma
di•plo-macy

di•plo-mas
dip-lo•mat
dip-lo-matic
dip-lo-mati-cally
dip•per

dip-ping
dip-stick
di•rect
di•rect-ing
di•rec-tion

d

53

di•rec-tional
di•rec-tive
di•rectly
di•rect-ness
di•rec-tor

di•rec-tor•ate
di•rec-to-ries
di•rec-tory
di•ri-gi•ble
dirt-ied

dirty
dis-abili-ties
dis-abili•ity
dis-able
dis-abling

dis-ad-van-tage
dis-ad-van-tages
dis-af-fec-tion
dis-agree
dis-agree-able

dis-agree•ing
dis-agree-ment
dis-allow
dis-al-low-ance
dis-al-low•ing

dis-ap-pear
dis-ap-pear-ance
dis-ap-pear•ing
dis-ap-point
dis-ap-point•ing

dis-ap-point-ment
dis-ap-proval
dis-ap-prove
dis•arm
dis-ar-ma-ment

dis-ar•ray
dis-as-sem-ble
dis-as-so-ci•ate
di•sas-ter
di•sas-trous

dis-avow
dis-band
dis-band•ing
dis•bar
dis-bar-ring

dis-be-lief
dis-be-lieve
dis-be-liever
dis-burse
dis-burse-ment

dis-burs•ing
dis-card
dis-card•ing
dis-cern
dis-cern-ible

dis-cern•ing
dis-cern-ment
dis-charge
dis-charges
dis-charg•ing

dis-ci•ple
dis-ci-pli-nar•ian
dis-ci-plin•ary
dis-ci-pline
dis-ci-plin•ing

dis-claim
dis-claimer
dis-close
dis-clos•ing
dis-clo-sure

disco
dis-cog-ra•phy
dis-color
dis-col-ored
dis-com-fort

dis-com-po-sure
dis-con-nect
dis-con-nect•ing
dis-con-nec-tion
dis-con-tent

dis-con-tent-ment
dis-con-tinu-ance
dis-con-tinue
dis-con-tin•ued
dis-con-tinu•ing

dis-cord
dis-cor-dance
dis-cor-dant
dis-co-theque
dis-count

dis-count•ing
dis-cour•age
dis-cour-age-ment
dis-cour-ages
dis-cour-ag•ing

dis-course
dis-cours•ing
dis-cour-te•ous
dis-cover
dis-cov-ered

dis-cov-erer
dis-cov-er•ies
dis-cov-er•ing
dis-cov•ery
dis-credit

dis-cred-ited
dis-cred-it•ing
dis-creet
dis-creetly
dis-crep-an-cies

dis-crep-ancy
dis-crete
dis-cre-tion
dis-cre-tion•ary
dis-crimi-nate

dis-crimi-nat•ing
dis-crimi-na-tion
dis-crimi-na-tory
dis•cus
dis-cuss

dis-cusses
dis-cuss•ing
dis-cus-sion
dis-dain
dis-ease

dis-em-bark
dis-em-bar-ka-tion
dis-em-body
dis-en-chant-ment
dis-en-fran-chise

dis-en-gage
dis-fa•vor
dis-fig•ure
dis-fig-ure-ment
dis-func-tion

dis-func-tional
dis-grace
dis-grace•ful
dis-grun-tled
dis-guise

dis-gust
dis-gust•ing
dis-heart-en•ing
dishes
di•shevel

dis-hon•est
dis-hon-esty
dis-honor
dis-hon-or-able
dis-hon-or-ably

dis-hon-ored
dish-washer
dis-il-lu-sion
dis-in-fect
dis-in-fec-tant

dis-in-for-ma-tion
dis-in-herit
dis-in-ter•est
dis-in-ter-ested
dis-join

disk
dis-kette
dis-like
dis-lo-cate
dis-lo-cat•ing

dis-lo-ca-tion
dis-lodge
dis-loyal
dis-loy-alty
dis•mal

dis-man•tle
dis-man-tling
dis•may
dis-mem•ber
dis-mem-ber-ment

dis-miss
dis-missal
dis-misses
dis-miss•ing
dis-mount

dis-mount•ing
dis-obe-di-ence
dis-obe-di•ent
dis-obey
dis-or•der

dis-or-derly
dis-or-ga-nize
dis-ori•ent
dis•own
dis-own•ing

dis-par•age
dis-par-age-ment
dis-par•ity
dis-pas-sion•ate
dis-patch

dis-patcher
dis-patch•ing
dis•pel
dis-pel-ling
dis-pen-sary

dis-pen-sa-tion
dis-pense
dis-penser
dis-pens•ing
dis-per-sion

dis-place
dis-place-ment
dis-play
dis-play•ing
dis-please

dis-pleas•ing
dis-plea-sure
dis-pos-able
dis-posal
dis-pose

dis-pos•ing
dis-po-si-tion
dis-pos-sess
dis-pos-ses-sion
dis-pro-por-tion

dis-pro-por-tional
dis-prov-able
dis-prove
dis-prov•ing
dis-pu-ta•ble

dis-pu-ta-tion
dis-pute
dis-put•ing
dis-quali-fi-ca-tion
dis-quali-fied

dis-qual•ify
dis-quali-fy•ing
dis-re-gard
dis-re-pair
dis-repu-ta•ble

dis-re-pute
dis-re-spect
dis-re-spect•ful
dis-rupt
dis-rupt•ing

dis-rup-tion
dis-rup-tive
dis-sat-is-fac-tion
dis-sat-is-fac-tory
dis-sat-is-fied

dis-sat-isfy
dis-sect
dis-sect•ing
dis-sec-tion
dis-sem•ble

dis-sem-bling
dis-semi-nate
dis-semi-nat•ing
dis-semi-na-tion
dis-sen-sion

dis-sent
dis-senter
dis-ser-ta-tion
dis-ser-vice
dis-si-dent

dis-simi•lar
dis-si-pate
dis-si-pa-tion
dis-solve
dis-solv•ing

dis-so-nance
dis-so-nant
dis-suade
dis-sua-sion
dis-tance

dis-tances
dis-tanc•ing
dis-tant
dis-taste
dis-taste•ful

dis-till
dis-til-late
dis-til-la-tion
dis-till•ery
dis-tinct

dis-tinc-tion
dis-tinc-tive
dis-tinctly
dis-tin-guish
dis-tin-guish-able

dis-tin-guished
dis-tin-guish•ing
dis-tort
dis-tort•ing
dis-tor-tion

dis-tract
dis-tract•ing
dis-trac-tion
dis-traught
dis-tress

dis-tress•ful
dis-tress•ing
dis-trib•ute
dis-trib-ut•ing
dis-tri-bu-tion

dis-tribu-tive
dis-tribu•tor
dis-tribu-tor-ship
dis-trict
dis-trust

dis-trust•ful
dis-turb
dis-tur-bance
dis-turb•ing
dis•use

ditches
ditto
divan
diver
di•verge

di•ver-gent
di•verg•ing
di•vers
di•verse
di•ver-si-fied

di•ver-sify
di•ver-sion
di•ver-sity
di•vert
di•vert-ing

di•vest
di•vest-ing
di•vid-able
di•vide
divi-dend

di•vider
di•vid-ing
di•vine
div•ing
di•vin-ity

di•vis-ible
di•vi-sion
di•vi-sor
di•vorce
di•vorcée

di•vorce-ment
di•vorces
di•vorc-ing
divot
di•vulge

di•vul-gence
diz-zily
diz-zi-ness
dizzy
do•able

doc•ile
do•cil-ity
docket
dock-eted
dock-et•ing

dock-ing
doc•tor
doc-toral
doc-tor•ate
doc-tors

doc-trinal
doc-trine
docu-ment
docu-men-tary
docu-men-ta-tion

docu-ment•ing
dodg-ing
dog•ged
dogma
dog-matic

dog-mati-cally
dog-ma-tism
dog-ma-tist
dog-ma-tize
dog-wood

dol-drums
dol•lar
dol-lars
dol-phin
do•main

do•mes-tic
do•mes-ti-cally
do•mes-ti-cate
do•mes-ti-ca-tion
do•mi-cile

do•mi-cili•ary
domi-nance
domi-nant
domi-nate
domi-nat•ing

domi-na-tion
domi-neer•ing
do•min-ion
do•nate
do•nat-ing

do•na-tion
don•key
donor
do•nors
door-bell

door-knob
door-stop
door-way
dor-mant
dor-mi-to-ries

dor-mi-tory
dos•age
dos-sier
dou•ble
dou-bles

dou-bling
dou•bly
doubted
doubter
doubt-ful

doubt-ing
doubt-less
dough-nut
dous-ing
dove-tail

dowel	drab-ness	dream-ing
dow-eled	drafted	dreary
dow-el•ing	draft-ing	dredg-ing
down-beat	dragged	drenched
down-cast	drag-ging	dressed
downed	drag-net	dresser
down-fall	dragon	dress-ers
down-grade	drag-ons	dresses
down-grading	drag-ster	dress-ing
down-hearted	drain-age	dressy
down-ing	drained	dried
down-line	drainer	drier
down-load	drain-ing	drifted
down-load-able	drama	drift-ing
down-loaded	dra-matic	drift-wood
down-load•ing	dra-mati-cally	drilled
down-pour	dra-ma-tist	driller
down-range	dra-ma-ti-za-tion	drill-ing
down-right	dra-ma-tize	drink-able
down-side	draped	drinker
down-size	drap-er•ies	drink-ing
down-siz•ing	drap-ery	dripped
down-stairs	drap-ing	drip-ping
down-stream	dras-tic	drive--in *(n.)*
down-time	dras-ti-cally	drivel
down-town	draw-back	driven
down-trend	drawee	driver
down-trod•den	drawer	driv-ers
down-turn	draw-ers	drive-way
down-ward	draw-ing	driv-ing
down-wind	dray-age	driz-zle
dowry	dread-ful	driz-zling
dozen	dread-fully	drome-dary
doz•ens	dreamed	drop-out *(n.)*
doz•ing	dreamer	dropped

drop-per
drop-ping
drought
drowned
drown-ing

drowsy
drudg-ery
drugged
drug-ging
drug-gist

drug-store
drummed
drum-mer
drum-ming
drum-roll

drum-stick
drunk-ard
drunken
drunk-en-ness
dryer

dry•ers
dry•ing
dual
dub•bing
du•bi-ous

duc•ats
duct
duc-tile
duel
du•eled

du•el-ing
du•el-ist
dues
duet
duf•fel

dug•out
dull-ness
duly
dumb-bell
dumb-waiter

dummy
dumped
dump-ing
dun-ga•ree
dun-geon

duo-de•nal
du•plex
du•plexer
du•plex-ing
du•pli-cate

du•pli-cated
du•pli-cat•ing
du•pli-ca-tion
du•pli-ca•tor
du•ra-bil•ity

du•ra-ble
du•ra-tion
du•ress
dur•ing
dust-cloth

dust-cover
dusted
dust-ing
dusty
du•ties

du•ti-ful
duty
dwarf-ish
dweller
dwell-ing

dwin-dle
dwin-dling
dyed
dye•ing
dyes

dying
dy•namic
dy•nami-cally
dy•nam-ics
dy•na-mite

dy•namo
dy•nasty
dys-func-tion
dys-func-tional
dys-lexia

eager
ea•gerly
eagle
ear-ache
ear-drum

ear•ful
ear-lier
ear-li•est
early
ear-mark

ear-mark•ing
ear-muff
earned
earner
earn-ers

ear-nest
ear-nestly
earn-ing
earn-ings
ear-phone

ear-piece
ear-plug
ear-rings
ear-shot
ear-split•ting

earthly
earth-quake
earth-shak•ing
earthy
easel

ea•sels
ease-ment
eas•ier
easi-est
eas•ily

easi-ness
eas•ing
Eas•ter
east-erly
east-ern

East-erner
east-ward
easy
easy-going
eat-able

eaten
eat•ery
eat•ing
eaves-drop
eaves-drop-ping

ec•cen-tric
ec•cen-tric•ity
ec•cle-si-as-ti•cal
eche-lon
echo

ech•oes
echo-ing
eclipse
eclips-ing
eclip-tic

eco-log-ical
ecolo-gist
ecol-ogy
econo-met-rics
eco-nomic

eco-nom-ical
eco-nomi-cally
eco-nom•ics
econo-mies
econo-mist

econo-mize
econo-miz•ing
econ-omy
eco-sphere
ec•stasy

ec•static
Ec•ua-dor
Ec•ua-doran
ecu-men-ical
edged

edge-wise
edg•ing
ed•ible
edict
edi-fi-ca-tion

edi-fice
edify
edi-fy•ing
edit
ed•ited

ed•it-ing
edi-tion
edi•tor
edi-to-rial
edi-to-ri-al•ize

edi-to-ri-al-iz•ing
edi-to-ri-ally
edi-tors
edu-ca•ble
edu-cate

edu-cat•ing
edu-ca-tion
edu-ca-tional
edu-ca-tion-ally
edu-ca-tive

edu-ca•tor
edu-ca-tors
ef•face
ef•face-ment
ef•fac-ing

ef•fect
ef•fected
ef•fect-ing
ef•fec-tive
ef•fec-tively

ef•fec-tive-ness
ef•fec-tual
ef•fec-tu•ate
ef•fer-ves-cence
ef•fer-ves-cent

ef•fi-ca-cious
ef•fi-cacy
ef•fi-ciency
ef•fi-cient
ef•fi-ciently

ef•figy
ef•fort
ef•fort-less
ef•ful-gence
ef•ful-gent

egg•nog
egg-plant
egg-shell
ego-cen-tric
ego-cen-tric•ity

ego-is•tic
ego-is-ti•cal
ego-ma•nia
ego-tist
ego-tis•tic

Egypt
Egyp-tian
eigh-teen
eighth
eight-ies

eighti-eth
eighty
ei•ther
eject
ejected

eject-ing
ejec-tion
elabo-rate
elabo-rately
elabo-ra-tion

elapse
elapses
elaps-ing
elas-tic
elas-tic•ity

elated
ela-tion
elbow
elbow-room
elder

el•derly
el•dest
elect
elect-ing
elec-tion

elec-tive
elec-tor
elec-toral
elec-tor•ate
elec-tric

elec-tri•cal
elec-tri-cian
elec-tric•ity
elec-tri-fi-ca-tion
elec-tri-fied

elec-trify
elec-tro-cute
elec-tro-cu-tion
elec-trode
elec-tro-jet

elec-tro-lyte
elec-tro-mag-netic
elec-tron
elec-tronic
elec-troni-cally

elec-tron•ics
elec-tro-plate
elec-tro-sen-si-tive
elec-tro-shock
elec-tro-static

ele-gance
ele-gant
ele-gantly
ele-ment
ele-men•tal

ele-men-tary
ele-phant
ele-vate
ele-vat•ing
ele-va-tion

ele-va•tor
eleven
elev-enth
elicit
elic-ited

elic-it•ing
eli-gi-bil•ity
eli-gi•ble
elimi-nate
elimi-nat•ing

elimi-na-tion
elimi-na•tor
elite
elixir
el•lipse

el•lip-sis
el•lip-tic
el•lip-ti•cal
elo-cu-tion
elon-gate

e

elon-gat•ing
elon-ga-tion
elope-ment
elop-ing
elo-quence

elo-quent
else-where
elu-ci-date
elu-ci-dat•ing
elu-ci-da-tion

elude
elud-ing
elu-sive
ema-ci•ate
ema-cia-tion

ema-nate
ema-na-tion
eman-ci-pate
eman-ci-pat•ing
eman-ci-pa-tion

emas-cu-late
emas-cu-lat•ing
em•balm
em•balmer
em•balm-ing

em•bank
em•bank-ment
em•bargo
em•bar-goes
em•bark

em•bark-ing
em•bar-rass
em•bar-rass•ing
em•bar-rass-ment
em•bassy

em•bat-tled
em•bed-ded
em•bel-lish
em•bel-lish-ment
em•bez-zle

em•bez-zle-ment
em•bez-zler
em•bez-zling
em•blem
em•bod-ied

em•bodi-ment
em•body
em•bo-lism
em•boss
em•boss-ing

em•brace
em•brac-ing
em•bryo
emcee
em•cee-ing

em•cees
em•er-ald
emerge
emer-gence
emer-gen-cies

emer-gency
emer-gent
emerges
emerg-ing
emer-iti

emeri-tus
emi-grant
emi-grate
emi-grat•ing
emi-gra-tion

emi-nence
emi-nent
em•is-sary
emis-sion
emit-ted

emit-ting
emo-tion
emo-tional
emo-tion-ally
emo-tion-less

em•pa-thy
em•peror
em•pha-ses
em•pha-sis
em•pha-size

em•pha-sizes
em•pha-siz•ing
em•phatic
em•phati-cally
em•phy-sema

em•pire
em•pir-ical
em•ploy
em•ploy-able
em•ployee

em•ployer
em•ploy-ing
em•ploy-ment
em•po-rium
em•power

em•pow-ered
em•pow-er•ing
emp-tied
emp-ties
emp-ti-ness

empty
emp-ty•ing
emu-late
emu-lat•ing
emu-la-tion

emu-la•tor
en•able
en•abling
enact
en•acted

en•act-ing
en•act-ment
enamel
enam-eled
enam-el•ing

en•am-ored
en•cased
en•case-ment
en•cas-ing
en•chant

en•chant-ing
en•chant-ment
en•chi-lada
en•ci-pher
en•ci-pher•ing

en•cir-cle
en•cir-cl•ing
en•close
en•clos-ing
en•clo-sure

en•code
en•coder
en•cod-ing
en•com-pass
en•com-passed

en•com-pass•ing
en•core
en•coun-ter
en•coun-ter•ing
en•cour-age

en•cour-ages
en•cour-ag•ing
en•croach
en•croach-ing
en•croach-ment

en•crypted
en•cryp-tion
en•crypts
en•cum-ber
en•cum-ber•ing

en•cum-brance
en•cy-clo-pe•dia
en•cy-clo-pe•dic
en•dan-ger
en•dan-ger•ing

en•dear
en•dear-ing
en•dear-ment
en•deavor
en•deav-ored

en•deav-or•ing
en•deav-ors
ended
end•ing
end-less

end-note
en•do-crine
en•do-cri-no-logic
en•do-cri-nolo-gist
en•dorse

en•dorse-ment
en•dorses
en•dors-ing
endow
en•dowed

en•dow-ing
en•dow-ment
en•dur-able
en•dur-ance
en•dure

en•dur-ing
ene-mies
enemy
en•er-getic
en•er-gize

en•er-gizer
en•er-giz•ing
en•ergy
en•fold
en•force

en•force-able
en•force-ment
en•forcer
en•forc-ing
en•fran-chise

en•fran-chis•ing
en•gage
en•gage-ment
en•gages
en•gag-ing

en•gag-ingly
en•gen-der
en•gine
en•gi-neer
en•gi-neer•ing

e

En•gland
En•glish
en•grave
en•graver
en•grav-ing

en•gross
en•gross-ing
en•gulf
en•gulf-ing
en•hance

en•hance-ment
en•hances
en•hanc-ing
enigma
en•join

en•join-ing
enjoy
en•joy-able
en•joy-ing
en•joy-ment

en•large
en•large-ment
en•larg-ing
en•lighten
en•light-ened

en•light-en•ing
en•light-en-ment
en•list
en•list-ing
en•list-ment

en•liven
en•liv-en•ing
en•mity
enor-mity
enor-mous

enor-mously
enough
en•plane
en•rage
en•rag-ing

en•rap-ture
en•rich
en•rich-ing
en•rich-ment
en•roll

en•rollee
en•roll-ing
en•roll-ment
en•sem-ble
en•shrine

en•shrin-ing
en•shroud
en•sign
en•slave
en•slave-ment

en•snare
en•snare-ment
ensue
en•sued
en•su-ing

en•sure
en•sur-ing
en•tail
en•tail-ing
en•tan-gle

en•tan-gle-ment
en•tan-gl•ing
enter
en•tered
en•ter-ing

en•ter-prise
en•ter-pris•ing
en•ter-tain
en•ter-tainer
en•ter-tain•ing

en•ter-tain-ment
en•throne
en•thused
en•thu-si•asm
en•thu-si•ast

en•thu-si-as•tic
en•tice
en•tice-ment
en•tic-ing
en•tire

en•tirely
en•tirety
en•ti-ties
en•ti-tle
en•ti-tle-ment

en•ti-tling
en•tity
en•tomb
en•tomb-ment
en•to-mo-log-ical

en•to-molo-gist
en•to-mol•ogy
en•tou-rage
en•trance
en•trance-ment

en•trant
en•trap
en•trap-ment
en•trap-ping
en•treat

en•treat-ies	en•vi-sion•ing	eques-trian
en•treaty	envoy	equi-dis-tance
en•tree	en•voys	equi-lib-rium
en•trench	en•vy-ing	equi-nox
en•trench-ment	en•zyme	equip
en•tre-pre-neur	epi-cen•ter	equip-ment
en•tries	epi-demic	equip-ping
en•trenched	epi-der•mal	eq•ui-ta•ble
en•trust	epi-der•mic	eq•uity
en•trusted	epi-der•mis	equiva-lence
en•trust-ing	epi-lepsy	equiva-lency
en•trust-ment	epi-lep•tic	equiva-lent
entry	epi-logue	equivo-cal
entry-way	epi-sode	equivo-cally
enu-mer•ate	epis-tle	equivo-cate
enu-mer-at•ing	epi-taph	equivo-ca-tion
enu-mera-tion	epit-ome	eradi-ca•ble
enu-mera-tive	epito-mize	eradi-cate
enu-mera•tor	epito-miz•ing	eradi-cat•ing
enun-ci•ate	epoch	eradi-ca-tion
enun-ci-at•ing	equa-ble	eradi-ca•tor
enun-cia-tion	equa-bly	eras-able
en•velop *(v.)*	equal	erase
en•ve-lope *(n.)*	equaled	eraser
en•vel-oped	equal-ing	eras-ers
en•vel-op•ing	equal-ity	erases
en•vel-op-ment	equal-iza-tion	eras-ing
en•vi-able	equal-ize	era-sure
en•vi-ably	equal-izes	erect
en•vied	equal-iz•ing	erec-tile
en•vi-ous	equally	erect-ing
en•vi-ron-ment	equate	erec-tion
en•vi-ron-men•tal	equa-tion	er•go-nom•ics
en•virons	equa-tor	erode
en•vi-sion	equa-to-rial	erod-ible

e

erod-ing
eroge-nous
ero-sion
er•rand
er•rant

er•rata
er•ratic
er•rati-cally
er•ra-tum
err•ing

er•ro•ne•ous
er•ro-ne-ously
error
er•rors
eru-dite

eru-di-tion
erupt
erup-tion
es•ca-late
es•ca-lat•ing

es•ca-la-tion
es•ca-la•tor
es•cap-able
es•ca-pade
es•cape

es•capee
es•cape-ment
es•cap-ing
es•cap-ism
es•cheat

es•chew
es•chew-ing
es•cort
es•cort-ing
es•crow

Es•kimo
Es•ki-mos
esopha-gus
es•pe-cial
es•pe-cially

es•pio-nage
es•pouse
es•pous-ing
es•quire
essay

es•says
es•sence
es•sen-tial
es•sen-tially
es•tab-lish

es•tab-lishes
es•tab-lish•ing
es•tab-lish-ment
es•tate
es•teem

es•ti-mate
es•ti-mat•ing
es•ti-ma-tion
es•ti-ma•tor
es•trange

es•trange-ment
es•tu-ary
etch-ing
eter-nal
eter-nally

eter-nity
ether
ethe-real
eth-ical
ethi-cally

eth•ics
Ethio-pia
Ethio-pian
eth•nic
eth-yl•ene

etio-log-ical
eti-quette
ety-mo-log-ical
ety-mol•ogy
eu•lo-gies

eu•lo-gize
eu•logy
eu•phe-mism
eu•phe-mize
eu•pho-ni•ous

eu•phony
eu•pho-ria
eu•reka
Eu•ro-dol-lars
Eu•rope

Eu•ro-pean
evacu-ate
evacu-at•ing
evacu-ation
evaded

evad-ing
evalu-ate
evalu-at•ing
evalu-ation
evalu-ative

evalu-ator
evan-ge-lism
evan-ge-list
evapo-rate
evapo-rat•ing

66

evapo-ra-tion	evo-lu-tion•ary	ex•cel-lent
evapo-ra-tive	evo-lu-tion•ist	ex•cel-ling
evapo-ra•tor	evolve	ex•cept
eva-sion	evolv-ing	ex•cept-ing
eva-sive	ex•ac-er•bate	ex•cep-tion
even-handed	ex•ac-er-bat•ing	ex•cep-tional
eve-ning	ex•ac-er-ba-tion	ex•cep-tion-ally
evenly	exact	ex•cerpt
event	ex•act-ing	ex•cess
event-ful	ex•actly	ex•cesses
even-tide	ex•ag-ger•ate	ex•ces-sive
even-tual	ex•ag-ger-at•ing	ex•ces-sively
even-tu-ally	ex•ag-gera-tion	ex•change
ever-lasting	exalt	ex•change-able
ever-more	ex•al-ta-tion	ex•chang-ing
every-body	ex•alted	ex•cise
every-day	ex•alt-ing	ex•cis-ing
every-one	ex•ami-na-tion	ex•ci-sion
every-place	ex•am-ine	ex•cit-able
every-thing	ex•am-iner	ex•cite
every-where	ex•am-in•ing	ex•cit-edly
evict	ex•am-ple	ex•cite-ment
evicted	ex•as-per•ate	ex•cit-ing
evict-ing	ex•as-per-at•ing	ex•claim
evic-tion	ex•as-pera-tion	ex•claim-ing
evi-dence	ex•ca-vate	ex•cla-ma-tion
evi-dences	ex•ca-vat•ing	ex•clama-tory
evi-denc•ing	ex•ca-va-tion	ex•clude
evi-dent	ex•ca-va•tor	ex•cluded
evi-den•tly	ex•ceed	ex•clud-ing
evinc-ible	ex•ceed-ing	ex•clu-sion
evo-ca•ble	ex•ceed-ingly	ex•clu-sive
evoke	excel	ex•clu-sively
evok-ing	ex•celled	ex•clu-sive-ness
evo-lu-tion	ex•cel-lence	ex•clu-siv•ity

e

ex•cre-ment
ex•crete
ex•cre-tion
ex•cru-ci•ate
ex•cru-ci-at•ing

ex•cru-cia-tion
ex•cur-sion
ex•cus-able
ex•cuse
ex•cuses

ex•cus-ing
exe-cut-able
exe-cute
exe-cut•ing
exe-cu-tion

exe-cu-tioner
ex•ecu-tive
ex•ecu-tor
ex•ecu-trix
ex•em-plary

ex•em-pli-fies
ex•em-plify
ex•empt
ex•emp-tion
ex•er-cise

ex•er-cises
ex•er-cis•ing
exert
ex•ert-ing
ex•er-tion

ex•hal-ant
ex•hale
ex•haust
ex•haust-ing
ex•haus-tion

ex•haus-tive
ex•hibit
ex•hib-ited
ex•hib-it•ing
ex•hi-bi-tion

ex•hi-bi-tion•ist
ex•hibi-tor
ex•hila-rate
ex•hila-ra-tion
ex•hort

ex•hor-ta-tion
ex•hort-ing
ex•hume
ex•hum-ing
exile

ex•iled
ex•il-ing
exist
ex•isted
ex•is-tence

ex•is-ten-tial•ism
ex•is-ten-tial•ist
ex•ist-ing
ex•ists
ex•ited

ex•it-ing
exo•dus
ex•on-er•ate
ex•on-er-at•ing
ex•on-era-tion

ex•or-bi-tant
ex•or-cise
ex•or-cism
ex•or-cist
exo-sphere

ex•otic
ex•pand
ex•pand-able
ex•pand-ing
ex•panse

ex•pan-sion
ex•pan-sion•ary
ex•pan-sive
ex•pa-tri•ate
ex•pa-tria-tion

ex•pect
ex•pec-tancy
ex•pec-tant
ex•pec-ta-tion
ex•pect-ing

ex•pe-di-ency
ex•pe-di•ent
ex•pe-di-ently
ex•pe-dite
ex•pe-dit•ing

ex•pe-di-tion
ex•pe-di-tious
ex•pe-di-tiously
ex•pe-di•tor
expel

ex•pelled
ex•pel-ling
ex•pend
ex•pend-able
ex•pend-ing

ex•pen-di-ture
ex•pense
ex•pens-ing
ex•pen-sive
ex•pe-ri-ence

ex•pe-ri-ences
ex•pe-ri-enc•ing
ex•peri-ment
ex•peri-men•tal
ex•peri-men-tally

ex•peri-mented
ex•peri-ment•ing
ex•pert
ex•per-tise
ex•pertly

ex•pi-ra-tion
ex•pire
ex•pired
ex•pir-ing
ex•plain

ex•plain-ing
ex•pla-na-tion
ex•plana-tory
ex•ple-tive
ex•pli-cate

ex•plicit
ex•plic-itly
ex•plic-it-ness
ex•plode
ex•plod-ing

ex•ploit
ex•ploi-ta-tion
ex•ploit-ing
ex•plo-ra-tion
ex•plor-atory

ex•plore
ex•plorer
ex•plor-ing
ex•plo-sion
ex•plo-sive

ex•po-nent
ex•po-nen-tial
ex•port
ex•por-ta-tion
ex•porter

ex•port-ing
ex•pose *(v.)*
ex•posé *(n.)*
ex•pos-ing
ex•po-si-tion

ex•posi-tive
ex•posi-tor
ex•posi-tory
ex•pos-tu-late
ex•pos-tu-lat•ing

ex•pos-tu-la-tion
ex•po-sure
ex•pound
ex•pound-ing
ex•press

ex•presses
ex•press-ing
ex•pres-sion
ex•pres-sive
ex•pressly

express-way
ex•pul-sion
ex•qui-site
ex•qui-sitely
ex•tend

ex•tend-able
ex•tend-ing
ex•ten-sion
ex•ten-sive
ex•ten-sively

ex•tent
ex•tenu-ate
ex•tenu-at•ing
ex•te-rior
ex•ter-mi-nate

ex•ter-mi-nat•ing
ex•ter-mi-na-tion
ex•ter-mi-na•tor
ex•ter-nal
ex•ter-nally

ex•tinct
ex•tinc-tion
ex•tin-guish
ex•tin-guisher
extol

ex•tolled
ex•tol-ling
ex•tort
ex•tor-tion
extra

ex•tract
ex•tract-ing
ex•trac-tion
ex•trac-tor
ex•tra-dite

ex•tra-di-tion
ex•tra-mari•tal
ex•tra-mu•ral
ex•tra-ne•ous
ex•traor-di-narily

ex•traor-di-nary
ex•trapo-late
ex•trapo-lat•ing
ex•trapo-la-tion
ex•tra-sen-sory

ex•trava-gance
ex•trava-gant
ex•trava-ganza
ex•treme
ex•tremely

fac-sim•ile
fac-tion
fac-tional
fac-tious
fac-ti-tious

ex•trem-ist
ex•tremi-ties
ex•trem-ity
ex•tri-cate
ex•tri-cat•ing

fable
fa•bled
fa•bles
fab•ric
fab-ri-cate

fac•tor
fac-to-ries
fac-tor•ing
fac-tors
fac-tory

ex•trin-sic
ex•tro-vert
ex•tru-sion
exu-ber-ance
exu-ber•ant

fab-ri-cat•ing
fab-ri-ca-tion
fab-ri-ca•tor
fab-rics
fabu-lous

fac-tual
fac-tu-ally
fac-ul-ties
fac-ulty
fad-dish

exult
ex•ul-tant
ex•ul-ta-tion
eye-brow
eyed

fa•cade
faced
faces
facet
fa•ce-tious

faded
fad•ing
Fahr-en-heit
failed
fail-ing

eye-glasses
eye•ing
eye-lash
eye•lid
eye--opener

fac•ets
fa•cial
fac•ile
fa•cili-tate
fa•cili-tat•ing

fail-ure
fainted
faint-hearted
faint-ing
fair

eye-sight
eye-sore
eye-tooth
eye-witness

fa•cili-ta-tion
fa•cili-ta•tor
fa•cili-ties
fa•cil-ity
fac•ing

fairer
fair-est
fair-ground
fairly
fair--minded

70

fair-ness	fa•mil-iar-iz•ing	farm-land
fair-way	fami-lies	far•row
faith-ful	fam•ily	far-sighted
faith-fully	fam•ine	far-sight-ed-ness
faith-ful-ness	fam•ish	far-ther
faith-less	fa•mous	far-thest
fak•ery	fa•mously	fas-ci-nate
fal-la-cies	fa•natic	fas-ci-nat•ing
fal-la-cious	fa•nat-ical	fas-ci-na-tion
fal-la-ciously	fa•nati-cism	fash-ion
fal-lacy	fan-cied	fash-ion-able
fall-away (n.)	fan-cier	fash-ion•ing
fallen	fan-cies	fasted
fal-li•ble	fan-ci•ful	fas•ten
fall-ing	fancy	fas-tened
fall-out (n.)	fan-fare	fas-tener
false-hood	fan-fold	fas-ten•ing
falsely	fan-ta-sies	faster
false-ness	fan-ta-size	fast-est
fal-setto	fan-ta-siz•ing	fas-tidi•ous
fal-si-fied	fan-tas•tic	fast-ing
fal-sify	fan-tasy	fatal
fal-si-fy•ing	far-ci•cal	fa•tal-ist
fal-sity	fare-well	fa•tal-is•tic
fal•ter	far-fetched	fa•tali-ties
fal-ter•ing	farmed	fa•tal-ity
fa•mil-iar	farmer	fa•tally
fa•mil-iar•ity	farm-ers	fate-ful
fa•mil-iar-iza-tion	farm-hand	fa•ther
fa•mil-iar•ize	farm-ing	fathom

fath-omed
fa•tigue
fa•tigu-ing
fat-ness
fat•ten

fat•ter
fatty
fau•cet
faulted
fault-finding

fault-ing
fault-less
faulty
favor
fa•vor-able

fa•vor-ably
fa•vored
fa•vor-ing
fa•vor-ite
fa•vor-it•ism

fax
fax•ing
feared
fear-ful
fear-ing

fear-less
fear-some
fea-si-bil•ity
fea-si•ble
feasted

feast-ing
feather
feather-bedding
feath-ered
fea-ture

fea-tur•ing
Feb-ru•ary
fed-eral
fed-er-al•ism
fed-er-al•ist

fed-er-ally
fed-er•ate
fed-er-at•ing
fed-era-tion
fee•ble

feeble-minded
feed-back
feed-ing
feeler
feel-ing

feign
feigned
feign-ing
feisty
fe•lici-tate

fe•lici-tat•ing
fe•lici-ta-tion
fe•lici-tous
fe•lic-ity
fe•line

fel•low
fel-low-ship
felon
felo-nies
fel•ony

fe•male
femi-nine
femi-nin•ity
femi-nist
fenced

fences
fenc-ing
fender
fend-ing
fer-ment

fer-mented
fer-men-ta-tion
fer-ment•ing
fe•ro-cious
fe•ro-ciously

fer-ried
ferry
ferry-boat
fer-tile
fer-til•ity

fer-til-iza-tion
fer-til•ize
fer-til-izer
fer-til-izes
fer-vent

fer-vently
fer•vor
fes-ti•val
fes-tive
fes-tivi-ties

fes-tiv•ity
fetal
fe•tish
fetus
fe•tuses

feu•dal
feud-ing
fever
fe•ver-ish
fewer

few•est
fi•ancé
fi•an-cée
fi•asco
fib•bing

fiber-board
fiber-glass
fiber--optic
fibula
fiche

fickle
fic-tion
fic-tional
fic-tion-al•ize
fic-ti-tious

fic-ti-tiously
fid•dle
fid-dler
fid-dling
fi•del-ity

fidget
fidg-eted
fidg-et•ing
fidg-ety
fi•du-ciary

fielded
fielder
field-ers
field-ing
fiend-ish

fiercely
fiery
fi•esta
fif-teen
fif-ties

fif-ti•eth
fifty
fighter
fight-ing
fig-ment

figu-ra-tive
figu-ra-tively
fig•ure
figure-head
fig-ures

figu-rine
fig-ur•ing
fila-ment
filed
file-name

filer
file-server
filet
fil•ial
fili-bus•ter

fili-bus-ter•ing
fil•ing
filled
filler
fill-ers

fil•let
fill-ing
filmed
film-ing
film-strip

fil•ter
fil-ter•ing
fil-tra-tion
final
fi•nale

fi•nal-ist
fi•nal-iza-tion
fi•nal-ize
fi•nal-iz•ing
fi•nally

fi•nance
fi•nances
fi•nan-cial
fi•nan-cially
fi•nan-cier

fi•nanc-ing
finder
find-ing
fined
finely

finer
fin•ery
fi•nesse
fin•est
fine--tune

fine--tuning
fin•ger
fin-ger•ing
finger-print
finis

fin•ish
fin-isher
fin-ishes
fin-ish•ing
fi•nite

fi•nitely
Fin-land
Fin-lander
fire-arm
fire-cracker

fired
fire-house
fire-place
fire-proof
fire-proofing

fire-side
fire-trap
fire-works
fir•ing
fir-ma-ment

firmed
firmer
firmly
firm-ness
firm-ware

first-hand
first-ling
firstly
first--rate
fis•cal

fis-cally
fished
fish-er•ies
fish-ery
fishes

fish-ing
fishy
fis-sion
fis-sure
fisti-cuffs

fis-tula
fit•ful
fit-fully
fit-ness
fit•ted

fit-test
fit-ting
fix-able
fix•ate
fix-at•ing

fixa-tion
fixed
fixer
fixes
fix•ing

fix-ture
fiz•zle
flab-bi-ness
flabby
flac-cid

flag-el-late
flag-el-la-tion
flagged
flag-ging
flag-pole

fla-grant
fla-grantly
flam-boy-ance
flam-boy-ancy
flam-boy•ant

flame-proof
flam-ing
flam-ma•ble
flank-ing
flan-nel

flap-ping
flared
flar-ing
flash-back
flash-bulb

flasher
flashes
flashi-ness
flash-ing
flash-light

flashy
flat-bed
flat-car
flat-foot
flat--footed

flatly
flat-ness
flat-ten
flat-ter
flat-tered

flat-terer
flat-ter•ing
flat-tery
flat-ware
flaunted

flaunt-ing
fla•vor
fla-vor•ful
fla-vor•ing
fla-vor-some

flawed
flaw-less
flea-bag
fledg-ing
fledg-ling

flee-ing
fleet-ing
fleshi-ness
fleshy
flexi-bil•ity

flex-ible	flood-plain	flu-ency
flex-ing	flood-water	flu•ent
flexi-time	floor-board	flu-ently
flex-time	floored	fluffi-ness
flex-ural	floor-ing	fluffy
flicker	floor-walker	fluid
flier	flop-pies	flu•ids
fli•ers	flop-pi-ness	flunk-ing
flies	floppy	fluo-res-cence
flighti-ness	flora	fluo-res-cent
flim-flam	flo•ral	fluo-ri-date
flim-sily	flo-res-cence	fluo-ri-dat•ing
film-si-ness	flo-res-cent	fluo-ri-da-tion
flimsy	flo-ri-cul-ture	fluo-ride
flinch-ing	Flor-ida	flur-ries
flip--flop	Flori-dan	flurry
flip-pancy	flo-rist	flushed
flip-pant	floss-ing	flushes
flipped	flo-ta-tion	flush-ing
flip-per	flo-tilla	flus-ter
flip-ping	flounc-ing	flus-ter•ing
flir-ta-tion	floun-der	flut-ter
flir-ta-tious	floun-der•ing	flut-ter•ing
flirted	flour	flut-tery
flirt-ing	flow-age	fly-catcher
floa-ta-tion	flow-chart	flyer
floated	flowed	fly•ers
floater	flower	fly•ing
float-ing	flow-ers	fly-leaf
flock-ing	flow-ery	fly-paper
flog-ging	flow-ing	foamed
flooded	flub-bing	foam-ing
flood-gate	fluc-tu•ate	foamy
flood-ing	fluc-tu-at•ing	focal
flood-light	fluc-tua-tion	fo•cal-ize

fo•cal-iz•ing
focus
fo•cused
fo•cuses
fo•cus-ing

fod•der
foggy
fog-horn
foi•ble
folded

folder
fold-ers
fold-ing
fold-out
fo•liage

fo•li-ate
fo•lia-tion
folio
fo•lios
folk-lore

folk-lor•ist
folksy
fol-li•cle
fol-licu•lar
fol-lies

fol•low
fol-lower
fol-low•ers
fol-low•ing
follow--up (n.)

fonder
fond-est
fondly
fond-ness
fon•due

food-stuff
fool-ery
fool-ing
fool-ish
fool-ishly

fool-proof
fools-cap
foot-age
foot-ball
footed

footer
foot-fall
foot-gear
foot-hill
foot-hold

foot-ing
foot-light
foot-locker
foot-loose
foot-note

foot-not•ing
foot-path
foot-print
foot-rest
foot-steps

foot-stool
foot-wear
for•age
for-ag•ing
foray

for-bear-ance
for•bid
for-bid•den
for-bid-ding
forced

force-ful
force-fully
for-ceps
forces
forc-ible

forc-ibly
forc-ing
fore-arm
fore-bears
fore-cast

fore-caster
fore-cast•ing
fore-close
fore-clos•ing
fore-clo-sure

fore-fin•ger
fore-front
forego
fore-go•ing
fore-gone

fore-ground
fore-hand
fore-head
for-eign
for-eigner

fore-judge
fore-most
fore-noon
fo•ren-sic
fore-part

fore-run•ner
fore-see
fore-see-able
fore-seen
fore-shadow

fore-sight	fork-lift	for-tify
fore-sight-ed-ness	for-lorn	for-ti-fy•ing
for•est	for•mal	for-tis-simo
fore-stall	form-al-de-hyde	for-ti-tude
fore-stall•ing	for-mali-ties	FORTRAN
for-es-ta-tion	for-mal•ity	for-tress
for-ester	for-mal•ize	for-tu-itous
for-estry	for-mal-iz•ing	for-tu•ity
for-ests	for-mally	for-tu-nate
fore-tell	for•mat	for-tu-nately
fore-thought	for-ma-tion	for-tune
fore-told	for-ma-tive	forty
for-ever	for-mat•ted	forum
fore-warn	for-mat-ting	fo•rums
fore-warn•ing	for•mer *(adj.)*	for-ward
fore-word	former *(n.)*	for-ward•ing
for-feit	for-merly	fos•sil
for-fei-ture	for-mi-da•ble	fos-sil-iza-tion
for-gave	form-ing	fos-sil•ize
forged	form-less	fos-sils
forger	for-mula	fos•ter
forg-er•ies	for-mu•las	fos-tered
forg-ery	for-mu-late	fos-ter•ing
for•get	for-mu-lat•ing	fouled
for-get•ful	for-mu-la-tion	foul-ing
for-get-ful-ness	for-sake	foun-da-tion
for-get-ting	for-saken	founded
forg-ing	for-sak•ing	founder *(n.)*
for-giv-able	forth-com•ing	foun-der *(v.)*
for-give	forth-right	foun-der•ing
for-given	for-ties	found-ers
for-give-ness	for-ti•eth	found-ing
for-giv•ing	for-ti-fi-ca-tion	found-ries
for•got	for-ti-fied	foundry
for-got•ten	for-ti-fies	foun-tain

f

four-teen
fox-hole
foyer
fra•cas
frac-tion

frac-tional
frac-tion-al•ize
frac-ture
frac-tur•ing
frag-ile

fra-gil•ity
frag-ment
frag-men-tary
frag-men-ta-tion
frag-ment•ing

fra-grance
fra-grant
fra-grantly
frailty
framed

framer
frame-work
fram-ing
France
fran-chise

fran-chi•see
fran-chises
fran-chis•ing
fran-chi•sor
frank-furter

frankly
frank-ness
fran-tic
fran-ti-cally
fra-ter•nal

fra-ter-nity
frat-er-nize
frat-ri-cide
fraudu-lence
fraudu-lent

fraudu-lently
free-bie
freed
free-dom
free-hand

free-ing
freely
free-standing
free-way
freezer

freez-ers
freezes
freez-ing
freight-age
freighter

freight-ers
freight-ing
French
frenzy
fre-quen-cies

fre-quency
fre-quent
fre-quently
fresco
freshen

fresh-ener
fresh-est
freshly
fresh-ness
fret-ful

fret-fully
fret-ting
fric-as•see
fric-tion
fric-tional

Fri•day
fried
friend-less
friend-li-ness
friendly

friend-ship
frier
frieze
frig-ate
frighten

fright-ened
fright-en•ing
fright-ful
frigid
fri-gid•ity

fri-vol•ity
frivo-lous
frolic
frol-icked
frol-ick•ing

front-age
fron-tal
fronted
fron-tier
front-ing

fron-tis-piece
frost-bite
frost-bitten
frosted
frost-ing

frosty
frowned
frown-ing
fro•zen
fruc-tose

fru•gal
fru-gal•ity
fru-gally
fruit-ful
fru-ition

fruit-less
frus-trate
frus-trat•ing
frus-tra-tion
fryer

fry•ing
fudg-ing
fu•eled
fu•el-ing
fu•gi-tive

ful-fill
ful-filled
ful-full•ing
ful-fill-ment
full-back

fuller
full-est
full-ness
full--time *(adj.)*
fully

ful-mi-nate
fum•ble
fum-bled
fum-bling
fu•mi-gate

fu•mi-ga-tion
fu•mi-ga•tor
func-tion
func-tional
func-tion-ally

func-tion•ing
fun-da-men•tal
fun-da-men-tal•ist
fun-da-men-tally
funded

fund-ing
fu•neral
fu•ne-real
fungi
fun-gi-cide

fun•gus
fun•nel
fun-nel•ing
fun-nels
fun-nier

fun-ni•est
funny
fur-bish
fur-bish•ing
fu•ri-ous

fur-lough
fur-nace
fur-nish
fur-nishes
fur-nish-ings

fur-ni-ture
furor
fur-rier
fur•row
furry

fur-ther
fur-ther•ing
fur-ther-more
fur-thest
fury

fused
fu•se-lage
fuses
fu•sion
fussi-ness

fu•tile
fu•til•ity
fu•ture
fu•tur-ist
fu•tur-is•tic

fuzzi-ness
fuzzy

G

gab-ar-dine
ga•bles
gad•get
gad-getry
Gaelic

gaf•fer
gagged
gag-ging
gai•ety
gained

gain-ful
gain-fully
gain-ing
gala
ga•lac-tic

gal-ax•ies
gal•axy
gal-lant
gal-lantry
gall-bladder

gal-ler•ies
gal-lery
gal•ley
gal-leys
gal-li-vant

gal•lon
gal•lop
gal-loped
gal-lop•ing
gal-lows

gall-stone
ga•lore
ga•loshes
gal-va-nize
gal-va-niz•ing

gam•ble
gam-bled
gam-bler
gam-bling
gan•der

gan-gling
gang-plank
gan-grene
gan-gre-nous
gang-ster

gang-way
gap-ping
ga•rage
gar-bage
gar•ble

gar•den
gar-dened
gar-de•nia
gar-den•ing
gar-gan-tuan

gar•gle
gar-gling
gar-land
gar•lic
gar-ment

gar•ner
gar-nish
gar-nish-ment
gar-ri•son
gar-ru-lous

gar•ter
gas-eous
gases
gashes
gas•ket

gas-kets
gaso-hol
gaso-line
gasped
gasp-ing

gassed
gas-si-ness
gas-sing
gas-tric
gas-tri•tis

gas-tro-nomic
gas-tro-nom-ical
gas-tronomy
gate-way
gather

gath-ered
gath-er•ing
gauged
gauges
gaug-ing

gavel
gav•els
ga•zebo
ga•zette
gaz•ing

geared
gear-ing
gela-tin
gelled
gem-olo-gist

gem-ology
gen•der
ge•nea-log-ical
ge•ne-alo-gist
ge•ne-al•ogy

gen-eral
gen-er-al•ist
gen-er-ali-ties
gen-er-al•ity
gen-er-al-iza-tion

gen-er-al•ize
gen-er-ally
gen-er•ate
gen-er-at•ing
gen-era-tion

gen-era•tor
ge•neric
ge•ner-ically
gen-er-os•ity
gen-er•ous

gen-er•ously	geo-ther•mic	giddy
ge•netic	ge•ri-at•ric	gifted
ge•net-ically	Ger•man	giga-bit
ge•nial	ger-mane	giga-byte
ge•nially	Ger-many	giga-hertz
geni-tal	ger-mi-cide	gi•gan-tic
ge•nius	ger-mi-nate	gig•gle
geno-cide	ger-mi-nat•ing	gig-gling
gen-tile	ger-mi-na-tion	gim-mick
gen•tle	ger-on-tolo-gist	gin•ger
gently	ger-on-tol•ogy	gin-gerly
genu-flect	gerry-mander	ging-ham
genu-flec-tion	ger•und	gin-gi-vi•tis
genu-ine	ge•stalt	gin-seng
genu-inely	ges-tate	gi•raffe
genus	ges-ta-tion	girded
ge•og-ra-pher	ges-ticu-late	girder
geo-graphic	ges-ticu-la-tion	gird-ing
geo-graph-ical	ges-ture	gir•dle
geo-graphi-cally	ges-tur•ing	give-away *(n.)*
ge•og-ra•phy	ge•sund-heit	given
geo-logic	get-away	giver
geo-log-ical	get-ting	giv•ing
geo-logi-cally	get--together *(n.)*	gizmo
ge•olo-gist	gey•ser	giz•mos
ge•ology	Ghana	giz-zard
geo-met•ric	Gha-nian	gla-cial
ge•ome-try	ghetto	gla-cier
geo-phys•ics	ghet-tos	glad-den
geo-poli-tics	ghostly	glad-dened
Geor-gia	ghost-writer	gladi-ator
Geor-gian	ghost-writing	gladly
geo-sta-tion•ary	ghoul-ish	glam-or•ize
geo-syn-chro-nous	gib-ber•ish	glam-or-iz•ing
geo-ther•mal	gid-di-ness	glam-or•ous

g

glam-our	glob-al-iza-tion	gnos-ti-cism
glances	glob-al•ize	gnu
glanc-ing	glob-al-iz•ing	goalie
glan-du•lar	glob-ally	goal-ies
glare-proof	globu-lar	goal-keeper
glar-ing	gloom-ily	goal-post
glasses	gloomi-ness	goal-tender
glass-ful	gloomy	goa•tee
glass-ily	glo-ries	gob•ble
glass-ware	glo-ri-fi-ca-tion	gob-bling
glassy	glo-ri-fied	go--between (n.)
glau-coma	glo-rify	gob•let
glazed	glo-ri-fy•ing	gob•lin
glazes	glo-ri•ous	god-hood
glaz-ier	glory	god-less
glaz-ing	glos-sa-ries	god-li-ness
gleam-ing	glos-sary	godly
gleaned	glossy	god-parent
glean-ing	glow-ing	god-send
glee-ful	glu-cose	goer
glider	glued	go--getter (n.)
glid-ing	glu•ing	gog•gle
glim-mer	glum-ness	gog-gling
glim-mer•ing	glu-ta-mate	going
glimpse	glu•ten	goi•ter
glimpses	glu-ten•ous	golden
glimps-ing	glut-ton	gold-en-rod
glis-ten	glut-ton•ous	gold-fish
glis-ten•ing	glut-tony	gold-smith
glitches	glyc-erin	golfer
glit-ter	gnarled	golf-ing
glit-ter•ing	gnarl-ing	go•nadal
glit-tery	gnash-ing	go•nad-ec-tomy
gloat-ing	gnaw-ing	go•nads
global	Gnos-tic	gon-dola

gon-do-lier
goner
good-bye
good--hearted
good-ies

goodly
good-ness
good-will
goofed
goofi-ness

goose-berry
goose-neck
go•pher
gored
gor-geous

gor-geously
gorg-ing
go•rilla
go•ril-las
gori-ness

gory
gos-ling
gos•pel
gos-sa•mer
gos•sip

gos-siper
gos-sip•ing
got•ten
gouges
goug-ing

gou-lash
gour-met
gov•ern
gov-er-nance
gov-erned

gov-ern•ing
gov-ern-ment
gov-ern-men•tal
gov-ern-men-tally
gov-er•nor

grabbed
grab-bing
grace-ful
grace-fully
grace-ful-ness

grac-ing
gra-cious
gra-ciously
gra-cious-ness
gra-da-tion

graded
grader
gra-di•ent
grad-ing
grad-ual

gradu-ally
gradu-ate
gradu-at•ing
gradu-ation
graf-fiti

graft-ing
grainy
gram-mar
gram-mar•ian
gram-mat-ical

gra-na-ries
gra-nary
grand-child
grand-chil-dren
grander

grand-est
gran-deur
gran-dilo-quence
gran-dilo-quent
gran-di•ose

gran-di-os•ity
gran-dioso
grand-par-ents
grand-stand
gran-ite

gra-nola
granted
grantee
grant-ing
grantor

granu-lar
granu-late
granu-lat•ing
granu-la-tion
gran-ule

grape-fruit
grape-vine
graphed
graphic
graph-ical

graphi-cally
graph-ics
graph-ing
graph-ite
grap-ple

grap-pling
grasped
grasp-ing
grassed
grasses

g

grass-hopper
grassy
grate-ful
grate-fully
grate-ful-ness

grati-fi-ca-tion
grati-fied
grati-fies
grat-ify
grati-fy•ing

grat-ing
gra•tis
grati-tude
gra-tu-ities
gra-tu-itous

gra-tu•ity
gravel
grav-eled
gravely
grave-side

grave-stone
grave-yard
gravi-sphere
gravi-tate
gravi-ta-tion

grav-ity
gravy
gray-ing
graz-ing
greas-ing

greasy
greater
great-est
greatly
great-ness

Gre-cian
Greece
greed-ily
greedi-ness
greedy

green-back
green-ery
green-house
green-ish
Green-land

Green-lander
green-room
greeted
greeter
greet-ing

gre-gari•ous
gre-gari-ously
grem-lin
Gre-nada
gre-nade

Gre-na-dian
grey-hound
grid-dle
grid-iron
griev-ance

griev-ant
grieved
griev-ing
griev-ous
grill-ing

grill-work
gri-mace
gri-mac•ing
grimly
grim-ness

grinder
grind-ing
grind-stone
grinned
grin-ning

grip-per
grip-ping
grisly
gris-tle
griz-zle

griz-zly
groan-ing
gro•cer
gro-cer•ies
gro-cery

groggy
groomed
groom-ing
groove
groovy

groped
grop-ing
grossed
gross-ing
grossly

gro-tesque
gro-tesquely
gro-tesque-ness
grotto
grouchi-ness

grouchy
grounded
grounder
ground-ing
ground-less

ground-work	guard-ian-ship	gulp-ing
grouped	guard-ing	gumbo
groupie	Gua-te-mala	gum-drop
group-ing	Gua-te-ma•lan	gummed
grovel	guava	gummy
grov-eled	gua•vas	gump-tion
grov-el•ing	gu•ber-na-to-rial	gum-shoe
grower	guer-rilla	gun-boat
grow-ers	guessed	gun-fire
grow-ing	guesses	gunned
growl-ing	guess-ing	gunny-sack
grown	guess-ti-mate	gun-shot
growth	guess-work	gun-slinger
grub-stake	Guiana	gun-smith
grudges	Guia-nan	gun-wale
grudg-ing	guid-ance	gup-pies
grudg-ingly	guide-book	guppy
gru-el•ing	guided	gur•gle
grue-some	guide-lines	gur-gling
gruff-ness	guide-post	gur•ney
grum-ble	guid-ing	gusher
grum-bling	guile-less	gush-ing
grump-ily	guil-lo-tine	gushy
grumpi-ness	guilt-less	gusto
grumpy	guilty	gutsy
grunted	Guinea	gut•ter
grunt-ing	Guin-ean	gut-ting
gua-ca-mole	guise	gut-tural
guar-an•tee	gui•tar	Guy•ana
guar-an-teed	gui-tar•ist	Guya-nese
guar-an-tee•ing	gui-tars	guz•zle
guar-an•tor	gull-ible	guz-zler
guar-anty	gul-lies	guz-zling
guarded	gully	gym-na-sium
guard-ian	gulped	gym-nast

gym-nas-tics
gy•ne-colo-gist
gy•ne-col•ogy
gypped
gyp•sum

gypsy
gy•rat-ing
gy•ra-tion
gy•ro-plane
gy•ro-scope

hab-er-dash•ery
ha•bili-tate
ha•bili-ta-tion
habit
ha•bi-tant

habi-tat
habi-ta-tion
hab•its
ha•bit-ual
ha•bitu-ally

ha•ci-enda
hacker
hack-ers
hack-ing
hack-ney

hack-neyed
hack-saw
had-dock
hag-gard
hag•gle

hag-gling
hailed
hail-ing
hail-stone
hail-storm

hair-cut
hair-cutting
hairdo
hair-dresser
hairi-ness

hair-line
hair-piece
hair-pin
hair-splitting
hairy

Haiti
Hai-tian
hal-cyon
hale
half-back

half-hearted
half-heart-edly
half-time
half-way
hali-but

hali-to•sis
hal-le-lu•jah
hall-mark
hal•low
Hal-low•een

hal-lu-ci-nate
hal-lu-ci-nat•ing
hal-lu-ci-na-tion
hal-lu-ci-na-tory
hal-lu-ci-no•gen

hal-lu-ci-no-genic
hall-way
halo
halted
hal•ter

halt-ing
halves
halv-ing
ham-burger
ham•let

ham•mer
ham-mer•ing
ham-mock
ham•per
ham-per•ing

ham-pers
ham-ster
ham-string
hand-bag
hand-ball

hand-bill
hand-book
hand-clasp
hand-cuffs
handed

hand-ed-ness
hand-ful
hand-held
handi-cap
handi-capped

handi-craft
handi-est
hand-ily
handi-work
hand-ker-chief

han•dle
handle-bar
han-dled
han-dling
hand-made

hand-out *(n.)*
hand-picked
hand-rail
hands-ful
hand-shake

hand-shaking
hand-some
hands--on
hand-stand
hand-writing

hand-written
handy
han•gar
hanged
hanger

hang-ers
hang-ing
hang--up *(n.)*
Ha•nuk-kah
hap-haz•ard

hap-haz-ardly
hap•pen
hap-pen•ing
hap-pen-stance
hap-pier

hap-pi•est
hap-pily
hap-pi-ness
happy
ha•rangue

ha•rass
ha•rasses
ha•rass-ing
ha•rass-ment
har•bor

har-bors
hard-back
hard-bound
hard--core *(adj.)*
harden

hard-ened
hard-en•ing
harder
hard-est
hard-headed

hard-hearted
hardly
hard-ness
hard-ship
hard-top

hard-ware
hard-wired
hard-wood
hardy
harem

harm-ful
harm-ing
harm-less
har-monic
har-mo-ni•ous

har-mo-ni-ously
har-mo-nize
har-mo-niz•ing
har-mony
har-ness

harp-ist
har-poon
harp-si-chord
har-ried
har•row

har-row•ing
harshly
har-vest
har-vester
har-vest•ing

hash-ing
hash-log
has•sle
has-sling
has-sock

haste
has•ten
has-tened
has-ten•ing
hast-ily

hasti-ness
hasty
hatch-back
hatched
hatch-ery

hatchet
hatch-ing
hate-ful
hate-ful-ness
hat•ing

ha•tred
haughty
haul-age
hauled
haul-ing

haunted
haunt-ing
haven
hav•ens
hav•ing

havoc
Ha•waii
Ha•wai-ian
hawked
hawk-ing

hay-field
hay-loft
hay-seed
hay-stack
hay-wire

haz•ard
haz-ard•ous
haz-ards
hazel
hazi-ness

haz•ing
hazy
head-ache
head-board
head-count

headed
header
head-ers
head-first
head-gear

head-hunter
head-ing
head-light
head-line
head-lock

head-master
head--on *(adj.)*
head-phones
head-quar-tered
head-quarters

head-rest
head-room
head-set
head-stone
head-strong

head-way
healed
healer
heal-ing
health-ful

health-ier
healthi-est
healthi-ness
healthy
heap-ing

hear-ing
hear-ken
hear-kened
hear-ken•ing
hear-say

hearse
heart-ache
heart-break
heart-breaking
heart-broken

heart-burn
heart-ened
heart-en•ing
heart-felt
hearti-est

heart-less
heart-rending
heart-sick
heart-throb
heart-warming

hearty
heated
heater
heat-ers
hea-then

heather
heat-ing
heaven
heav-enly
heav-ens

heav-en-ward
heavier
heavi-est
heavily
heavy--duty

heavy--handed
heavy-hearted
heavy-set
He•brew
heck-ler

heck-ling
hec•tic
hec-to-graph
heeded
heed-ing

heed-less
heel-ing
hefty
heifer
heif-ers

heighten	he•mo-philic	heroin
height-ened	hem-or-rhage	hero-ine
height-en•ing	hem-or-rhag•ing	hero-ism
Heim-lich	hem-or-rhoids	her•pes
hei-nous	he•mo-stat	her-ring
hei-nously	he•mo-static	her-self
heir-loom	hence-forth	hesi-tancy
heist	hepa-ti•tis	hesi-tant
heisted	hep-ta•gon	hesi-tate
heist-ing	her•ald	hesi-tat•ing
he•li-cop•ter	her-aldry	hesi-ta-tion
he•li-pad	herbal	het-ero-ge-ne•ity
he•li-port	herb-al•ist	het-ero-ge-neous
he•lium	her-bi-cide	heu-ris•tic
hello	Her-cu-lean	hexa-deci•mal
hel•met	herded	hexa-gon
hel-mets	herd-ing	hex-ago•nal
helped	here-abouts	hia•tal
helper	here-after	hia•tus
help-ers	hereby	hi•ber-nate
help-ful	he•redi-tary	hi•ber-nat•ing
help-fully	he•red-ity	hi•ber-na-tion
help-ful-ness	herein	hi•bus-cus
help-ing	her•esy	hic•cup
help-less	here-tic	hic-cup•ing
help-lessly	he•ret-ical	hick-ory
help-less-ness	here-to-fore	hid•den
help-mate	here-with	hide-away
he•ma-tolo-gist	heri-tage	hid-eous
he•ma-tol•ogy	her•mit	hide-out
hemi-sphere	her•nia	hid•ing
hemi-spheric	her-ni-ated	hi•er-ar-chi•cal
hemmed	her-ni-at•ing	hi•er-ar•chy
he•mo-glo•bin	he•roes	hi•ero-glphy•ics
he•mo-philia	he•roic	high-brow

higher
high-est
high-light
high-lighting
highly

high-ness
high--rise *(adj.)*
high-way
hi•jack
hi•jacker

hi•jack-ing
hik•ing
hi•lari-ous
hi•lar-ity
hill

hill-billy
hill-side
hilly
him-self
hin•der

hin-der•ing
hin-ders
hind-quarter
hin-drance
hind-sight

hinges
hing-ing
hinted
hint-ing
hip•pie

Hip-po-cratic
hip-po-pota•mus
hired
hir•ing
His-panic

his-ta-mine
his-to-gram
his-to-rian
his-toric
his-tor-ical

his-tori-cally
his-tori-ric•ity
his-to-ries
his-to-ri-og-ra-pher
his-to-ri-og-ra•phy

his-tory
hitch-hiker
hitch-hik•ing
hitch-ing
hither

hith-er-most
hith-erto
hit-ting
hoa•gie
hoa-gies

hoarded
hoard-ing
hoarsely
hoarse-ness
hoary

hoaxes
hob-bies
hob•ble
hob-bles
hob-bling

hobby
hob-by•ist
hob•nob
hockey
hock-ing

hodge-podge
hoe•ing
hogged
hog-ging
hog-gish

hog--tie
hog-wash
hoisted
hoister
hoist-ing

holder
hold-ers
hold-ing
hold-out *(n.)*
hold-over *(n)*

holdup *(n.)*
holi-day
ho•lis-tic
hol-lan-daise
hol•low

hol-low-ness
holly
holly-hock
ho•lo-caust
ho•lo-graph

ho•lo-graphic
ho•lo-gra•phy
hol-stein
hol-ster
hom•age

hom•bre
home-bound
home-coming
home-grown
home-land

home-less	honey	hor-ren-dous
home-like	honey-bee	hor-ri•ble
home-li-ness	honey-moon	hor-ri•bly
homely	hon•ing	hor•rid
home-made	honor	hor-ridly
home-maker	hon-or-able	hor-rify
home-making	hon-or-ably	hor-ri-fy•ing
ho•meo-pathic	hono-raria	hor•ror
ho•me-opa•thy	hono-rar•ium	hors d'oeuvre
home-owner	hon-or•ary	horse-back
homer	hon-ored	horse-hide
home-room	hon-oree	horse-play
home-sick	hon-or•ing	horse-power
home-site	hon•ors	hor-ta-tory
home-spun	hood-lum	hor-ti-cul-tural
home-stead	hood-wink	hor-ti-cul-ture
home-stretch	hooked	hor-ti-cul-tur•ist
home-town	hook-ing	hosed
home-work	hookup	hoses
homey	hoopla	ho•siery
ho•mi-cidal	hoo•ray	hos•ing
ho•mi-cide	hoped	hos-pice
ho•mo-ge-ne•ity	hope-ful	hos-pi-ta•ble
ho•mo-ge-neous	hope-fully	hos-pi•tal
ho•moge-nize	hope-less	hos-pi-tal•ity
ho•moge-niz•ing	hope-lessly	hos-pi-tal-iza-tion
hom-onym	hope-less-ness	hos-pi-tal•ize
ho•mo-phone	hop•ing	hos-pi-tal-iz•ing
hon•cho	hop•per	hos-tage
Hon-du•ran	hop-ping	hosted
Hon-du•ras	ho•ri-zon	hos•tel
honed	hori-zon•tal	hos-telry
hon•est	hori-zon-tally	hos-tile
hon-estly	hor-mone	host-ing
hon-esty	horo-scope	hot-cake

h

91

hotel	howl-ing	hu•mid-ity
ho•tels	huck-ster	hu•mili-ate
hot-head	hud•dle	hu•mili-at•ing
hot-house	hud-dling	hu•mili-ation
hot-line	huffi-ness	hu•mil-ity
hot•ter	huffy	hummed
hot-test	hug-ga•ble	hum-ming
hot-zone	hug-ging	hu•mon-gous
hounded	human	humor
hound-ing	hu•mane	hu•mor-ist
hour-glass	hu•manely	hu•mor-less
hourly	hu•man-ism	hu•mor-ous
house-boat	hu•man-ist	hump-back
house-breaking	hu•man-is•tic	hunch-back
house-broken	hu•mani-tar•ian	hunches
house-cleaning	hu•mani-ties	hun-dred
housed	hu•man-ity	hundred-weight
house-ful	hu•man-ize	Hun-garian
house-hold	hu•man-iz•ing	Hun-gary
house-holder	hu•manly	hun•ger
house-keeper	hu•man-ness	hun-gered
house-keeping	hu•man-oid	hun-ger•ing
house-parents	hum•ble	hun-grily
houses	hum-ble-ness	hun•gry
house-wares	hum-blest	hunter
house-warming	hum-bling	hunt-ing
house-work	hum•bly	hur•dle
hous-ing	hum-drum	hur-dling
hovel	hu•merus	hurled
hov•els	humid	hurl-ing
hover	hu•midi-fi-ca-tion	hur•rah
Hover-craft	hu•midi-fier	hur-ri-cane
hov-ered	hu•midi-fies	hur-ried
hov-er•ing	hu•mid-ify	hur-riedly
how-ever	hu•mid-ify•ing	hurry

hur-ry•ing
hurt-ful
hurt-ing
hus-bandry
hush-ing

husk-ing
husky
hus•tle
hus-tling
hy•brid

hy•drant
hy•drate
hy•drau-lic
hy•dro-car•bon
hy•dro-chlo•ric

hy•dro-elec-tric
hy•dro-elec-tri•cal
hy•dro-gen
hy•drome-ter
hy•dro-plane

hy•dro-pon•ics
hy•dro-static
hy•drox-ide
hyena
hye•nas

hy•giene
hy•gienic
hy•gieni-cally
hy•gien-ist
hym•nal

hymn-book
hy•per-ac-tive
hy•per-bole
hy•per-card
hy•per-crit-ical

hy•per-golic
hy•per-me•dia
hy•per-sonic
hy•per-space
hy•per-ten-sion

hy•phen
hy•phen-ate
hy•phen-at•ing
hy•phen-ation
hyp-no•sis

hyp-notic
hyp-no-tism
hyp-no-tist
hyp-no-tize
hyp-no-tiz•ing

hy•po-chon-dria
hy•po-chon-driac
hy•poc-risy
hypo-crite
hypo-crit-ical

hy•po-der•mal
hy•po-der•mic
hy•po-der•mis
hy•pos-ta-tize
hy•pos-ta-tiz•ing

hy•pote-nuse
hy•po-ther•mia
hy•po-ther•mic
hy•pothe-ses
hy•pothe-sis

hy•pothe-size
hy•po-thet-ical
hy•po-theti-cally
hyp•oxia
hys-ter-ec-tomy

hys-te•ria
hys-teric
hys-ter-ical
hys•ter•ics

Ibe•ria
Ibe-rian
ice-berg
Ice-land
Ice-lander

Ice-lan•dic
ici•cle
icing
icon
icono-clast

Idaho
Ida-hoan
idea
ideal
ide-al•ism

ide-al•ist
ide-al-is•tic
ide-ally
iden-ti•cal
iden-ti-fi-able

iden-ti-fi-ca-tion
iden-ti-fied
iden-ti-fier
iden-ti-fies
iden-tify

iden-ti-fy•ing	il•leg-ible	imag-in•ing
iden-ti-ties	il•leg-ibly	im•bal-ance
iden-tity	il•le-giti-macy	im•be-cile
ideo-logi-cally	il•le-giti-mate	im•bibe
ide-ol•ogy	il•licit	imi-ta•ble
idiom	il•lic-itly	imi-tate
id•io-syn-crasy	Il•li-nois	imi-tat•ing
idiot	Il•li-noisan	imi-ta-tion
idi-otic	il•lit-er•acy	imi-ta-tive
idle-ness	il•lit-er•ate	imi-ta•tor
idling	ill-ness	im•macu-late
idol	il•log-ical	im•ma-te-rial
idola-ter	il•logi-cally	im•ma-ture
idola-trous	il•lu-mi-nate	im•ma-tu-rity
idola-try	il•lu-mi-nat•ing	im•mea-sur-able
idol-ize	il•lu-mi-na-tion	im•me-diacy
idol-iz•ing	il•lu-sion	im•me-di•ate
idyl-lic	il•lu-sion•ary	im•me-di-ately
igloo	il•lu-sion•ist	im•me-mo-rial
ig•loos	il•lu-sive	im•mense
ig•nit-able	il•lus-trate	im•mensely
ig•nite	il•lus-trat•ing	im•men-sity
ig•nit-ing	il•lus-tra-tion	im•merge
ig•ni-tion	il•lus-tra-tive	im•merse
ig•no-rance	il•lus-tra•tor	im•mers-ing
ig•no-rant	il•lus-tri•ous	im•mer-sion
ig•nore	image	im•mi-grant
ig•nor-ing	im•ag-ery	im•mi-grate
iguana	images	im•mi-grat•ing
il•le-gal	imag-in-able	im•mi-gra-tion
il•le-gali-ties	imagi-nary	im•mi-nent
il•le-gal•ity	imagi-na-tion	im•mi-nently
il•le-gal•ize	imagi-na-tive	im•mo-bil•ity
il•le-gally	imag-ine	im•mo-bi-lize
il•legi-bil•ity	im•ag-ing	im•mo-bi-liz•ing

im•mod-est
im•moral
im•mo-rali-ties
im•mo-ral•ity
im•mor-tal

im•mor-tal•ity
im•mor-tal•ize
im•mor-tally
im•mov-able
im•mune

im•mu-nity
im•mu-nize
im•mu-niz•ing
im•mu-nology
im•mure

im•mur-ing
im•mu-ta•ble
im•pact
im•pact-ing
im•pair

im•pair-ing
im•pair-ment
im•panel
im•pan-eled
im•pan-el•ing

im•par-ity
im•part
im•par-tial
im•par-tially
im•part-ing

im•pass-able
im•passe
im•pas-sion
im•pas-sive
im•pa-tience

im•pa-tient
im•pa-tiently
im•peach
im•peach-ment
im•pec-ca-bil•ity

im•pec-ca•ble
im•ped-ance
im•pede
im•pedi-ment
impel

im•pelled
im•pel-ling
im•pend
im•pend-ing
im•pene-tra•ble

im•pera-tive
im•per-cep-ti•ble
im•per-cep-tive
im•per-fect
im•per-fec-tion

im•per-fectly
im•pe-rial
im•pe-ri-al•ism
im•pe-ri-al•ist
im•pe-ri-al-is•tic

im•peril
im•per-ish-able
im•per-ma-nent
im•per-me-able
im•per-sonal

im•per-son-al•ize
im•per-son-ally
im•per-son•ate
im•per-son-at•ing
im•per-son-ation

im•per-son-ator
im•per-ti-nence
im•per-ti-nent
im•per-turb-able
im•petu-ous

im•petu-ous-ness
im•pe-tus
im•pinge
im•pinge-ment
im•ping-ing

imp•ish
im•pla-ca•ble
im•plant
im•plan-ta-tion
im•plant-ing

im•plau-si•ble
im•ple-ment
im•ple-mented
im•ple-ment•ing
im•pli-cate

im•pli-cat•ing
im•pli-ca-tion
im•plicit
im•plic-it-ness
im•plic-ity

im•plied
im•plies
im•plore
im•plor-ing
imply

im•ply-ing
im•po-lite
im•port
im•por-tance
im•por-tant

im•por-ta-tion	im•pres-sion-is•tic	in•ac-cu-ra-cies
im•porter	im•pres-sive	in•ac-cu-racy
im•port-ing	im•print	in•ac-cu-rate
im•por-tune	im•print-ing	in•ac-tion
im•pose	im•prison	in•ac-tive
im•poses	im•pris-oned	in•ac-tiv•ity
im•pos-ing	im•pris-on•ing	in•ade-qua-cies
im•po-si-tion	im•pris-on-ment	in•ade-quacy
im•pos-si-bil•ity	im•prob-able	in•ade-quate
im•pos-si•ble	im•promptu	in•ade-quately
im•pos-tor	im•proper	in•ad-mis-si•ble
im•po-tence	im•prop-erly	in•ad-ver-tence
im•po-tency	im•pro-pri•ety	in•ad-ver-tent
im•po-tent	im•prove	in•ad-ver-tently
im•pound	im•prove-ment	in•ad-vis-able
im•pound-ing	im•prov-ing	in•alien-able
im•pound-ment	im•pro-vise	in•al-ter-able
im•pov-er•ish	im•pro-vis•ing	inane
im•pov-er-ished	im•pru-dence	in•ani-mate
im•prac-ti-ca•ble	im•pru-dent	in•ap-pli-ca•ble
im•prac-ti•cal	im•pru-dently	in•ap-pre-cia•ble
im•prac-ti-cal•ity	im•pugn	in•ap-pre-cia-tive
im•pre-cise	im•pulse	in•ap-proach-able
im•preg-na•ble	im•pul-sive	in•ap-pro-pri•ate
im•preg-nate	im•pul-sive-ness	in•ap-pro-pri-ately
im•preg-nat•ing	im•pu-nity	in•ap-ti-tude
im•preg-na-tion	im•pure	in•ar-gu-ably
im•press	im•pu-ri-ties	in•ar-ticu-late
im•presses	im•pu-rity	in•as-much
im•press-ible	im•pu-ta-tion	in•at-ten-tive
im•press-ing	im•pute	in•au-di•ble
im•pres-sion	im•put-ing	in•au-gu•ral
im•pres-sion-able	in•abil-ity	in•au-gu-rate
im•pres-sion•ism	in ab-sen•tia	in•au-gu-rat•ing
im•pres-sion•ist	in•ac-ces-si•ble	in•au-gu-ra-tion

in•aus-pi-cious
in•born
in•bound
in•bred
in•breed

in•breed-ing
in•cal-cu-la•ble
in•can-des-cence
in•can-des-cent
in•ca-pa•ble

in•ca-paci-tate
in•ca-paci-tated
in•ca-paci-tat•ing
in•ca-paci-ta-tion
in•ca-paci-ties

in•ca-pac•ity
in•car-cer•ate
in•car-cer-at•ing
in•car-cera-tion
in•car-nate

in•cau-tious
in•cense
in•cens-ing
in•cen-tive
in•cep-tion

in•ces-sant
in•cest
in•ces-tu•ous
inches
inch-ing

in•ci-dence
in•ci-dent
in•ci-den•tal
in•ci-den-tally
in•cin-er•ate

in•cin-er-at•ing
in•cin-era-tion
in•cin-era•tor
in•cipi-ent
in•cise

in•ci-sion
in•ci-sive
in•ci-sively
in•ci-sor
in•cite

in•cit-ing
in•clem-ency
in•clem-ent
in•cli-na-tion
in•cline

in•clin-ing
in•clud-able
in•clude
in•clud-ing
in•clu-sion

in•clu-sive
in•clu-sively
in•cog-nito
in•co-her-ence
in•co-her•ent

in•co-her-ently
in•com-bus-ti•ble
in•come
in•com-ing
in•com-pa-ra•ble

in•com-pat-ible
in•com-pe-tence
in•com-pe-tency
in•com-pe-tent
in•com-plete

in•com-pli-ance
in•com-pli-ant
in•con-ceiv-able
in•con-ceiv-ably
in•con-clu-sive

in•con-gru-ence
in•con-gru•ent
in•con-gru•ity
in•con-gru•ous
in•con-se-quent

in•con-sid-er•ate
in•con-sis-tence
in•con-sis-ten-cies
in•con-sis-tency
in•con-sis-tent

in•con-sol-able
in•con-spicu•ous
in•con-test-able
in•con-ti-nence
in•con-ti-nent

in•con-ve-nience
in•con-ve-nienced
in•con-ve-nient
in•con-ve-niently
in•cor-po-rate

in•cor-po-rat•ing
in•cor-po-ra-tion
in•cor-rect
in•cor-ri-gi•ble
in•cor-rupt

in•cor-rupt-ible
in•cor-rup-tion
in•crease
in•creases
in•creas-ing

in•creas-ingly
in•cred-ible
in•cred-ibly
in•cre-du-lity
in•credu-lous

in•credu-lously
in•cre-ment
in•cre-men•tal
in•cre-ment•ing
in•crimi-nate

in•crimi-nat•ing
in•crimi-na-tion
in•cu-bate
in•cu-ba-tion
in•cu-ba•tor

in•cum-bency
in•cum-bent
incur
in•curred
in•cur-ring

in•debted
in•debt-ed-ness
in•de-cen-cies
in•de-cency
in•de-cent

in•de-ci-pher-able
in•de-ci-sion
in•de-ci-sive
in•de-co•rum
in•deed

in•de-fati-ga•ble
in•de-fen-si•ble
in•de-fin-able
in•defi-nite
in•defi-nitely

in•del-ible
in•deli-cacy
in•deli-cate
in•dem-ni-fied
in•dem-nify

in•dem-ni-fy•ing
in•dem-nity
in•dent
in•den-ta-tion
in•dent-ing

in•den-tion
in•den-ture
in•de-pen-dence
in•de-pen-dent
in•de-pen-dently

in•de-scrib-able
in•de-struc-ti•ble
in•de-ter-mi-nate
index
in•dexed

in•dexes
in•dex-ing
India
In•dian
In•di-ana

In•di-anan
in•di-cate
in•di-cat•ing
in•di-ca-tion
in•dica-tive

in•di-ca•tor
in•di-ces
in•dict
in•dict-ing
in•dict-ment

in•dif-fer-ence
in•dif-fer•ent
in•dif-fer-ently
in•dige-nous
in•di-gent

in•di-gest-ible
in•di-ges-tion
in•dig-nant
in•dig-na-tion
in•dig-ni-ties

in•dig-nity
in•digo
in•di-rect
in•di-rectly
in•dis-cern-ible

in•dis-creet
in•dis-creetly
in•dis-crete
in•dis-cre-tion
in•dis-crimi-nate

in•dis-pens-able
in•dis-posed
in•dis-tinct
in•dite
in•di-vid•ual

in•di-vidu-al•ism
in•di-vidu-al•ist
in•di-vidu-al-is•tic
in•di-vidu-al•ize
in•di-vidu-ally

in•di-vid-uals
in•di-vis-ible
In•do-china
Indo--Chinese
in•doc-tri-nate

in•doc-tri-na-tion
in•do-lence
in•do-lent
in•domi-ta•ble
In•do-ne•sia

In•do-ne-sian
in•door
in•du-bi-ta•bly
in•duce
in•duce-ment

in•duc-ing
in•duct
in•ducted
in•ductee
in•duct-ing

in•duc-tion
in•duc-tive
in•dulge
in•dul-gence
in•dul-gent

in•dulg-ing
in•dus-trial
in•dus-tri-al•ism
in•dus-tri-al•ist
in•dus-tri-al•ize

in•dus-tri-ally
in•dus-tries
in•dus-tri•ous
in•dus-try
ine-bri•ate

ine-bria-tion
in•ed-ible
in•edu-ca•ble
in•ef-fec-tive
in•ef-fec-tual

in•ef-fi-cien-cies
in•ef-fi-ciency
in•ef-fi-cient
in•ef-fi-ciently
in•elas-tic•ity

in•eli-gi•ble
in•elo-quent
inept
in•ep-ti-tude
in•eptly

in•ept-ness
in•equali-ties
in•equal-ity
in•eq-ui-ta•ble
in•eq-ui-ta•bly

in•eq-ui-ties
in•eq-uity
inert
in•er-tia
in•es-cap-able

in•es-cap-ably
in•es-sen-tial
in•es-ti-ma•ble
in•evi-ta•ble
in•ex-act

in•ex-ac-ti-tude
in•ex-cus-able
in•ex-haust-ible
in•ex-pen-sive
in•ex-pe-ri-enced

in•ex-plain-able
in•fal-li•ble
in•fa-mous
in•famy
in•fant

in•fan-tile
in•fan-tries
in•fan-try
in•fatu-ate
in•fatu-at•ing

in•fatu-ation
in•fea-si•ble
in•fect
in•fec-tion
in•fec-tious

infer
in•fer-ence
in•fer-en-tial
in•fe-rior
in•fe-ri-or•ity

in•fer-nal
in•ferno
in•ferred
in•fer-ring
in•fer-til•ity

in•fest
in•fes-ta-tion
in•fest-ing
in•fi-del
in•fi-del•ity

in•field
in•fielder
in•fil-trate
in•fil-trat•ing
in•fil-tra-tion

in•fil-tra•tor
in•fi-nite
in•fi-nitely
in•fini-tesi•mal
in•fini-tive

in•fin-ity
in•firm
in•fir-mary
in•fir-mity
in•flam-ma•ble

in•flam-ma-tion
in•flam-ma-tory
in•flate
in•flat-ing
in•fla-tion

in•fla-tion•ary
in•flec-tion
in•flexi-bil•ity
in•flex-ible
in•flict

in•flict-ing
in•flic-tion
in•flo-res-cence
in•flu-ence
in•flu-ences

in•flu-enc•ing
in•flu-en-tial
in•flu-enza
in•flux
in•form

in•for-mal
in•for-mal•ity
in•for-mally
in•for-mant
in•for-ma-tion

in•for-ma-tional
in•for-ma-tive
in•former
in•form-ing
in•frac-tion

infra-red
infra-struc-ture
in•fre-quent
in•fre-quently
in•fringe

in•fringe-ment
in•fring-ing
in•fu-ri•ate
in•fu-ri-at•ing
in•fuse

in•fus-ing
in•fu-sion
in•ge-nious
in•ge-nue
in•ge-nu•ity

in•genu-ous
in•gest
in•gest-ing
in•ges-tion
in•ges-tive

in•glo-ri•ous
ingot
in•grain
in•grain-ing
in•grate

in•gra-ti•ate
in•gra-ti-at•ing
in•gra-tia-tion
in•grati-tude
in•gre-di•ent

in•gress
in•grown
in•habit
in•hab-it•ant
in•hab-it•ing

in•hale
in•haler
in•hal-ing
in•her-ent
in•her-ently

in•herit
in•heri-tance
in•her-ited
in•her-it•ing
in•hibit

in•hib-it•ing
in•hi-bi-tion
in•hos-pi-ta•ble
in•hu-man
in•hu-mane

in•iq-ui-tous
in•iq-uity
ini-tial
ini-tial•ing
ini-tial•ize

ini-tial-iz•ing
ini-tially
ini-ti•ate *(v.)*
ini-tiate *(n.)*
ini-ti-at•ing

ini-tia-tion
ini-tia-tive
ini-tia-tory
in•ject
in•ject-ing

in•jec-tion
in•junc-tion
in•junc-tive
in•jure
in•ju-ries

in•jur-ing
in•ju-ri•ous
in•jury
in•jus-tice
in•kling

in•laid
in•land
inlay
in•lay-ing
inlet

in•lets
in•mate
in•nate
in•nately
inner

inner-most
in•ning
inn-keeper
in•no-cence
in•no-cent

in•no-cently
in•nocu-ous
in•no-vate
in•no-vat•ing
in•no-va-tion

in•no-va-tive
in•no-va•tor
in•nu-endo
in•nu-mer-able
in•ocu-late

in•ocu-lat•ing
in•ocu-la-tion
in•of-fen-sive
in•op-er-able
in•op-por-tune

in•or-di-nate
in•or-di-nately
in•or-ganic
in•or-gani-cally
in-patient

input
in•put-ting
in•quest
in•quire
in•qui-ries

in•quir-ing
in•quiry
in•qui-si-tion
in•quisi-tive
in•roads

in•sane
in•sani-tary
in•san-ity
in•sa-tia•ble
in•scribe

in•scrib-ing
in•scrip-tion
in•scru-ta•ble
in•seam
in•sect

in•sec-ti-cide
in•se-cure
in•se-cu-rity
in•sen-si•ble
in•sen-si-tive

in•sepa-ra•ble
in•sert
in•sert-ing
in•ser-tion
in--service

in•side
in•sidi-ous
in•sight
in•sight-ful
in•sig-nia

in•sig-nifi-cant
in•sig-nifi-cantly
in•sin-cere
in•sin-cer•ity
in•sinu-ate

in•sinu-at•ing
in•sinu-ation
in•sipid
in•sist
in•sis-tence

in•sis-tent
in•sist-ing
in•so-far
in•so-late
in•so-la-tion

in•so-lence
in•so-lent
in•sol-uble
in•sol-vency
in•sol-vent

in•som-nia
in•som-niac
in•so-much
in•spect
in•spect-ing

in•spec-tion
in•spec-tor
in•spi-ra-tion
in•spi-ra-tional
in•spire

i

in•spir-ing
in•sta-bil•ity
in•stall
in•stal-la-tion
in•stall-ing

in•stall-ment
in•stance
in•stant
in•stan-ta-neous
in•stan-ta-neously

in•stantly
in•state
in•stead
in•step
in•sti-gate

in•sti-gat•ing
in•sti-ga-tion
in•sti-ga•tor
in•still
in•still-ing

in•stinct
in•stinc-tive
in•stinc-tively
in•sti-tute
in•sti-tuted

in•sti-tut•ing
in•sti-tu-tion
in•sti-tu-tional
in•struct
in•structed

in•struct-ing
in•struc-tion
in•struc-tional
in•struc-tive
in•struc-tor

in•stru-ment
in•stru-men•tal
in•stru-men-tally
in•sub-or-di-nate
in•sub-stan-tial

in•suf-fer-able
in•suf-fi-cient
in•suf-fi-ciently
in•su-late
in•su-lated

in•su-lat•ing
in•su-la-tion
in•su-lin
in•sult
in•sult-ing

in•sur-able
in•sur-ance
in•sure
in•surer
in•sur-ers

in•sur-gence
in•sur-gency
in•sur-gent
in•sur-ing
in•sur-mount-able

in•sur-rec-tion
in•sur-rec-tion•ist
in•tact
in•take
in•tan-gi•ble

in•te-ger
in•te-gral
in•te-grate
in•te-grat•ing
in•te-gra-tion

in•te-gra-tive
in•te-gra•tor
in•teg-rity
in•tel-lect
in•tel-lec-tual

in•tel-lec-tu-ally
in•tel-li-gence
in•tel-li-gent
in•tel-li-gently
in•tel-li-gi•ble

in•tem-per•ate
in•tend
in•tend-ing
in•tense
in•tensely

in•ten-si-fied
in•ten-sify
in•ten-si-fy•ing
in•ten-sity
in•ten-sive

in•ten-sively
in•tent
in•ten-tion
in•ten-tional
inter *(v.)*

in•ter-act
in•ter-act•ing
in•ter-ac-tion
in•ter-ac-tive
in•ter-agency

in•ter-block
in•ter-cede
in•ter-ced•ing
in•ter-cept
in•ter-cept•ing

in•ter-cep-tion
in•ter-cep•tor
in•ter-ces-sion
in•ter-change
in•ter-city

in•ter-col-le-giate
in•ter-com
in•ter-com-pany
in•ter-con-nect
in•ter-course

in•ter-cul-tural
in•ter-de-pen-dent
in•ter-dict
in•ter-dict•ing
in•ter-dic-tion

in•ter-di-vi-sion
in•ter-est
in•ter-ested
in•ter-est•ing
in•ter-est-ingly

in•ter-face
in•ter-fa-cial
in•ter-fac•ing
in•ter-faith
in•ter-fere

in•ter-fered
in•ter-fer-ence
in•ter-fer•ing
in•ter-ga-lac•tic
in•ter-globu•lar

in•terim
in•te-rior
in•ter-ject
in•ter-ject•ing
in•ter-jec-tion

in•ter-leaf
in•ter-leav•ing
in•ter-lock
in•ter-lude
in•ter-lu•nar

in•ter-mar-riage
in•ter-marry
in•ter-me-di•ary
in•ter-ment
in•ter-mezzo

in•ter-mi-na•ble
in•ter-min•gle
in•ter-min-gling
in•ter-mis-sion
in•ter-mit-tent

in•ter-mit-tently
in•ter-mo-lecu•lar
in•ter-moun-tain
in•tern
in•ter-nal

in•ter-nal•ize
in•ter-nal-iz•ing
in•ter-nally
in•ter-na-tional
in•ter-na-tion-ally

in•tern-ing
in•ter-nist
in•tern-ment
in•tern-ship
in•ter-of-fice

in•ter-op-er-able
in•ter-or-bital
in•ter-per-sonal
in•ter-plane-tary
in•ter-po-late

in•ter-po-lat•ing
in•ter-po-la-tion
in•ter-pret
in•ter-pre-ta-tion
in•ter-pre-ta-tive

in•ter-preted
in•ter-preter
in•ter-pret•ing
in•ter-pre-tive
in•ter-ra-cial

in•ter-rec•ord
in•terred
in•ter-re-lated
in•ter-ring
in•ter-ro-gate

in•ter-ro-gated
in•ter-ro-gat•ing
in•ter-ro-ga-tion
in•ter-roga-tive
in•ter-ro-ga•tor

in•ter-roga-tory
in•ter-rupt
in•ter-rupt•ing
in•ter-rup-tion
in•ter-rup-tive

in•ter-scho-las•tic
in•ter-school
in•ter-sect
in•ter-sect•ing
in•ter-sec-tion

in•ter-sec-tional
in•ter-seg-ment
in•ter-space
in•ter-sperse
in•ter-spers•ing

in•ter-sper-sion
in•ter-state
in•ter-stel•lar
in•ter-twine
in•ter-twin•ing

in•ter-user
in•ter-val
in•ter-vene
in•ter-ven•ing
in•ter-ven-tion

in•ter-view
in•ter-viewer
in•ter-view•ing
in•ter-wo•ven
in•tes-tacy

in•tes-tate
in•tes-ti•nal
in•tes-tines
in•ti-macy
in•ti-mate

in•ti-mately
in•ti-mat•ing
in•timi-date
in•timi-dat•ing
in•timi-da-tion

in•tol-er-ance
in•tol-er•ant
in•tone
in•toxi-cant
in•toxi-cate

in•toxi-cat•ing
in•toxi-ca-tion
in•toxi-ca-tive
in•tra-cel-lu•lar
in•tra-city

in•tra-com-pany
in•tra-mo-lecu•lar
in•tra-mu•ral
in•tra-mus-cu•lar
in•tran-si-tive

in•tra-of-fice
in•tra-state
in•tra-ve-nous
in•trepid
in•tri-ca-cies

in•tri-cacy
in•tri-cate
in•trigue
in•trigu-ing
in•trin-sic

in•trin-si-cally
in•tro-duce
in•tro-duces
in•tro-duc•ing
in•tro-duc-tion

in•tro-duc-tory
in•tro-ject
in•tro-jec-tion
in•tro-spect
in•tro-spec-tion

in•tro-spec-tive
in•tro-ver-sion
in•tro-vert
in•trude
in•truder

in•trud-ing
in•tru-sion
in•tru-sive
in•tu-ition
in•tu-itive

in•un-date
in•un-dat•ing
in•un-da-tion
inure
in•ured

in•ur-ing
in•vade
in•vader
in•vad-ers
in•vad-ing

in•va-lid (n.)
in•valid (adj.)
in•vali-date
in•vali-dat•ing
in•vali-da-tion

in•valu-able
in•vari-able
in•va-sion
in•va-sive
in•vent

in•vent-ing
in•ven-tion
in•ven-tive
in•ven-tor
in•ven-to-ried

in•ven-to-ries
in•ven-tory
in•ven-to-ry•ing
in•verse
in•ver-sion

in•vert
in•ver-te-brate
in•verter
in•vert-ing
in•vest

in•ves-ti-gate
in•ves-ti-gat•ing
in•ves-ti-ga-tion
in•ves-ti-ga-tive
in•ves-ti-ga•tor

in•ves-ti-ga-tory
in•vest-ing
in•ves-ti-ture
in•vest-ment
in•ves-tor

in•vigo-rate
in•vigo-rat•ing
in•vigo-ra-tion
in•vin-ci•ble
in•vio-late

in•vis-ible
in•vi-ta-tion
in•vi-ta-tional
in•vite
in•vi-tee

in•vit-ing
in•vo-ca-tion
in•voice
in•voices
in•voic-ing

in•voke
in•vok-ing
in•vol-un-tary
in•vo-lute
in•volve

in•volve-ment
in•volv-ing
in•ward
in•wardly
io•dine

ionic
ion-iza-tion
ion•ize
ion-iz•ing
iono-sphere

iono-spheric
iota
Iowa
Iowan
Iran

Ira-nian
Iraq
Iraqi
irate
irately

Ire-land
iri-des-cence
iri-des-cent
Irish
ironed

ironic
iron-ical
iro-nies
iron-ing
iron-worker

iron-works
irony
ir•ra-di•ate
ir•ra-di-at•ing
ir•ra-tio•nal

ir•ra-tio-nally
ir•re-fut-able
ir•regu-lar
ir•regu-lari-ties
ir•regu-lar•ity

ir•rele-vance
ir•rele-vancy
ir•rele-vant
ir•re-li-gious
ir•repa-ra•ble

ir•re-place-able
ir•re-sist-ible
ir•reso-lute
ir•re-spon-si•ble
ir•rev-er-ence

ir•rev-er•ent
ir•re-vers-ible
ir•revo-ca•ble
ir•ri-gate
ir•ri-gat•ing

ir•ri-ga-tion
ir•ri-ta•ble
ir•ri-tant
ir•ri-tate
ir•ri-tat•ing

ir•ri-ta-tion
is•land
is•lander
isle
iso-late

iso-lat•ing
iso-la-tion
iso-la-tion•ist
iso-met-rics
Is•rael

Is•raeli
Is•ra-el•ite
issu-ance
issue
is•sued

is•su-ing
Ital-ian
italic
itali-cize
itali-ciz•ing

Italy
itch-ing
item
item-ize
item-izes

item-iz•ing
it•er-ate
it•era-tion
it•era-tive
itin-er•ant

itin-er-ar•ies
itin-er•ary
its *(possessive)*
it's *(it is)*
it•self

ivo-ries
ivory

jabbed
jackal
jacket
jack-ets
jack-hammer

jack-knife
jack-knifing
jack-pot
jack-rabbit
Ja•cuzzi

jag•ged
jag-ged-ness
jag-gies
jag•uar
jail

jail-break
jailed
jailer
ja•lop-ies
ja•lopy

Ja•maica
Ja•mai-can
jam-bo•ree
jammed
jam-ming

jan•gle
jan-gling
jani-tor
jani-to-rial
Janu-ary

Japan
Japa-nese
jar•gon
jarred
jar-ring

jas-mine
jas•per
jaun-dice
Java
Ja•va-nese

jave-lin
jaw-bone
jaw-breaker
Jay-cee
jay-walk

jay-walker
jay-walking
jazzy
jeal-ous
jeal-ously

jeal-ousy
jeans
jeered
jeer-ing
jelled

jel-lied
jel-lies
jelly
jelly-bean
jeop-ar-dize

jeop-ar-diz•ing
jeop-ardy
jer•sey
jet-liner
jet-port

jet-ting
jet-ti•son
jewel
jew-eled
jew-eler

jew-elry
jew•els
Jew•ish
Jewry
jiffy

jig•gle
jig-gling
jig•saw
jilted
jilt-ing

jim-mied
jim-my•ing
jin•gle
jin-gling
jinx-ing

jit•ney
jitter-bug
jitter-bugging
jit-tery
job•ber

job-bers
job-less
job-less-ness
jockey
jock-eyed

jock-ey•ing
jocu-lar
jocu-lar•ity
jogged
jog•ger

jog-gers
jog-ging
joined
joiner
join-ing

jointly
joker
jok•ers
jok•ing
jok-ingly

jolly
jolted
jolt-ing
Jor•dan
Jor-da-nian

jos•tle
jos-tled
jos-tling
jour-nal
jour-nal•ism

jour-nal•ist
jour-nal-is•tic
jour-nal•ize
jour-nal-iz•ing
jour-ney

jour-neyed
jour-ney•ing
jousted
joust-ing
jo•vial

jo•vi-al•ity
joy•ful
joy-fully
joy-ful-ness
joy•ous

joy-ously
joy-ride
joy-stick
ju•bi-lant
ju•bi-la-tion

ju•bi-lee
judged
judges
judge-ship
judg-ing

judg-ment
judg-men•tal
ju•di-ca-tory
ju•di-cial
ju•di-ciary

ju•di-cious
ju•di-ciously
judo
jug-ger-naut
jug•gle

jug-gled
jug-gler
jug-gling
jugu-lar
juicer

juices
juic-ing
juicy
juke-box
July

jum•ble
jum-bling
jumped
jumper
jump-ers

jump-ing
jumpy
junc-tion
junc-ture
June

jun•gle
ju•nior
ju•ni-per
jun•ket
jun-ket•ing

jun-kets
junk-yard
junta
Ju•pi-ter
ju•ries

ju•ris-dic-tion
ju•ris-dic-tional
ju•ris-pru-dence
ju•ris-pru-dent
ju•rist

juror
ju•rors
jury
jus-tice
jus-tices

jus-ti-fi-able
jus-ti-fi-ca-tion
jus-ti-fied
jus-ti-fies
jus-tify

jus-ti-fy•ing
jut•ted
jut-ting
ju•ve-nile
jux-ta-po-si-tion

ka•lei-do-scope
ka•mi-kaze
kan-ga•roo
Kan•san
Kan•sas

ka•rate
ka•ty-did
kayak
kay•aks
kazoo

ka•zoos
keenly
keeper
keep-ing
keep-sake

ken•nel
Ken-tuckian
Ken-tucky
Kenya
Ke•nyan

ker-chief
ker•nel
kern-ing
kero-sene
ket•tle

kettle-drum
ket-tles
key-board
key-boarding
keyed

key-hole
key•ing
key-less
key-lock
key-note

key-noting
key•pad
key-punch
key-punching
key-word

khaki
kib-butz
kick-back
kicked
kicker

kick-ing
kick-off (n.)
kick-stand
kid•ded
kid•der

kid-ding
kid•nap
kid-napped
kid-nap•per
kid-nap-ping

kid•ney
kid-neys
killed
killer
kill-ers

kill-ing
kiln
ki•lo-byte
kilo-cy•cle
ki•lo-gram

ki•lo-hertz
ki•lo-me•ter
kilo-watt
ki•mono
kinder

kin-der-gar•ten
kin-der-gart•ner
kind-hearted
kin•dle
kin-dling

kindly
kind-ness
kin-dred
ki•ne-scope
ki•ne-sics

ki•ne•sis
kin-es-thetic
ki•netic
king-dom
kins-folks

kin-ship
kiss-able
kissed
kiss-ing
kitchen

kitch-en-ette
kitch-ens
kit•ten
kit-tens
kit-ties

knap-sack
knead-ing
knee-cap
knick-knack
knife

knifed
knight
knighted
knight-hood
knight-ing

knit-ted
knit-ting
knives
knobby
knock-down (n.)

knocked
knock-ing
knock-out (n.)
knot-hole
knot-ted

knot-ting
know--how
know-ing
know-ingly
knowl-edge

knowl-edge-able
knowl-edged
knuckle
knuckle-ball
knuck-ling

koala
Korea
Ko•rean
ko•sher
kudos

kum-quat

label
la•beled
la•bel-ing
la•bels
labor

labo-ra-to-ries
labo-ra-tory
la•bored
la•borer
la•bor-ing

la•bo-ri•ous
la•bo-ri•ously
la•bors
laby-rinth
lac-er•ate

lac-era-tion
lacka-dai-si•cal
lacked
lackey
lack-eys

lack-ing
lack-lus•ter
la•conic
la•coni-cally
lac-quer

la•crosse
lad•der
lad-ders
laden
la•dies

lad•ing
ladle
la•dles
lady-bug
lady-finger

lady-like
lag-gard
lag-ging
la•goon
la•guna

laity
lake-shore
lake-side
lal-ly-gag
La•maze

lam-baste
lam-bast•ing
lame-brain
lame-ness
la•ment

la•men-ta•ble
lam-en-ta-tion
la•ment-ing
lami-nate
lami-nat•ing

lami-na-tion
lami-na•tor
lamp-light
lam-poon
lam-poon•ist

lamp-shade
lanced
lancer
lanc-ing
landed

land-fill
land-holder
land-ing
land-locked
land-mark

land-owner
land-scape
land-scap•ing
land-slide
land-ward

lan-guage
lan-guages
lan-guid
lan-guidly
lan-guish

lan-guish•ing
lanky
lano-lin
lan-tern
Laos

Lao-tian
lapel
lap•ful
lapi-dary
Lap-land

Lap-lander
lapped
lap-ping
lapsed
lapses

laps-ing
lap•top
lar-ce-nist
lar-ceny
largely

larger
larg-est
lariat
lari-ats
lark-spur

larva
lar•vae
lar-yn-gi•tis
lar•ynx
las-civi•ous

laser
laser-jet
lashed
lash-ing
lasso

las-soed
las-so•ing
lasted
last-ing
lastly

latches
latch-ing
latch-key
latch-string
lately

la•tency
la•tent
later
lat-eral
lat-er-ally

lat•est
latex
lather
lath-ered
lath-er•ing

Latin
lati-tude
lati-tu-di•nal
la•trine
lat•ter

lat-tice
lattice-work
Lat•via
Lat-vian
laud-able

lau-da-tory
lauded
laud-ing
laugh-able
laugh-ing

laugh-ter
launched
launcher
launches
launch-ing

laun-der
laun-der•ing
laun-dries
Laun-dro-mat
laun-dry

lau-re•ate
lau•rel
lava-tory
lav-en•der
lav•ish

lav-ish•ing
law--abiding
law-breaker
law•ful
law-less

law-maker
law-making
law-suit
law•yer
law-yers

laxa-tive
lax•ity
lay-away (n.)
layer
lay-ered

lay-er•ing
lay•off (n.)
lay•out (n.)
lay-over (n.)
la•zily

la•zi-ness
lazy
leaded
leaden
leader

lead-ers
lead-er-ship
lead-ing
lead-work
leaf-ing

leaf-let
league
leak-age
leaked
leak-ing

leak-proof
leaky
lean-ing
lean-ness
leap-frog

leap-ing
learned
learner
learn-ing
leased

lease-holder
leases
leas-ing
leather
leather-neck

leath-ery
leaven
leav-ing
Leba-nese
Leba-non

lech-er•ous
lech-ery
leci-thin
lec-tern
lec-ture

lec-turer
lec-tur•ing
led•ger
led-gers
leech-ing

lee-ward
lee•way
left-ist
left-over
lega-cies

leg•acy
legal
le•gal-ese
le•gal-is•tic
le•gal-ities

le•gal-ity
le•gal-iza-tion
le•gal-ize
le•gal-iz•ing
le•gally

le•gato
leg•end
leg-end•ary
leg-ging
leg-horn

legi-bil•ity
leg-ible
leg-ibly
le•gion
le•gion-ary

le•gion-naire
leg-is-late
leg-is-lat•ing
leg-is-la-tion
leg-is-la-tive

111

leg-is-la•tor
leg-is-la-tors
leg-is-la-ture
legit
le•giti-macy

le•giti-mate
le•giti-mately
le•giti-ma-tize
leg-room
le•gume

leg-work
lei-sure
lei-surely
lemon
lem-on-ade

lem•ons
lender
lend-ing
lengthen
length-ened

length-en•ing
length-wise
lengthy
le•niency
le•nient

lenses
leop-ard
leo-tard
lep-re-chaun
lep-rosy

lep-rous
les-bian
le•sion
les•see
les-sees

lessen
less-ened
less-en•ing
less-ens
lesser

les•son
les-sons
les•sor
let-down (n.)
le•thal

le•thar-gic
leth-argy
let•ter
letter-head
let-ter•ing

let-ters
let-ting
let-tuce
leu-ke•mia
levee

level
lev-eled
lev-el•ing
lev•els
lever

le•ver-age
lev•ied
lev•ies
levi-tate
levi-tat•ing

levi-ta-tion
lev•ity
levy-ing
lewd-ness
lexi-cog-ra-pher

lexi-cog-ra•phy
lexi-con
lia-bili-ties
lia-bil•ity
li•able

li•ai-son
libel
li•bel-ing
li•bel-ous
lib-eral

lib-er-al•ism
lib-er-al•ize
lib-er-al-iz•ing
lib-er-ally
lib-er•ate

lib-er-at•ing
lib-era-tion
lib-era•tor
lib-er-ties
lib-erty

li•brar-ian
li•brar-ies
li•brary
Libya
Libyan

li•cense
li•censes
li•cens-ing
licked
lick-ing

lico-rice
lied
lien
lien-holder
lieu

lieu-ten•ant	lilac	linked
life-blood	lil•ies	link-ing
life-boat	lily	li•no-leum
life-guard	lim•ber	Li•no-type
life-less	limbo	lin-seed
life-line	lime-ade	li•poma
life-saver	lime-light	lip-reading
life-saving	lim-er•ick	lip-stick
life-time	lime-stone	liq-ue-fac-tion
lifted	limit	liq-ue-fi-able
lift-ing	limi-ta-tion	liq-ue-fied
lift--off	lim-ited	liq-uefy
liga-ment	lim-it•ing	liq-ue-fy•ing
li•ga-tion	lim-it-less	li•queur
lighten	lim•its	liq•uid
light-en•ing	lim-ou-sine	liq-ui-date
ligh-ter	limp-ing	liq-ui-dat•ing
light--headed	lin•age	liq-ui-da-tion
light-hearted	linch-pin	liq-ui-da•tor
light-house	lin•eal	li•quidi-ties
light-ing	lin•ear	li•quid-ity
lightly	line-backer	liq-uid•ize
light--minded	lined	liq-uid-iz•ing
light-ning	linen	li•quor
light-weight	liner	listed
lik-able	lineup	lis•ten
liked	lin•ger	lis-tener
like-li•est	lin-ge•rie	lis-ten•ing
like-li-ness	lin-ger•ing	lis-tens
likely	lin-gers	list-ing
liken	lin-guist	list-less
lik-ened	lin-guis•tic	list-lessly
like-ness	lini-ment	lit•any
like-wise	lin•ing	liter
lik•ing	link-age	lit-er•acy

lit-eral	loaded	lock-out (n.)
lit-er-ally	loader	lock-smith
lit-er•ary	load-ing	lock-step
lit-er•ate	loaf-ers	lockup (n.)
lit-era-ture	loaf-ing	lo•co-mo-tion
li•ters	loaned	lo•co-mo-tive
lith-ium	loaner	lo•cust
litho-graph	loan-ing	lo•cu-tion
li•thog-ra•phy	loathe	lode-star
liti-ga•ble	loath-ing	lodges
liti-gant	loath-some	lodg-ing
liti-gate	loaves	loft-ily
liti-ga-tion	lob-bied	loga-rithm
li•ti-gious	lob-bies	loges
lit•ter	lobby	logged
litter-bug	lob-by•ing	log•ger
lit-ter•ing	lob-by•ist	log-ging
lit-ters	lo•bot-omy	logic
lit•tle	lob-ster	log-ical
lit-urgy	local	logi-cally
liv-able	lo•cale	lo•gis-ti•cal
lived	lo•cal-ity	lo•gis-ti-cally
live-lier	lo•cal-ize	lo•gis-ti-cian
live-li•est	lo•cal-iz•ing	lo•gis-tics
live-li-hood	lo•cally	logo
lively	lo•cate	log--off
liven	lo•cat-ing	log--on
liver	lo•ca-tion	log--out
liv-er-wurst	lo•ca-tor	loi•ter
liv•ery	locked	loi-terer
live-stock	locker	lol-li•pop
livid	locket	lolly-gag
liv-id-ness	lock-ing	lone-li-ness
liv•ing	lock-jaw	lonely
liz•ard	lock-nut	loner

lone-some
longed
lon•ger
lon-gest
lon-gev•ity

long-hand
long-ing
long-ingly
lon-gi-tude
lon-gi-tu-di•nal

lon-gi-tu-di-nally
long--range
long--standing
long--suffering
long--term

looked
looker
look-ing
look-out
loom-ing

loop-back
looped
loop-hole
loop-ing
loose

loose--leaf
loosely
loosen
loos-ened
loos-en•ing

loos-ens
looted
looter
loot-ers
loot-ing

lopped
lop-ping
lop-sided
lo•qua-cious
lo•quac-ity

lose
loser
los•ers
loses
los•ing

losses
lo•tion
lot-ter•ies
lot-tery
louder

loud-est
loudly
loud-mouth
loud-speaker
Loui-si•ana

Loui-si-an•ian
lounged
lounges
loung-ing
lou•ver

lov-able
loved
love-lier
love-li•est
love-li-ness

lovely
lover
lov•ing
lov-ingly
low-down *(n.)*

lower
lower-case
low-ered
low-er•ing
low•est

low-land
low-li-ness
lowly
loyal
loy-ally

loy-al-ties
loy-alty
loz-enge
luau
lu•bri-cant

lu•bri-cate
lu•bri-cat•ing
lu•bri-ca-tion
lucid
lu•cidly

luck-ier
lucki-est
luck-ily
lucky
lu•cra-tive

lu•di-crous
lug-gage
lugged
lug-ging
luke-warm

lul-la-bies
lul-laby
lulled
lum-bago
lum•bar

lum•ber
lum-ber•ing
lumber-jack
lumber-yard
lu•mi-nance

lu•mi-nary
lu•mi-nes-cence
lu•mi-nes-cent
lu•mi-nous
lumped

lump-ing
lu•nacy
lunar
lu•na-tic
lun-cheon

lunches
lunch-ing
lunch-room
lunges
lung-ing

lus-cious
lus-ciously
lusted
lus•ter
lus-ter-less

lust-ful
lust-fully
lust-ily
lust-ing
lus-trous

luxu-ri•ant
luxu-ries
luxu-ri•ous
lux•ury
ly•ceum

lying
lym-phatic
lym-phoid
lynch-ing
lyric

lyr-ical
lyri-cist

ma•ca-bre
mac-adam
maca-roni
maca-roon
Mach

ma•chete
ma•chine
ma•chin-ery
ma•chin-ist
macro

macro--command
mac-ro-cosm
mac•ros
mad•den
mad-den•ing

ma•de-moi-selle
mad-house
madly
mad-ness
mad-ri•gal

mael-strom
mae-stro
mafia
maga-zine
magic

mag-ical
magi-cally
ma•gi-cian
mag-is-tracy
mag-is-trate

mag-na-nim•ity
mag-nani-mous
mag-ne-sium
mag•net
mag-netic

mag-ne-tism
mag-ne-tize
mag-ne-tiz•ing
mag-neto
mag-ni-fi-ca-tion

mag-ni-fi-cent
mag-nifi-cently
mag-ni-fied
mag-ni-fier
mag-nify

mag-ni-fy•ing
mag-ni-tude
mag-no•lia
mag•pie
mag--stripe

ma•ha-raja
ma•hog-any
mail-able
mail-bag
mail-box

mail-boxes
mailed
mailer
mail-ers
mail-ing

mail-room
Maine
Mainer
main-frame
main-land

main-lander
main-line *(v.)*
main-lining
mainly
main-stay

main-stream
main-streaming
main-tain
main-tain•ing
main-te-nance

ma•jes-tic
ma•jes-ti•cal
ma•jes-ti-cally
maj-esty
major

ma•jored
ma•jor-ing
ma•jori-ties
ma•jor-ity
ma•jors

maker
mak•ers
make-shift
makeup *(n.)*
mak•ing

mal-ad-just-ment
mal•ady
mal-aise
mala-prop•ism
ma•laria

Ma•laya
Ma•layan
Ma•lay-sia
Ma•lay-sian
mal-con-tent

ma•levo-lent
mal-fea-sance
mal-formed
mal-func-tion
mal-func-tion•ing

mal•ice
ma•li-cious
ma•li-ciously
ma•lign
ma•lig-nancy

ma•lig-nant
ma•lign-ing
mal-lea•ble
mal•let
mal-nour-ished

mal-nu-tri-tion
mal-prac-tice
mal-treat
mal-treat•ing
mal-treat-ment

mambo
mam•mal
mam-mo-gram
mam-mog-ra•phy
mam-moth

man-acle
man•age
man-age-able
man-age-ment
man-ager

mana-ge-rial
man-ag•ers
man-ages
man-ag•ing
man-date

man-dat•ing
man-da-tory
man-do•lin
ma•neu-ver
ma•neu-vered

ma•neu-ver•ing
man•ger
man•gle
man-gling
mango

man-goes
man-handle
man-handling
mania
ma•niac

ma•nia-cal
ma•ni-acs
mani-cure
mani-cur•ing
mani-cur•ist

mani-fest
mani-fes-ta-tion
mani-fest•ing
mani-festly
mani-festo

mani-fold
ma•nila
ma•nipu-late
ma•nipu-lat•ing
ma•nipu-la-tion

ma•nipu-la-tive
ma•nipu-la•tor
Mani-toba
Mani-toban
man-ne-quin

man•ner
man-ner•ism
man-nerly
man-ners
manor

man•ors
man-sion
man-slaughter
man•tel
mantel-piece

man•tle
man-tles
man•ual
manu-ally
man-uals

manu-fac-ture
manu-fac-turer
manu-fac-tur•ing
ma•nure
manu-script

maple
mapped
map-ping
mara-thon
ma•rauder

mar•ble
mar-bles
March
marched
marches

march-ing
mar-ga-rine
mar-ga-rita
mar•gin
mar-ginal

mar-gin-ally
mar-gins
mari-gold
mari-juana
ma•rina

mari-nade
mari-nate
mari-nat•ing
ma•rine
mari-ner

mari-onette
mari-tal
mari-time
mark-down *(n.)*
marked

mark-edly
marker
mark-ers
mar•ket
mar-ket-able

mar-keted
mar-ket•ing
market-place
mar-kets
mark-ing

markup *(n.)*
ma•roon
ma•roon-ing
mar-quee
marred

mar-riage
mar-riage-able
mar-ried
mar-ries
mar•row

marry
mar-ry•ing
mar-shal
mar-shal•ing
marshes

marsh-mal•low
marshy
mar-tial
mar-tial•ing
Mar-tian

mar-ti•net
mar-tini
mar•tyr
mar-tyr•dom
mar•vel

mar-vel•ing
mar-vel•ous
mar-vels
Mary-land
Mary-lander

mas•cot
mas-cu-line
mas-cu-lin•ity
mashed
mash-ing

masked
mask-ing
mas-och•ism
mas-och•ist
mason

118

Ma•son-ite
ma•sonry
mas-quer•ade
mas-quer-ades
mas-quer-ad•ing

Mas-sa-chu-setts
mas-sa•cre
mas-sa-cres
mas-sage
mas-sages

mas-sag•ing
masses
mas-sive
mas-tec-tomy
mas•ter

mas-ter•ful
mas-ter•ing
master-mind
master-piece
mas-ters

mas-tery
mast-head
mas-ti-cate
mas-ti-cat•ing
mas-ti-ca-tion

mast-odon
mas-toid
mata-dor
match-book
matched

matches
match-ing
match-less
match-maker
ma•te-rial

ma•te-ri-al•ism
ma•te-ri-al•ist
ma•te-ri-al-is•tic
ma•te-ri-al•ize
ma•te-ri-al-izes

ma•te-ri-al-iz•ing
ma•te-ri-ally
ma•te-ri•als
ma•ter-nal
ma•ter-nally

ma•ter-nity
mathe-mat-ical
mathe-mati-cally
mathe-ma-ti-cian
mathe-mat•ics

mati-nee
mat•ing
ma•tri-arch
ma•tri-ar•chy
ma•tri-cide

ma•tricu-late
ma•tricu-lat•ing
ma•tricu-la-tion
mat-ri-mo-nial
mat-ri-mony

ma•trix
ma•tron
mat•ted
mat•ter
mat-ters

mat-ting
mat-tress
matu-rate
matu-rat•ing
matu-ra-tion

matu-ra-tional
ma•ture
ma•turely
ma•ture-ness
ma•tur-ing

ma•tu-rity
matzo
maud-lin
mauled
maul-ing

mau-so-leum
mav-er•ick
maxim
maxi-mal
maxi-mi-za-tion

maxi-mize
maxi-miz•ing
max•ims
maxi-mum
Maya

Mayan
maybe
may•hem
may-on-naise
mayor

may-oral
may-or-alty
may•ors
meadow
meadow-land

mea•ger
mea-gerly
mea-ger-ness
meal-time
me•an-der

m

me•an-der•ing
mean-ing
mean-ing•ful
mean-ing-less
mean-time

mean-while
mea-sles
mea•sly
mea-sur-able
mea-sure

mea-sure-ment
mea-sur•ing
meat-ball
me•chanic
me•chan-ical

me•chani-cally
me•chan-ics
mecha-nism
mecha-nize
mecha-nizes

mecha-niz•ing
medal
med-al•ist
me•dal-lion
med•als

med•dle
med-dler
med-dles
meddle-some
med-dling

media
me•dial
me•dian
me•di-ate
me•di-at•ing

me•dia-tion
me•dia-tor
medic
med-ical
medi-cally

medi-care
medi-cate
medi-cat•ing
medi-ca-tion
me•dici-nal

medi-cine
med•ics
me•di-eval
me•di-eval•ism
me•dio-cre

me•di-oc-rity
medi-tate
medi-tat•ing
medi-ta-tion
medi-ta-tive

Medi-ter-ra-nean
me•dium
med•ley
meek-ness
meet-ing

meeting-house
mega-byte
mega-cy•cle
mega-hertz
mega-lo-ma•nia

mega-phone
mega-watt
mel-an-cho•lia
mel-an-cholic
mel-an-choly

melee
me•lees
mel•low
mel-low•ing
me•lodic

melo-dies
me•lo-di•ous
melo-drama
melo-dra-matic
mel•ody

melon
mel•ons
melt-down
melted
melt-ing

mem•ber
mem-ber-ship
mem-brane
me•mento
me•men-tos

mem•oir
mem-oirs
memo-ra-bilia
memo-ra•ble
memo-randa

memo-ran•dum
me•mo-rial
me•mo-ri-al•ize
me•mo-ri-al-iz•ing
memo-ries

memo-rize
memo-riz•ing
mem•ory
memos
men•ace

men-aces
men-ac•ing
me•nag-erie
mended
mend-ing

me•nial
me•nially
men-in-gi•tis
meno-pausal
meno-pause

men-strual
men-stru•ate
men-stru-at•ing
men-strua-tion
men•tal

men-tal•ist
men-tal•ity
men-tally
men-thol
men-tho-lated

men-tion
men-tion•ing
men•tor
menu
mer-can-tile

mer-ce-nary
mer-chan-dise
mer-chan-diser
mer-chan-dises
mer-chan-dis•ing

mer-chant
mer-ci•ful
mer-ci-fully
mer-ci-less
mer-cury

mercy
merely
mer•est
merged
merger

merg-ers
merges
merg-ing
me•rid-ian
merit

mer-ited
mer-it•ing
meri-to-ri•ous
mer•its
mer-maid

mer-ri•est
mer-rily
mer-ri-ment
merry-maker
merry-making

meshed
meshes
mesh-ing
mes-meric
mes-mer•ize

me•so-sphere
mes•quite
mes-sage
mes-sag•ing
mes-sen•ger

mess-ing
messy
meta-bolic
meta-bol-ical
me•tabo-lism

meta-car•pal
meta-car•pus
metal
meta-lan-guage
me•tal-lic

met-al-lur•gic
met-al-lur-gi•cal
met-al-lur-gist
met-al-lurgy
metal-worker

meta-phor
meta-phys-ical
meta-phys•ics
meta-tar•sal
meta-tar•sus

me•teor
me•te-or•ite
me•teo-ro-logic
me•teo-ro-log-ical
me•teo-rolo-gist

me•teo-rol•ogy
meter
me•tered
me•ter-ing
me•ters

metes
meth-ane
method
me•thodic
me•thod-ical

meth-od-olog-ical
meth-od-olo-gies
meth-od-ol•ogy
meth-ods
methyl

m

me•ticu-lous
met•ric
met-ri•cal
met-ri-cally
metro

metro-liner
met-ro-nome
me•tropo-lis
met-ro-poli•tan
met•tle

met-tle-some
Mexi-can
Mexico
mez-za-nine
Michi-gan

Michi-gan•der
micro
mi•cro-ana-lyst
mi•crobe
mi•crobes

mi•cro-bi-ol•ogy
mi•cro-blast
Mi•cro-card
mi•cro-cas-sette
mi•cro-chip

mi•cro-cir-cuit
mi•cro-code
mi•cro-com-puter
mi•cro-copy
mi•cro-cosm

mi•cro-disk
mi•cro-dis-kette
mi•cro-farad
mi•cro-fiche
mi•cro-film

mi•cro-filmed
mi•cro-film•ing
mi•cro-form
mi•cro-graph
mi•cro-graph•ics

mi•cro-graphy
mi•cro-grav•ity
mi•cro-groove
mi•cro-im-ages
mi•cro-lith

mi•cro-me•ter
mi•cron
mi•cro-or-gan•ism
mi•cro-phone
mi•cro-phon•ics

mi•cro-pro-gram
mi•cro-reader
mi•cros
mi•cro-scope
mi•cro-scopic

mi•cro-sec•ond
mi•cro-space
mi•cro-watt
mi•cro-wave
mid•air

mid-af-ter-noon
mid•day
mid•dle
Mid--east
midget

midg-ets
mid--life
mid-night
mid-point
mid-range

mid-riff
mid-sec-tion
mid-seg-ment
mid-se•mes•ter
mid-size

mid-stream
mid-sum•mer
mid-term
mid•way
mid-week

Mid-west
Mid-western
Mid-west-erner
mid-wife
mid-wifery

mid-win•ter
mid-year
might-ily
mighty
mi•gnon

mi•graine
mi•grant
mi•grate
mi•grates
mi•grat-ing

mi•gra-tion
mi•gra-tory
mil•dew
mildly
mild-ness

mile-age
mile-post
mile-stone
mili-ary
mi•lieu

mili-tancy
mili-tant
mili-ta-rist
mili-ta-ris•tic
mili-ta-rize

mili-ta-riz•ing
mili-tary
mili-tate
mili-tat•ing
mi•li-tia

milk-ing
mil-len•nia
mil-len-nial
mil-len-nium
miller

mil•let
mil•li-am•pere
mil•li-gram
mil•li-me•ter
mil-li•ner

mil-li-nery
mill-ing
mil-lion
mil-lion-aire
mil•li-sec•ond

mill-work
mill-wright
mimeo
mim-eo-graph
mim-eo-graph•ing

mimic
mim-icked
mim-icker
mim-ick•ing
mim-icry

mim•ics
minc-ing
minded
mind-ful
mind-ing

mind-less
mind-lessly
mined
miner
min-eral

min-er-al•ize
min-er-al-iz•ing
min-er-alo-gist
min-er-alogy
min-er•als

min•ers
min•gle
min-gling
min-ia-ture
min-ia-tur•ize

min-ia-tur-iz•ing
mini-cas-sette
mini-com-puter
mini-course
mini-dis-kette

mini-floppy
mini-mal
mini-mize
mini-miz•ing
mini-mum

min•ing
mini-se•ries
min-is•ter
min-is-te-rial
min-is-ter•ing

min-is-tra-tion
min-is-tries
min-is•try
Min-ne-sota
Min-ne-so•tan

min•now
minor
mi•nori-ties
mi•nor-ity
mi•nors

min-strel
minted
mint-ing
minu-end
min•uet

minus
mi•nus-cule
mi•nuses
min•ute (n.)
mi•nute (adj.)

mi•nutely
mi•nu-tia
mir-acle
mi•racu-lous
mi•racu-lously

mi•rage
mired
mir•ror
mir-ror•ing
mis-ad•ven-ture

mis-aligned
mis-align-ment
mis-al-li-ance
mis-an-thrope
mis-ap-pre-hend

m

mis-be•have
mis-be•hav•ing
mis-be•hav•ior
mis-be•lief
mis-cal•cu-lated

mis-cal•cul-at•ing
mis-cal•cu-la-tion
mis-car-riage
mis-car-ried
mis-carry

mis-cel-la-neous
mis-chief
mis-chie-vous
mis-chie-vous-ness
mis-clas-sify

mis-con-ceive
mis-con-cep-tion
mis-con-duct
mis-con-strue
mis-count

mis-count•ing
mis•cue
mis-deal
mis-deed
mis-de-meanor

miser
mis-er-able
mi•serly
mis•ery
mis-fire

mis•fit
mis-for-tune
mis-giv-ings
mis-guided
mis-han-dled

mis•hap
mis-in•form
mis-in•ter-pret
mis-in•ter-preted
mid-judge

mis-judg•ing
mis-la•bel
mis-la•bel-ing
mis-laid
mis•lay

mis-lead
mis-lead•ing
mis-man•age
mis-man-age-ment
mis•man-ag•ing

mis-match
mis-match•ing
mis-no•mer
mis-place
mis-place-ment

mis-plac•ing
mis-print
mis-print•ing
mis-pro-nounce
mis-quote

mis-quot•ing
mis-read
mis-rep-re-sent
mis-rep-re-sented
mis-routed

mis-rule
mis•sal
missed
mis-sent
misses

mis-sile
mis-silry
miss-ing
mis-sion
mis-sion-ar•ies

mis-sion•ary
Mis-sis-sippi
Mis-sis-sip-pian
mis-sive
Mis-souri

Mis-sou-rian
mis-spell
mis-spell•ing
mis-state
mis-state-ment

mis-stat•ing
mis-step
mis-take
mis-taken
mis-tak-enly

mis•ter
mis•tle-toe
mis-took
mis-treat
mis-treat•ing

mis-treat-ment
mis-trial
mis-trust
mis-trust•ing
misty

mis-type
mis-typ•ing
mis-un•der-stand
mis-un•der-stood
mis•use

mis-used	mod-el•ing	mois-tur-izes
mis-us•ing	mod•els	mois-tur-iz•ing
miter	modem	molar
miti-gate	mo•dems	mo•lars
miti-gat•ing	mod-er•ate	mo•las-ses
miti-ga-tion	mod-er-ately	molded
miti-ga-tory	mod-er-at•ing	mold-ing
mit-tens	mod-era-tion	moldy
mix-able	mod-era•tor	mo•lecu-lar
mixed	mod•ern	mole-cule
mixer	mod-ern-iza-tion	mole-hill
mix•ers	mod-ern•ize	mo•lest
mixes	mod-ern-izes	mo•les-ta-tion
mix•ing	mod-ern-iz•ing	mo•lester
mix-ture	mod•est	mo•lest-ing
mix--up (n.)	mod-estly	molly-coddle
mne-monic	mod-esty	molly-coddling
mne-mon•ics	modi-fied	mol•ten
moan-ing	modi-fier	mol-tenly
mo•bile	modi-fies	molt-ing
mo•bil-ity	mod•ify	mo•ment
mo•bi-lize	modi-fy•ing	mo•men-tarily
mo•bi-lizes	modu-lar	mo•men-tary
mo•bi-liz•ing	modu-late	mo•men-tous
mob-ster	modu-lat•ing	mo•men-tously
moc-ca•sin	modu-la-tion	mo•men-tum
moc-ca-sins	modu-la•tor	mon-arch
mocked	mod•ule	mon-ar-chies
mock-ery	mod-ules	mon-ar-chism
mock-ing	moisten	mon-ar-chist
mocking-bird	moist-ened	mon-ar•chy
mock-ingly	moist-ener	mon-as-tery
mock--up	moist-en•ing	mon-au•ral
model	mois-ture	Mon•day
mod-eled	mois-tur•ize	Mon-days

mone-tary
money
mon•eys
money-wise
Mon•gol

Mon-go•lia
Mon-go-lian
Mon-gol•oid
mon-grel
moni-tor

moni-tor•ing
moni-tory
mon•key
mon-keyed
mon-key•ing

mon-keys
mono-chrome
mono-cle
mon-ocu•lar
mo•noga-mist

mo•noga-mous
mo•nog-amy
mono-gram
mono-gram-ming
mono-graph

mono-lith
mono-lithic
mono-logue
mono-plane
mo•nopo-lies

mo•nopo-list
mo•nopo-lis•tic
mo•nopo-lize
mo•nopo-lizes
mo•nopo-liz•ing

mo•nop-oly
mono-rail
mono-syl-la•bic
mono-syl-la•ble
mono-tone

mo•noto-nous
mo•not-ony
mon-sei-gnor
mon-soon
mon-ster

mon-stros•ity
mon-strous
mon-tage
Mon-tana
Mon-tanan

month-lies
monthly
monu-ment
monu-men•tal
monu-men-tally

moodi-ness
moody
moon-beam
moon-light
moon-lighting

moon-scope
moon-shine
moon-struck
moon-tracking
moon-walk

moped
mo•peds
mop•pet
mop-pets
mop-ping

moral
mo•rale
mor-al•ist
mo•ral-ity
mor-al•ize

mor-al-iz•ing
mor-ally
mora-to-rium
mor•bid
mor-bidly

more-over
mores
morgue
morn-ing
Mo•roc-can

Mo•rocco
moron
mo•ronic
mo•rons
mo•rose

mor-phia
mor•phine
mor•sel
mor-sels
mor•tal

mor-tali-ties
mor-tal•ity
mor-tally
mor-tals
mor•tar

mortar-board
mort-gage
mort-gages
mort-gag•ing
mort-gagor

mor-ti-cian	motor-bike	moved
mor-ti-fi-ca-tion	motor-boat	move-ment
mor-ti-fied	motor-cade	mover
mor-tify	motor-cycle	mov•ers
mor-ti-fy•ing	mo•tored	movie
mor-tise	mo•tor-ing	mov•ies
mor-tu•ary	mo•tor-ist	mov•ing
mo•saic	mo•tor-ize	mowed
Mos•lem	mo•tor-izes	mower
Mos-lems	mo•tor-iz•ing	mow•ers
mos-quito	motor-scooter	mow•ing
mos-qui-toes	motto	mu•ci-lage
mostly	mot-toes	muck-rake
motel	mould-ing	muck-raker
mo•tels	mount	muck-rak•ing
moth-ball	moun-tain	mucus
mother	moun-tain•eer	mud-died
mother-board	moun-tain-side	mud•dle
moth-ered	moun-tain•ous	muddy
moth-er•ing	moun-te-bank	mud-dy•ing
mother-land	mounted	mud-slinger
moth-erly	mount-ing	mud-slinging
moth-proofed	mourned	muf•fin
motif	mourner	muf-fins
mo•tifs	mourn-ful	muf•fle
mo•tion	mourn-ing	muf-fler
mo•tion-ing	mouse-trap	muf-fling
mo•tion-less	mousse	mugged
mo•ti-vate	mous-tache	mug•ger
mo•ti-vates	mouthed	mug-ging
mo•ti-vat•ing	mouth-ful	muggy
mo•ti-va-tion	mouth-ing	mu•latto
mo•ti-va-tional	mouth-piece	mul-berry
mo•tive	mouth-wash	mulched
motor	mov-able	mulch-ing

mul•ti-ac•cess
mul•ti-ad•dress
mul•ti-chan-nel
mul•ti-col-ored
mul-ti-col•umn

mul•ti-com-puter
mul•ti-copy
mul•ti-cul-tural
mul•ti-drop
mul-ti-eth•nic

mul•ti-fac-eted
mul•ti-form
mul•ti-func-tional
mul•ti-lan-guage
mul•ti-lay-ered

mul•ti-level
mul•ti-lin-gual
mul•ti-linked
mul•ti-me•dia
mul•ti-mil-lion

mul•ti-na-tional
mul•ti-part
mul•ti-party
mul•ti-path
mul•ti-plat-form

mul-ti•ple
mul•ti-plex
mul•ti-plex•ing
mul•ti-plexor
mul-ti-pli-cand

mul-ti-pli-ca-tion
mul-ti-plic•ity
mul-ti-plied
mul-ti-plier
mul-ti-plies

mul-ti•ply
mul-ti-ply•ing
mul•ti-point
mul•ti-port
mul•ti-pro-ces•sor

mul•ti-pro-pel-lant
mul•ti-pur-pose
mul•ti-sec-tion
mul•ti-sen-sory
mul•ti-sided

mul•ti-sta-tion
mul•ti-tape
mul•ti-task•ing
mul•ti-thread•ing
mul-ti-tude

mul•ti-user
mul•ti-val•ued
mul•ti-ven•dor
mul-ti-vi•ta-min
mum•ble

mum-bles
mum-bling
mum-mi-fied
mum-mi-fies
mum-mify

mum-mi-fy•ing
mumps
munches
munch-ing
mun-dane

mu•nici-pal
mu•nici-pali-ties
mu•nici-pal•ity
mu•nici-pally
mu•ni-tion

mural
mu•ral-ist
mu•rals
mur•der
mur-derer

mur-der•ing
mur-der•ous
mur-ders
mur•mur
mur-mur•ing

mur-murs
mus-ca•tel
mus•cle
mus-cles
mus-cling

mus-cu•lar
mu•seum
mu•se-ums
mush-room
mush-rooming

music
mu•si-cal
mu•si-cally
mu•si-cian
mu•si-co-log-ical

mu•si-colo-gist
mu•si-col•ogy
mus•ket
mus-ke-teer
mus-ketry

musk-melon
musk-rat
Mus•lim
mus•lin
mus•sel

mus-tache	mys-te-ri-ous-ly	nan-nies
mus-tang	mys-tery	nanny
mus-tard	mys•tic	nano-sec•ond
mus•ter	mys-ti•cal	nap•kin
mus-ter•ing	mys-ti-cism	nap-kins
mus-ters	mys-ti-fied	napped
musti-ness	mys-tify	nap-ping
musty	mys-ti-fy•ing	nar-cis-sism
mu•ta-ble	mys-tique	nar-cis-sist
mu•tant	myth-ical	nar-cis•sus
mu•tate	mytho-log-ical	nar-cotic
mu•ta-tion	mytho-logi-cally	nar-cot•ics
muted	my•tholo-gies	nar-rate
mutely	my•thology	nar-rat•ing
mute-ness		nar-ra-tion
mu•ti-late		nar-ra-tive
mu•ti-lates		nar-ra•tor
mu•ti-lat•ing		nar•row
mu•ti-la-tion		narrow-band
mu•ti-neer		nar-rowed
mu•ti-nous		nar-rower
mu•tiny	nabbed	nar-row•ing
mut•ter	nab-bing	nar-rowly
mut-ters	nadir	nar-row-ness
mut•ton	nagged	nasal
	nag-ging	
mu•tual		na•sally
mu•tu-ally	nailed	nas-tily
muz•zle	nail-ing	nas-ti-ness
muz-zling	naive	nasty
myo•pia	na•ively	natal
	naked	
myo•pic		na•tally
myr•iad	na•ked-ness	na•ta-to-rium
my•self	namely	na•tion
mys-ter•ies	name-plate	na•tional
mys-te-ri•ous	name-sake	na•tion-al•ism
	nam•ing	

129

na•tion-al•ist
na•tion-al-is•tic
na•tion-ali-ties
na•tion-al•ity
na•tion-al•ize

na•tion-al-izes
na•tion-ally
na•tion-hood
na•tion-wide
na•tive

na•tivi-ties
na•tiv-ity
natu-ral
natu-ral•ism
natu-ral•ist

natu-ral-is•tic
natu-ral-iza-tion
natu-ral•ize
natu-ral-iz•ing
natu-rally

na•ture
na•tu-ro-path
na•tu-ro-pathic
naugh-tily
naugh-ti-ness

naughty
nau•sea
nau-se•ate
nau-se-at•ing
nau-seous

nau-ti•cal
nau-ti•lus
naval
navel
na•vies

navi-ga•ble
navi-gate
navi-gat•ing
navi-ga-tion
navi-ga-tional

navi-ga•tor
navi-ga-tors
Ne•an-der-thal
nearby
neared

nearer
near-est
near-ing
nearly
near-sighted

near-sight-ed-ness
neatly
neat-ness
Ne•braska
Ne•bras-kan

neb•ula
nebu-lae
nebu-lous
nec-es-sar•ily
nec-es-sary

ne•ces-si-tate
ne•ces-si-tat•ing
ne•ces-si-ties
ne•ces-sity
neck-er-chief

neck-lace
neck-line
neck-tie
neck-wear
nec•tar

nec-tar•ine
needed
need-ful
need-ing
nee•dle

nee-dled
needle-point
need-less
need-lessly
needle-work

needy
ne•fari-ous
ne•gate
ne•gat-ing
ne•ga-tion

nega-tive
nega-tively
nega-tiv•ism
ne•glect
ne•glect-ful

ne•glect-ful-ness
ne•glect-ing
neg-li•gee
neg-li-gence
neg-li-gent

neg-li-gi•ble
ne•go-tia•ble
ne•go-ti•ate
ne•go-ti-at•ing
ne•go-tia-tion

ne•go-tia•tor
neigh-bor
neigh-bor-hood
neigh-bor•ing
neigh-bor-li-ness

neigh-borly
nei-ther
neme-sis
neo-clas-si•cal
neo-clas-si-cism

neo-lith
neo-lithic
neon
Nepal
Ne•pali

nephew
neph-ews
nepo-tism
nepo-tis•tic
ner•vous

ner-vously
ner-vous-ness
nervy
nested
nest-ing

nes•tle
nes-tled
nes-tling *(v.)*
nest-ling *(n.)*
netbios

neth-er-most
net•ted
net-ting
net•tle
net-work

net-working
neu•ral
neu-ral•gia
neu-ral•gic
neu-ri•tis

neu•ro-bi•ol-ogy
neu•ro-chem-ical
neu•ro-chem•ist
neu•ro-logic
neu•ro-log-ical

neu•ro-logi-cally
neu-rolo-gist
neu-rol•ogy
neu•ron
neu•ro-pathic

neu-ropa•thy
neu-ro•ses
neu-ro•sis
neu•ro-sur-geon
neu•ro-sur-gery

neu•ro-sur-gi•cal
neu-rotic
neu•ter
neu-tral
neu-tral•ity

neu-tral•ize
neu-tral-izer
neu-tron
Ne•vada
Ne•va-dan

never
never-more
never-the-less
new-born
new-comer

newer
new•est
new-fan-gled
new-found
New-found-land

New-found-lander
New Hamp-shire
New Jer•sey
New Jer-seyan
newly

new•ly-wed
New Mexico
New Mexi-can
new-ness
news-break

news-cast
news-caster
news-cast•ing
news-hound
news-letter

news-paper
new-speak
news-print
news-reel
news-room

news-stand
news-worthy
New York
New Yorker
nib•ble

nib-bling
Nica-ra•gua
Nica-ra-guan
nicely
nicer

nic•est
nice-ties
nicety
niche
nicked

n

nickel	ni•trous	nomi-nal
nick-els	nit•wit	nomi-nally
nick-el-odeon	nixed	nomi-nate
nick-name	nix•ing	nomi-nat•ing
nick-nam•ing	Nobel	nomi-na-tion
nico-tine	No•bel-ist	nomi-na-tive
niece	no•bili-ties	nomi-na•tor
nifty	no•bil-ity	nomi-nee
Ni•ge-ria	noble	nomi-nee
Ni•ge-rian	no•ble-ness	non-abra-sive
		non-ab•sor-bent
night-cap	nobly	non-ad•dict-ing
night-club	no•bod-ies	non-ad•dic-tive
night-fall	no•body	non-ad•he-sive
night-gown	noc-tur•nal	non-ad•mis-si•ble
night-in-gale	noc-tur-nally	non-ag•gres-sion
nightly	noc-turne	non-al•co-holic
night-mare	nodal	non-al•ler-genic
night-time	nod-ally	non-ap•pli-ca•ble
night-wear	nod•ded	non-as•so-ci-ated
ni•hil-ism	nod-ding	non-at•ten-dance
ni•hil-ist	node	non-bind•ing
ni•hil-is•tic	nodu-lar	non-break-able
nim•ble	nod•ule	non-can-cer•ous
nine-teen	noel	non-car-bon-ated
nine-ti•eth	noise	non-cha-lant
ninety	noise-less	non-cha-lantly
ninth	noise-maker	non-com•bat
nipped	noises	non-com-bat•ant
nip-ping	nois-ily	non-com-mer-cial
nippy	noisi-ness	non-com-mit•tal
nit-pick	noisy	non-com-mit•ted
nit-picker	nomad	non-com-pli-ance
ni•trate	no•madic	non-com-pli-cated
ni•tro-gen	no•mads	non-con-fi-dence
ni•tro-glyc-erin	no•men-cla-ture	non-con-fi-den-tial

non-con-for-mance
non-con-form•ing
non-con-form•ist
non-con-for-mity
non-con-tact

non-con-ta-gious
non-con-tribu-tory
non-con-vert-ible
non-cor-rod•ing
non-credit

non-crit-ical
non-dairy
non-de•duct-ible
non-de•script
non-dis-clo-sure

non-drinker
non-drink•ing
non-du-ra•ble
non-elec-tronic
non-en•ti-ties

non-en•tity
non-es•sen-tial
none-such
non-ex•clu-sive
non-ex•empt

non-ex•is-tent
non•fat
non-fic-tion
non-fic-tional
non-for-fei-ture

non-haz-ard•ous
non-im•pact
non-lin•ear
non-mail-able
non-mem•ber

non-me•tal-lic
non-op•er-at•ing
non-par-tici-pant
non-par-ti•san
non-pay•ing

non-pay-ment
non-per-ish-able
non-plused
non-poi-son•ous
non-po•rous

non-pre-cious
non-pro-ce-dural
non-pro-duc-tive
non-profit
non-re•cov-er-able

non-re•fund-able
non-resi-dent
non-re•stric-tive
non-sched-uled
non-sense

non-sen-si•cal
non-sex•ist
non-skid
non-smoker
non-smok•ing

non-stan-dard
non-stick
non-stop
non-sup-port
non-tax-able

non-tech-ni•cal
non-toxic
non-trans-fer-able
non-vio-lent
non-vola-tile

non-voter
noo•dle
noon-day
noon-time
nooses

Nor•dic
nor•mal
nor-mal-cies
nor-malcy
nor-mal•ity

nor-mal-iza-tion
nor-mal•ize
nor-mal-ized
nor-mally
nor-ma-tive

normed
North Caro-lina
North Dakota
North Da•ko-tan
north-east

north-east-erly
north-eastern
north-east-ward
north-east-wardly
north-erly

north-ern
North-erner
north-ward
north-wardly
north-west

north-west-erly
north-western
Nor•way
Nor-we-gian
nose-bleed

n

nose-dive (n.)
nos•ily
nos-tal•gia
nos-tal•gic
nos-tal-gi-cally

nos-tril
nos-trum
no•ta-ble
no•ta-ries
no•ta-ri-za-tion

no•ta-rize
no•ta-riz•ing
no•tary
no•ta-tion
notched

note-book
noted
note-pad
note-paper
note-wor•thy

noth-ing
no•tice-able
no•ticed
no•tices
no•tic-ing

no•ti-fi-ca-tion
no•ti-fied
no•ti-fies
no•tify
no•ti-fy•ing

not•ing
no•tion
no•to-ri•ety
no•to-ri•ous
no•to-ri-ously

nou•gat
nou-gats
nour-ish
nour-ish•ing
nour-ish-ment

nova
novel
nov-el•ist
nov-el•ize
nov-el-iz•ing

no•vella
nov•els
nov-el-ties
nov-elty
No•vem-ber

nov•ice
No•vo-cain
no•where
nox-ious
noz•zle

nu•ance
nu•clear
nu•clei
nu•cleus
nudg-ing

nud•ism
nud•ist
nu•dity
nug•get
nui-sance

nul-li-fied
nul-lify
nul-li-fy•ing
numbed
num•ber

num-ber•ing
num-bers
numb-ing
numb-ness
nu•mer-able

nu•meral
nu•mer-als
nu•mer-ate
nu•mer-at•ing
nu•mera-tion

nu•mera-tor
nu•meric
nu•mer-ical
nu•meri-cally
nu•mer-ous

nu•mis-ma-tist
nun-nery
nup-tial
nursed
nurs-er•ies

nurs-ery
nurses
nurs-ing
nur-ture
nur-tur•ing

nut-cracker
nut•meg
nu•tri-ent
nu•tri-tion
nu•tri-tional

nu•tri-tion-ally
nu•tri-tion•ist
nu•tri-tious
nu•tri-tiously
nu•tri-tive

nut-shell
nut-ti-ness
nutty
nuz•zle
nuz-zles

nuz-zling
nylon

oases
oasis
oat-meal
ob•bli-gato
obe-di-ence

obe-di•ent
obe-di-ently
obei-sance
obei-sant
obese

obe-si-ties
obe-sity
obey
obey-ance
obeyed

obey-ing
obitu-ar•ies
obitu-ary
ob•ject
ob•ject-ing

ob•jec-tion
ob•jec-tion-able
ob•jec-tive
ob•jec-tively
ob•jec-tive-ness

ob•jec-tiv•ity
ob•late
ob•la-tion
ob•li-gate
ob•li-gat•ing

ob•li-ga-tion
ob•li-ga-tional
obliga-tory
oblige
oblig-ing

oblig-ingly
oblique
obliquely
oblit-er•ate
oblit-er-at•ing

oblit-era-tion
oblit-era-tive
obliv-ion
oblivi-ous
ob•long

ob•nox-ious
ob•nox-iously
ob•nox-ious-ness
oboe
obo•ist

ob•scene
ob•scenely
ob•sceni-ties
ob•scen-ity
ob•scure

ob•scurely
ob•scur-ing
ob•scu-rity
ob•serva-able
ob•ser-vance

ob•ser-vant
ob•ser-va-tion
ob•ser-va-to-ries
ob•ser-va-tory
ob•serve

ob•server
ob•serv-ing
ob•sess
ob•ses-sion
ob•ses-sive

ob•ses-sively
ob•ses-sive-ness
ob•so-lesce
ob•so-les-cence
ob•so-les-cent

ob•so-lete
ob•sta-cle
ob•step-er•ous
ob•stet-ric
ob•stet-ri•cal

ob•stet-ri-cally
ob•ste-tri-cian
ob•stet-rics
ob•sti-nacy
ob•sti-nate

ob•sti-nately
ob•struct
ob•struct-ing
ob•struc-tion
ob•struc-tive

O

ob•struc-tively	ocean	of•fen-sive
ob•tain	ocean-front	offer
ob•tain-able	oce-anic	of•fered
ob•tain-ing	ocean-og-ra-pher	of•fer-ing
ob•tru-sive	ocean-og-ra-phic	of•fers
ob•tru-sively	ocean-og-ra•phy	off-hand
ob•tuse	oceans	of•fice
ob•vi-ous	oc•ta-gon	of•fi-cer
ob•vi-ously	oc•tago-nal	of•fi-cial
oc•ca-sion	oc•tane	of•fi-cially
oc•ca-sional	oc•tave	of•fi-ci•ate
oc•ca-sion-ally	Oc•to-ber	of•fi-ci-ates
oc•ci-dent	oc•to-ge-nar•ian	of•fi-ci-at•ing
oc•ci-den•tal	oc•topi	of•fi-cia-tion
oc•clude	oc•to-pus	of•fi-cia•tor
oc•clud-ing	ocu•lar	of•fi-cious
oc•clu-sion	ocu-list	of•fi-ciously
oc•clu-sive	odd-ball	off•ing
oc•cult	odd•ity	off--line
oc•cult-ism	oddly	off•set
oc•cult-ist	odd-ness	off-shoot
oc•cu-pancy	odi•ous	off-shore
oc•cu-pant	odi-ously	off-side
oc•cu-pa-tion	odome-ter	off-spring
oc•cu-pa-tional	odor	often
oc•cu-pa-tion-ally	odor-if-er•ous	Ohio
oc•cu-pied	odor-less	Ohioan
oc•cu-pies	odor-ous	ohm
oc•cupy	od•ys-sey	ohm-me•ter
oc•cu-py•ing	off-cast	oiled
occur	of•fend	oil-skin
oc•curred	of•fender	oily
oc•cur-rence	of•fend-ers	oint-ment
oc•cur-ring	of•fend-ing	Okla-homa
oc•curs	of•fense	Okla-ho•man

olden
older
old•est
old--fashioned
old•ies

ol•fac-tion
ol•fac-tory
oli-gar•chy
oli-gop•oly
olive

ol•ives
olym-piad
Olym-pian
Olym-pic
om•buds-man

om•elet
omens
omi-nous
omi-nously
omis-sion

omit-ted
omit-ting
om•nipo-tence
om•nipo-tent
om•ni-pres•ent

om•ni-science
om•ni-scient
on--board
on•col-ogy
on•com-ing

one-ness
oner-ous
one-self
one--sided
on•go-ing

onion
on•ions
onion-skin
on--line
on•looker

on•rush
on--screen
onset
on•slaught
on•to-log-ical

on•tol-ogy
on•ward
onyx
opaque
open

opened
opener
open-ers
open-ing
openly

open-ness
opera
op•er-able
op•er-and
op•er-ant

op•eras
op•er-ate
op•er-ates
op•er-atic
op•er-at•ing

op•era-tion
op•era-tional
op•era-tion-ally
op•era-tive
op•era-tor

op•er-etta
oph-thal-mo-logic
oph-thal-molo-gist
oph-thal-mol•ogy
oph-thal-mo-scope

opi•ate
opin-ion
opin-ion-ated
opium
opos-sum

op•po-nent
op•por-tune
op•por-tun•ist
op•por-tu-ni-ties
op•por-tu-nity

op•pose
op•poses
op•pos-ing
op•po-site
op•po-si-tion

op•press
op•presses
op•press-ing
op•pres-sion
op•pres-sive

op•pres-sor
opted
optic
op•ti-cal
op•ti-cian

op•tics
op•ti-mal
op•ti-mism
op•ti-mist
op•ti-mis•tic

0

op•ti-mize
op•ti-mum
opt•ing
op•tion
op•tional

op•tions
op•tome-trist
op•tome-try
opu-lence
opu-lent

or•acle
oral
orally
or•ange
orat-ing

ora-tion
ora•tor
ora-tor-ical
ora-to•rio
ora-tory

or•bicu-lar
orbit
or•bital
or•bited
or•bit-ing

or•bits
or•chard
or•ches-tra
or•ches-tral
or•ches-trally

or•ches-trate
or•ches-trat•ing
or•ches-tra-tion
or•chid
or•dain

or•dain-ing
or•deal
order
or•dered
or•der-ing

or•derly
or•ders
or•di-nal
or•di-nance
or•di-narily

or•di-nary
or•di-nate
or•di-na-tion
ord-nance
Ore•gon

Ore-go-nian
organ
or•ganic
or•gani-cally
or•gan-ism

or•gan-ist
or•ga-ni-za-tion
or•ga-ni-za-tional
or•ga-nize
or•ga-nizer

or•ga-niz•ing
or•gans
ori•ent
ori-en•tal
ori-en-ta-tion

ori-ent•ing
ori•gin
origi-nal
origi-nal•ity
origi-nally

origi-nate
origi-nates
origi-nat•ing
origi-na-tion
origi-na•tor

ori-gins
ori•ole
or•na-ment
or•na-mental
or•na-men-ta-tion

or•na-ment•ing
or•nate
or•nately
or•nate-ness
or•ni-thol•ogy

or•phan
or•phan-age
orth-odon•tic
orth-odon-tics
orth-odon-tist

or•tho-dox
or•tho-doxy
or•tho-graphic
or•tho-gra•phy
or•tho-pe-di-cally

or•tho-pe-dics
or•tho-pe-dist
or•tho-scopic
or•thot-ics
or•tho-tist

os•cil-late
os•cil-lat•ing
os•cil-la-tion
os•cil-la•tor
os•cil-lo-scope

os•mo-ses
os•mo-sis
os•si-fi-ca-tion
os•sify
os•ten-si•ble

os•ten-si•bly
os•ten-sive
os•ten-sively
os•ten-ta-tion
os•ten-ta-tious

os•teo-path
os•teo-pathic
os•te-opa•thy
os•tra-cism
os•tra-cize

os•tra-cizes
os•tra-ciz•ing
os•trich
other
oth•ers

other-wise
ounces
our-self
our-selves
ousted

oust-ing
out•age
out•bid
out-bid-ding
out-board

out-bound
out-break
out-burst
out-cast
out-class

out-come
out-cries
out•cry
out-dated
out-dis-tance

outdo
out-doors
outer
outer-most
outer-wear

out-field
out-fielder
out•fit
out-fit•ted
out-fit-ting

out-flank
out•fox
out-go•ing
out-grow
out-grown

out-guess
out•ing
out-land•ish
out-last
out-last•ing

out•law
out-lawed
out•lay
out•let
out-line

out-lin•ing
out-live
out-liv•ing
out-look
out-ly•ing

out-ma-neu•ver
out-moded
out-num•ber
out-num-bered
out-patient

out-per-formed
out-post
out-pour•ing
out•put
out-put-ting

out-rage
out-ra-geous
out-ra-geously
out-rag•ing
out-rank

out-rank•ing
out-reach
out-rig•ger
out-right
out•run

out-run-ning
out-score
out-scor•ing
out-sell
out-sell•ing

out•set
out-side
out-skirts
out-smart
out-sold

out-spo•ken
out-stand•ing
out-stretched
out-stretch•ing
out-ward

O

out-wardly
out-wear
out-weigh
out-weigh•ing
out•wit

out-wit•ted
out-wit-ting
ovar-ian
ova-ries
ovary

ova-tion
over-abun-dance
over-achiever
over-act
over-act•ing

over-ac•tive
over-age
over-all
over-anx-ious
over-bear•ing

over-board
over-bur•den
over-came
over-cast
over-charge

over-charg•ing
over-coat
over-come
over-com•ing
over-com-pen-sate

over-con-fi-dence
over-cooked
over-cor-rect
over-crit-ical
over-crowded

over-crowd•ing
overdo
over-dose
over-dos•ing
over-draft

over-draw
over-draw•ing
over-drawn
over-drive
over-due

over-eat
over-eat•ing
over-flow
over-flow•ing
over-growth

over-hand
over-haul
over-head
over-hear
over-hear•ing

over-joyed
over-kill
over-laid
over-land
over-lapped

over-lap-ping
over-lay
over-lay•ing
over-load
over-load•ing

over-look
over-look•ing
overly
over-night
over-nighter

over-paid
over-pass
over-passes
over-pay
over-pay•ing

over-pay-ment
over-play
over-power
over-price
over-priced

over-pric•ing
over-quali-fied
over-rate
over-rat•ing
over-re•act

over-re•act•ing
over-re•ac-tion
over-rid•den
over-ride
over-rid•ing

over-rule
over-rul•ing
over-run
over-seas
over-see

over-see•ing
over-seen
over-shadow
over-shad-ow•ing
over-shoes

over-sight
over-sized
over-sleep
over-slept
over-sold

over-spend
over-spend•ing
over-spent
over-stated
over-stay

over-stepped
over-step-ping
over-stocked
over-stock•ing
over-strike

over-strik•ing
over-stuff
overt
over-take
over-throw•ing

over-time
overtly
over-tone
over-ture
over-turned

over-turn•ing
over-uti-li-za-tion
over-view
over-weight
over-whelmed

over-whelm•ing
over-worked
over-work•ing
over-write
over-writ•ing

ovu-late
ovu-lat•ing
ovu-la-tion
owed
owing

owned
owner
own•ers
own-er-ship
own•ing

oxen
ox•fords
oxi-dant
oxi-da-tion
oxide

oxi-dize
oxi-dizer
oxi-dizes
oxi-diz•ing
oxy•gen

oys•ter
oys-ters
ozone
ozon-iz•ing
ozo-no-sphere

paced
pace-maker
pacer
paces
pace-setter

pace-setting
pa•cific
pa•cifi-cist
paci-fied
paci-fier

paci-fies
paci-fism
paci-fist
pac•ify
pac-ify•ing

pac•ing
pack-age
pack-ager
pack-ages
pack-ag•ing

packed
packer
pack-ers
packet
pack-ets

pack-ing
pact
pad•ded
pad-dies
pad-ding

pad•dle
pad-dles
pad-dling
pad-lock
pad-lock•ing

pagan
pa•gan-ism
pa•gan-ize
pa•gans
pag-eant

pag-eantry
pag-eants
paged
pager
pag•ers

p

pages
pagi-nate
pagi-nates
pagi-nat•ing
pagi-na-tion

pag•ing
pa•goda
paid
pail-ful
pained

pain-ful
pain-fully
pain-ing
pain-killer
pain-less

pains-tak•ing
pains-tak-ingly
paint-brush
painted
painter

paint-ers
paint-ing
paired
pair-ing
pais-ley

pa•ja-mas
Pa•ki-stan
Pa•ki-stani
pal•ace
pal-at-able

pala-tal
pala-tal•ize
pal•ate
paled
pale-face

pale-ness
Pal-es-tine
Pal-es-tin•ian
pal-ette
pali-mony

pal-la-dium
pall-bearer
pal•let
pal-let-ized
pal•lor

palmed
pal-metto
palm-ing
palm-ist
palm-istry

palo-mino
pal-pa•ble
pal-pi-tate
pal-pi-tates
pal-pi-tat•ing

pal-pi-ta-tion
pal-sied
palsy
pal•try
pam•per

pam-per•ing
pam-pers
pam-phlet
pana-cea
Pan•ama

Pana-ma-nian
pana-tela
pan-cake
pan-creas
pan-cre-atec-tomy

pan-cre-atic
panda
pan•das
pan-de-mo-nium
pan•der

pan-der•ing
panel
pan-eled
pan-el•ing
pan-el•ist

pan•els
pan-han•dle
pan-han-dler
panic
pan-icked

pan-ick•ing
pan-ning
pan-orama
pan-oramic
pan-the•ism

pan-the•ist
pan-ther
pant-ing
pan-to-mime
pan-to-mim•ist

pan-tries
pan•try
pants
pant-suit
panty hose

panty-waist
pa•pacy
papal
pa•paya
paper

paper-back
pa•pered
pa•perer
paper-hanger
paper-hanging

pa•per-ing
pa•pers
paper-weight
paper-work
pa•pyri

pa•py-rus
par-able
para-chute
para-chut•ing
para-chut•ist

pa•rade
pa•rades
pa•rad-ing
para-di-sa-ical
para-di-sa-ically

para-dise
para-dox
para-dox-ical
para-doxi-cally
par-af•fin

para-gli•der
para-gon
para-graph
para-graph•ing
Para-guay

Para-guayan
para-le•gal
par-al•lax
par-al•lel
par-al-lel•ing

par-al-lel•ism
par-al-lelo-gram
pa•raly-sis
para-lyze
para-lyz•ing

para-medic
para-med-ical
para-med•ics
pa•rame-ter
para-met•ric

para-mount
para-noia
para-noid
para-pet
para-pher-na•lia

para-phrase
para-phras•ing
para-ple•gia
para-ple•gic
para-pro-fes-sional

para-psy-chol•ogy
para-site
para-sol
para-trooper
par•cel

par-cel•ing
par-cels
parch-ment
par•don
par-don•ing

par-dons
pared
pare-go•ric
par•ent
par-ent•age

pa•ren-tal
pa•ren-the•ses
pa•ren-the•sis
par-en-thetic
par-en-thet-ical

par-en-theti-cally
par-ent-hood
par-ents
par•ing
Paris

par•ish
par-ishes
pa•rish-io•ner
Pa•ri-sian
par•ity

parka
par•kas
parked
park-ing
park-way

par•lay
par-layed
par-lay•ing
par-lia-ment
par-lia-men-tary

par•lor
pa•ro-chial
paro-died
paro-dies
paro-dist

par•ody
par-ody•ing
pa•role
pa•rolee
pa•roles

p

pa•rol-ing
par•rot
par-rot•ing
parse
parsed

parses
par-si-mo-ni•ous
par-si-mony
pars-ing
pars-ley

pars-nip
par•son
par-son•age
par-take
par-taken

par-taker
par-tak•ing
parted
par-tial
par-tal•ity

par-tially
par-tici-pant
par-tici-pate
par-tici-pates
par-tici-pat•ing

par-tici-pa-tion
par-tici-pa•tor
par-tici-pa-tory
par-ti-ci•ple
par-ti•cle

par-ticu•lar
par-ticu-lar•ity
par-ticu-larly
par-tied
par-ties

part-ing
par-ti•san
par-ti-tion
par-ti-tion•ing
partly

part-ner
part-ner-ship
par-took
part--time
part-way

party
par-ty•ing
pas•cal
pass-able
pas-sage

passage-way
pass-book
passé
passed
pas-sen•ger

pas-sen-gers
passer
passer•by
passers•by
passes

pass-ing
pas-sion
pas-sion•ate
pas-sive
pas-sively

pas-siv•ist
Pass-over
pass-port
pasta
pass-word

pasted
pas•tel
pas-tels
pastes
pas-teur-iza-tion

pas-teur•ize
pas-teur-izes
pas•teur-iz•ing
pas-time
pas•tor

pas-to-rale
pas-trami
past-ries
pastry
pas-ture

pas-tur•ing
patched
patches
patch-ing
patch-work

patchy
pat•ent
pat-ented
pat-ent•ing
pat-ently

pat-ents
pa•ter-nal
pa•ter-nally
pa•ter-nity
pa•thetic

patho-logic
patho-log-ical
patho-logi-cally
pa•tholo-gies
pa•tholo-gist

pa•thol-ogy	paunchy	peace-maker
pa•thos	pau•per	peace-time
pa•tience	pau-pers	peaches
pa•tient	paused	peachy
pa•tiently	pauses	peaked
patio	paus-ing	peaked-ness
pa•tios	paved	peak-ing
pa•tri-arch	pave-ment	pealed
pa•tri-ar-chal	paves	peal-ing
pa•tri-ar•chy	pa•vil-ion	pea•nut
pat-ri-mony	pav•ing	pea-nuts
pa•triot	paw•ing	pearly
pa•tri-otic	pawn-broker	peas-ant
pa•tri-oti-cally	pawn-broking	peb•ble
pa•trio-tism	pawned	peb-bles
pa•trol	pawn-ing	pecan
pa•trol-ling	pawn-shop	pe•cans
pa•tron	pay-able	pec-ca-dillo
pa•tron-age	pay-back	pec•tin
pa•tron-ize	pay-check	pec-to•ral
pa•tron-izes	pay•day	pe•cu-liar
pa•tron-iz•ing	payee	pe•cu-liar•ity
pat-sies	pay•ees	pe•cu-liarly
patsy	payer	pe•cu-ni•ary
pat•ted	pay•ers	peda-gogic
pat•ter	pay•ing	peda-gog-ical
pat-ter•ing	pay-load	peda-gogi-cally
pat-tern	pay-ment	peda-gogue
pat-terned	pay•off *(n.)*	peda-gogy
pat-ties	pay•ola	pedal
pat-ting	pay•out	ped-aled
patty	pay-roll	ped-al•ing
pau-city	peace-able	ped•als
paunch	peace-ful	ped•ant
paunchi-ness	peace-fully	pe•dan-tic

p

ped•dle
ped-dler
ped-dling
ped-es•tal
pe•des-trian

pe•di-at•ric
pe•dia-tri-cian
pe•di-at-rics
pedi-cure
pedi-gree

pedi-ment
peeked
peek-ing
peeled
peel-ing

peep-hole
peep-ing
peer-age
peer-ing
peer-less

pee-ving
pee-vish
pee-vishly
pegged
peg-ging

Pe•king
Pe•king-ese
peli-can
pel•let
pel-let•ize

pel-let-iz•ing
pelted
pelt-ing
pel•vic
pel•vis

penal
pe•nal-ize
pe•nal-izes
pe•nal-iz•ing
pen-al-ties

pen-alty
pen-ance
pen-chant
pen•cil
pen-cil•ing

pen-cils
pen-dant
pend-ing
pen-du•lum
pene-tra•ble

pene-trant
pene-trate
pene-trates
pene-trat•ing
pene-tra-tion

pene-tra-tive
pene-tra•tor
pen-guin
peni-cil•lin
pen-in-sula

pen-in-su•lar
peni-tence
peni-tent
peni-ten-tia-ries
peni-ten-tiary

pen-man-ship
pen-nant
penned
pen-nies
pen-ni-less

pen-ning
Penn-syl-va•nia
Penn-syl-va-nian
penny
penny-weight

pe•nolo-gist
pe•nol-ogy
pen-sion
pen-sioner
pen-sion•ing

pen-sive
pen-sively
pen-ta•gon
pen-tago•nal
pen-tame•ter

pen-tath•lon
pent-house
pe•nu-ri•ous
pe•nu-ri-ously
pen•ury

peon
peo-nies
peons
peony
peo•ple

peo-pling
pep•per
pep-per•ing
pep-per-mint
pep-per•oni

pep-pers
pep-pery
peppy
pep•sin
pep•tic

per-am•bu-late
per-am•bu-lat•ing
per-am•bu-la-tion
per-am•bu-la-tor
per annum

per-cale
per cap•ita
per-ceiv-able
per-ceiv-ably
per-ceive

per-ceives
per-ceiv•ing
per-cent
per-cent•age
per-cen-tile

per-cep-ti-bil•ity
per-cep-ti•ble
per-cep-tion
per-cep-tive
per-cep-tively

per-cep-tive-ness
per-cep-tual
per-cep-tu-ally
per-chance
perched

perches
perch-ing
per-co-late
per-co-lates
per-co-lat•ing

per-co-la-tion
per-co-la•tor
per-cus-sion
per-cus-sion•ist
per-cus-sive

per diem
per-di-tion
pe•ren-nial
pe•ren-nially
per-fect

per-fected
per-fect•ing
per-fec-tion
per-fec-tion•ist
per-fectly

per-fidi•ous
per-fidy
per-fo-rate
per-fo-rat•ing
per-fo-ra-tion

per-fo-ra•tor
per-form
per-for-mance
per-former
per-form•ers

per-form•ing
per-fume
per-fum•ery
per-func-tory
per-fuse

per-fus•ing
per-fu-sion
per-haps
peri-gee
peril

per-il•ous
per-il-ously
per•ils
pe•rime-ter
peri-na•tal

pe•riod
pe•ri-odic
pe•ri-od-ical
pe•ri-odi-cally
pe•ri-od-ic•ity

peri-odon•tal
peri-odon-tics
peri-odon-tist
peri-odon-tol•ogy
pe•ri-ods

pe•riph-eral
pe•riph-er•als
pe•riph-ery
peri-scope
per•ish

per-ish-able
per-ishes
per-ish•ing
per-jure
per-jurer

per-jur•ers
per-jures
per-ju-ries
per-jur•ing
per-jury

perk-ier
perki-ness
perky
per-ma-frost
per-ma-nence

per-ma-nency
per-ma-nent
per-ma-nently
per-me-able
per-me•ate

p

per-me-ates
per-me-at•ing
per-me-ation
per-mis-si•ble
per-mis-sion

per-mis-sive
per-mis-sive-ness
per•mit
per-mit•ted
per-mit-ting

per-mu-ta-tion
per-mu-ta-tional
per-ni-cious
per-ni-ciously
per-ox•ide

per-pen-dicu•lar
per-pe-trate
per-pe-trat•ing
per-pe-tra-tion
per-pe-tra•tor

per-pet•ual
per-pet-ually
per-petu•ate
per-petu-ates
per-petu-at•ing

per-petu-ation
per-petu-ator
per-pe-tu-ities
per-pe-tu•ity
per-plex

per-plexes
per-plex•ing
per-plex-ities
per-plex•ity
per-qui-site

per se
per-se-cute
per-se-cutes
per-se-cut•ing
per-se-cu-tion

per-se-cu•tor
per-se-ver-ance
per-se-vere
per-se-ver•ing
per-sim•mon

per•sist
per-sis-tence
per-sis-tent
per-sis-tently
per-sist•ing

per-snick•ety
per•son
per-sona
per-son-able
per-son•age

per-sonal
per-son-ali-ties
per-son-al•ity
per-son-al•ize
per-son-al-izes

per-son-al-iz•ing
per-son-ally
per-soni-fi-ca-tion
per-soni-fied
per-soni-fies

per-son•ify
per-son-ify•ing
per-son•nel
per-sons
per-spec-tive

per-spi-ca-cious
per-spi-ca-ciously
per-spicu•ous
per-spicu-ously
per-spi-ra-tion

per-spire
per-spir•ing
per-suade
per-suad•ing
per-sua-sion

per-sua-sive
per-sua-sively
per-sua-sive-ness
per-tain
per-tain•ing

per-ti-nence
per-ti-nent
per-turb
per-tur-ba-tion
per-turb•ing

Peru
pe•rusal
pe•ruse
pe•ruses
pe•rus-ing

Pe•ru-vian
per-vade
per-vades
per-vad•ing
per-va-sion

per-va-sive
per-va-sive-ness
per-verse
per-versely
per-ver-sion

per-ver-sity	pet-ti-coat	Phil-har-monic
per-ver-sive	pet-ti-ness	philo-den-dron
per-vert	pet-ting	phi-lolo-gist
per-vert•ing	petty	phi-lol•ogy
peso	petu-lance	phi-loso-pher
pesos	petu-lant	philo-sophic
pes-si-mism	pe•tu-nia	philo-soph-ical
pes-si-mist	pew•ter	philo-sophi-cally
pes-si-mis•tic	phan-tom	phi-loso-phies
pes•ter	pha-raoh	phi-loso-phize
pes-ter•ing	phari-see	phi-loso-phiz•ing
pes-ters	phar-ma-ceu-ti•cal	phi-loso•phy
pes-ti-cide	phar-ma-ceu-tics	phlegm
pes-ti-lence	phar-ma-cies	pho•bia
petal	phar-ma-cist	pho-bias
pet-aled	phar-ma-colo-gist	pho•bic
pet•als	phar-ma-col•ogy	phone
pe•tered	phar-macy	pho-neme
pe•ter-ing	phar-ynx	pho-netic
pe•tite	phase	pho-neti-cally
pe•ti-tion	phase-out *(n.)*	pho-ne-ti-cian
pe•ti-tioned	phaser	pho-net•ics
pe•ti-tioner	phases	pho-ni-cally
pet-ri-fied	phas-ing	pho-nics
pet-ri-fies	pheas-ant	pho-nies
pet-rify	phe-nomena	phon-ing
pet-ri-fy•ing	phe-nome•nal	pho-no-graph
pet•ro-chem-ical	phe-nome•non	pho-no-graphic
pet•rol	phi-lan•der	pho-nolo-gist
pe•tro-leum	phi-lan-derer	pho-nol•ogy
pet-ro-logic	phi-lan-der•ing	pho•to-cell
pet-ro-logi-cally	phil-an-thropic	pho•to-chem-ical
pe•trolo-gist	phil-an-throp-ical	pho•to-chem•ist
pe•trol-ogy	phi-lan-thro-pist	pho•to-cop•ied
pet•ted	phi-lan-thropy	pho•to-cop•ier

pho•to-cop•ies
pho•to-copy
pho•to-copy•ing
pho•to-elec-tric
pho•to-emis-sion

pho•to-en•grave
pho•to-en•graver
photo-finish
pho•to-ge•nic
pho•to-graph

pho•to-graphed
pho-tog-ra-pher
pho•to-graphic
pho•to-graph•ing
pho-tog-ra•phy

pho•to-gra-vure
pho•to-ki•ne-ses
pho•to-ki•ne-sis
pho•to-ki-netic
pho•to-mask

pho•to-mask•ing
pho•ton
pho•to-play
pho•tos
pho•to-sphere

pho•to-stat
pho•to-static
pho•to-syn-the•sis
pho•to-type•set
phrase

phrase-ol•ogy
phrases
phras-ing
phys-ical
physi-cally

phy-si-cian
physi-cist
phys-ics
physi-olog-ical
physi-olo-gist

physi-ol•ogy
phys-io-thera-pist
phys-io-ther•apy
phy-sique
pia-nis-simo

pia-nist
piano
pia•nos
pica
pic-colo

pic-co•los
picked
picker
picket
pick-ted

pick-eter
pick-et•ing
pick-ets
pick-ing
pickle

pick-led
pick-les
pick-pocket
picky
pic•nic

pic-nicked
pic-nick•ing
pic-nics
pi•co-sec•ond
pic-to-graph

pic-to-rial
pic-to-ri-ally
pic-to-ri•als
pic-ture
pic-tur-esque

pic-tur•ing
pieced
piece-meal
pieces
piece-work

piece-worker
piec-ing
pierced
pierces
pierc-ing

pierc-ingly
piety
pi•geon
pigeon-hole
pigeon-holing

pig-gish
pig-gish-ness
piggy
piggy-back
pig-headed

pig-ment
pig-men-tary
pig-men-ta-tion
pig-mented
pigmy

pig•pen
pig-skin
pig•sty
pig-tail
pilaf

pi•las-ter
piled
pileup *(n.)*
pil•fer
pil-fer•age

pil-ferer
pil-fer•ing
pil-grim
pil-grim•age
pil•ing

pil-lage
pil-lag•ing
pil•lar
pil•low
pillow-case

pil-lows
pil-lowy
pilot
pi•loted
pi•lot-ing

pi•lots
pi•mento
pim•ple
pim-ples
pim•ply

pin-afore
pin-ball
pinches
pinch-ing
pin-cushion

pine-apple
pin-feather
pinged
ping-ing
pin-head

pin-hole
pin•ion
pin-ion•ing
pin•kie
pin-na•cle

pinned
pin-ning
pi•nochle
pin-point
pin-pointing

pin-prick
pin-stripe
pio-neer
pio-neer•ing
pious

pi•ously
piped
pipe dream
pipe-line
piper

pip•ing
pip--squeak
pique
piqu-ing
pi•racy

pi•ra-nha
pi•rate
pi•rated
pi•rates
pi•rat-ing

pir-ou-ette
pir-ou-ett•ing
pis-ta-chio
pis•til
pis•tol

pis•ton
pitched
pitcher
pitches
pitch-fork

pitch-ing
pite-ous
pite-ously
pit-fall
pit•ied

pit•ies
piti-ful
piti-less
pit-tance
pit•ted

pi•tu-itary
pity
pity-ing
pivot
piv-otal

piv-oted
piv-ot•ing
pixel
pix•els
pixie

pizza
piz•zas
piz-zazz
piz-ze•ria
piz-zi-cato

pla-ca•ble
plac-ard
plac-ard•ing
pla-cate
pla-cat•ing

p

pla-ca-tion
pla-cebo
placed
place-kick
place-ment

pla-centa
places
placid
plac-idly
plac-ing

pla-gia-rism
pla-gia-rist
pla-gia-ris•tic
pla-gia-rize
pla-gia-riz•ing

pla-giary
plague
plagu-ing
plainly
plain-ness

plain-spoken
plain-tiff
plain-tive
plain-tively
planed

planer
planet
plane-tar•ium
plane-tary
plane-toid

plan-ets
plank-ing
planned
plan-ner
plan-ning

plant
plan-ta-tion
planted
planter
plant-ers

plant-ing
plaque
plasma
plas-ter
plaster-board

plas-terer
plas-ter•ing
plas-tic
plas-tic•ity
plas-ti-cize

pla-teau
plated
plate-ful
plate-maker
plate-making

platen
plat-form
plat-ing
plati-num
platitude

pla-tonic
pla-toon
plat-ted
plat-ter
plat-ting

plau-dit
plau-si-bil•ity
plau-si•ble
play-able
play-acted

play-acting
play-back (n.)
play-bill
played
player

play-ers
play-ful
play-fully
play-ful-ness
play-ground

play-house
play-ing
play-mate
play--off (n.)
play-pen

play-room
play-thing
play-time
play-wright
plaza

pla•zas
pleaded
plead-ing
pleas
pleas-ant

pleas-antly
pleas-ant-ries
pleas-antry
pleased
pleases

pleas-ing
pleas-ingly
plea-sur-able
plea-sure
pleated

pleat-ing
plebe
ple-be•ian
plebi-scite
pledged

pledges
pledg-ing
ple-nary
plen-te•ous
plen-ti•ful

plenty
pleu-risy
Plexi-glass
plexus
pli-able

pli-ancy
pli•ant
pli•ers
plighted
plod-ded

plod-ding
plopped
plop-ping
plot-tage
plot-ted

plot-ter
plot-ting
plowed
plow-ing
plucked

pluck-ing
plugged
plug-ger
plug-ging
plug--in

plumbed
plumber
plumb-ers
plumb-ing
plum-ing

plum-met
plum-met•ing
plun-der
plun-derer
plun-der•ing

plunger
plung-ers
plunges
plung-ing
plu•ral

plu-ral•ism
plu-ral-is•tic
plu-rali-ties
plu-ral•ity
plu-ral-iza-tion

plu-ral•ize
plu-rals
pluses
plushly
plushy

plu-to-crat
plu-to-cratic
plu-to-nium
ply•ing
ply-wood

pneu-matic
pneu-mati-cally
pneu-mo•nia
pneu-monic
poached

poacher
poach-ers
poach-ing
pocket
pocket-book

pock-eted
pock-et•ful
pock-et•ing
pocket-knife
pocket-knives

pock-ets
pock-mark
pock-marked
po•dia-trist
po•dia-try

po•dium
po•diums
poem
poet
po•etic

po•et-ical
po•etry
po•grom
poi-gnancy
poi-gnant

poi-gnantly
poin-set•tia
pointed
point-edly
point-ed-ness

pointer
point-ers
point-ing
point-less
point-lessly

p

point-less-ness
poised
poises
pois-ing
poi•son

poi-soned
poi-son•ing
poi-son•ous
poi-sons
poker

pok•ing
Po•land
polar
po•lar-ity
po•lar-ize

po•lar-iz•ing
Po•lar-oid
pole-cat
po•lice
po•lices

poli-cies
po•lic-ing
pol•icy
policy-holder
polio

pol•ish
Pol•ish
pol-ishes
pol-ish•ing
po•lite

po•litely
po•lite-ness
poli-tic
po•lit-ical
po•liti-cally

poli-ti-cian
po•liti-cize
po•liti-ciz•ing
poli-tick
poli-tick•ing

poli-tics
polka
polled
pol•len
pol-li-nate

pol-li-nates
pol-li-nat•ing
pol-li-na-tion
pol-li-na•tor
poll-ing

poll-ster
pol-lut•ant
pol-lute
pol-luted
pol-lut•ing

pol-lu-tion
polo
pol-ter-geist
poly-es•ter
poly-eth-yl•ene

po•lyga-mist
po•lyga-mous
po•lyg-amy
poly-glot
poly-gon

po•lygo-nal
poly-graph
poly-mer
poly-meric
po•ly-mer-iza-tion

poly-pro-pyl•ene
pol•yps
poly-syl-labic
poly-syl-la•ble
poly-tech•nic

poly-the•ism
poly-the•ist
pome-gran•ate
pom•mel
pom-mel•ing

pom-pa-dour
pomp-ous
pon•cho
pon•der
pon-der•ing

pon-der•ous
pon-ders
po•nies
pon-tiff
pon-tifi-cate

pony
pony-tail
poo•dle
pooled
pool-ing

poorer
poor-est
poor-house
poorly
pop-corn

popped
pop•per
pop-pies
pop-ping
poppy

poppy-cock
popu-lace
popu-lar
popu-lar•ity
popu-lar•ize

popu-lar-iz•ing
popu-larly
popu-late
popu-lated
popu-lat•ing

popu-la-tion
popu-list
popu-lous
pop--up
por-ce-lain

porches
por-cu-pine
pored
por•ing
por-nog-ra-pher

por-no-graphic
por-nog-ra•phy
po•rous
po•rous-ness
por-poise

por-ridge
por-ta-bil•ity
por-ta•ble
por-tage
por-tages

por-tag•ing
por•tal
por-tals
ported
por-tend

por-ten-tous
por•ter
port-fo•lio
port-hole
por-tico

por-tion
por-tion•ing
port-li-ness
portly
por-trait

por-trai-ture
por-tray
por-trayal
por-tray•ing
por-trays

Por-tu•gal
Por-tu-guese
posed
poses
pos•ing

posit
pos-ited
po•si-tion
po•si-tion•ing
posi-tive

posi-tively
posi-tron
pos•its
posse
pos-sess

pos-sesses
pos-sess•ing
pos-ses-sion
pos-ses-sive
pos-ses-sively

pos-ses-sive-ness
pos-sessor
pos-si-bili-ties
pos-si-bil•ity
pos-si•ble

pos-si•bly
pos•sum
post-ado-les-cent
post-age
postal

post-bel•lum
post-box
post-card
post-date
post-dated

post-doc-toral
posted
poster
pos-te-rior
pos-ter•ity

post-ers
post-gradu•ate
post-hu-mous
post-hu-mously
post-hyp-notic

post-ing
post-lude
post-mark
post-mark•ing
post-master

post me•ri-diem
post-mor•tem
post-na•sal
post-op•era-tive
post-paid

p

post-pone
post-pone-ment
post-pon•ing
post-pro-ces•sor
post-script

post-sec-ond•ary
post-test
post-test•ing
pos-tu-late
pos-tu-lat•ing

pos-tu-la-tion
pos-tural
pos-ture
pos-tur•ing
post-war

posy
po•ta-bil•ity
po•ta-ble
pot•ash
po•tas-sium

po•tato
po•ta-toes
pot-bellied
pot-belly
po•tency

po•tent
po•ten-tial
po•ten-tially
po•tently
pot-hole

po•tion
pot-luck
pot-pourri
pot-shot
pot-tage

pot•ted
pot•ter
pot-tery
pot-ting
poul-tice

poul-try
pounces
pounc-ing
pound-age
pounded

pound-ing
poured
pour-ing
pout-ing
pov-erty

pow•der
pow-der•ing
pow-ders
pow-dery
power

pow-ered
pow-er•ful
power-house
pow-er•ing
pow-er-less

power--off
power--on
power pack
pow•ers
power--up

pow•wow
prac-ti-ca-bil•ity
prac-ti-ca•ble
prac-ti•cal
prac-ti-cal•ity

prac-ti-cally
prac-tice
prac-tices
prac-tic•ing
prac-ti•cum

prac-ti-tio•ner
prag-matic
prag-mati-cally
prag-ma-tism
prag-ma-tist

prai-rie
praised
praise-worthy
prais-ing
prances

pranc-ing
prank-ster
prayer
prayer-ful
prayer-fully

prayer-ful-ness
prayers
pray-ing
preached
preacher

preach-ers
preaches
preach-ing
preachy
pre-ad•just

pre-ad•just-ment
pre-ad•mis-sion
pre-ado-les-cence
pre-ado-les-cent
pre-adop-tion

pre-am•ble
pre-ar•ranged
pre-as•sem-ble
pre-as•sem-bling
pre-as•sem-bly

pre-as•sign
pre-au•tho-rized
pre-bill•ing
pre-can-cer•ous
pre-cari•ous

pre-cari-ously
pre-cau-tion
pre-cau-tion•ary
pre-cede
pre-ce-dence

pre-ce-dent *(adj.)*
prece-dent *(n.)*
pre-cedes
pre-ced•ing
pre-cept

pre-cep-tive
pre-cinct
pre-cious
preci-pice
pre-cipi-tant

pre-cipi-tate
pre-cipi-tat•ing
pre-cipi-ta-tion
pre-cipi-tous
pre-cipi-tously

pré•cis
pre-cise
pre-cisely
pre-cise-ness
pre-ci-sion

pre-clude
pre-clud•ing
pre-clu-sion
pre-co-cious
pre-co-cious-ness

pre-coc•ity
pre-con-ceived
pre-con-ceiv•ing
pre-con-cep-tion
pre-con-di-tion

pre-con-struct
pre-cooked
pre-cur•sor
pre-cur-sory
pre-date

pre-dat•ing
preda-tor
preda-tory
pre-de•cease
pre-de•ceas-ing

pre-des-ti-na-tion
pre-des-tine
pre-de•ter-mine
pre-dica-ment
predi-cate

predi-cat•ing
predi-ca-tion
pre-dict
pre-dict-able
pre-dict•ing

pre-dic-tion
pre-dic-tive
pre-dic•tor
pre-dis-pose
pre-dis-pos•ing

pre-dis-po-si-tion
pre-domi-nance
pre-domi-nant
pre-domi-nantly
pre-domi-nat•ing

pre-domi-na-tion
pre-elec-tion
pree-mie
pre-emi-nence
pre-emi-nent

pre-emi-nently
pre-empt
pre-empted
pre-empt•ing
pre-emp-tion

pre-emp-tive
pre-en•roll-ment
pre-ex•ist
pre-ex•is-tence
pre-ex•ist•ing

pre•fab
pre-fab-ri-cate
pre-fab-ri-cat•ing
pre-fab-ri-ca-tion
pref-ace

pref-aces
pref-ac•ing
prefa-tory
pre•fer
pref-er-able

pref-er-ably
pref-er-ence
pref-er-en-tial
pre-ferred
pre-fer-ring

pre-fers
pre•fix
pre-fixes
pre-flight
pre-formed

pre-game
preg-nancy
preg-nant
pre-heat
pre-heat•ing

pre-his-toric
pre-his-tory
pre-judge
pre-judg•ing
preju-dice

preju-dices
preju-di-cial
preju-dic•ing
prel-ate
pre-launch

pre•law
pre-limi-nar•ies
pre-limi-nary
pre-lude
pre-mari•tal

pre-ma•ture
pre-ma•turely
pre•med
pre-medi-cine
pre-medi-tate

pre-medi-tat•ing
pre-medi-ta•tion
pre-mier
pre-miere
pre-mieres

pre-mier•ing
prem-ise
pre-mium
pre-mi•ums
pre-mo-ni-tion

pre-mor•tal
pre-na•tal
pre-oc•cu-pa-tion
pre-oc•cu-pied
pre-paid

prepa-ra-tion
pre-para-tive
pre-pa-ra-tory
pre-pare
pre-pared-ness

pre-par•ing
pre•pay
pre-pay•ing
pre-pay-ment
pre-pon-der-ance

pre-pon-der•ant
prepo-si-tion
prepo-si-tional
pre-pos-sess
pre-pos-sess•ing

pre-pos-ter•ous
prepped
prep-ping
pre-pro-ces•sor
pre-pro-duc-tion

pre-pro-gram
pre-pu•bes-cence
pre-pu•bes-cent
pre-re•cord
pre-reg-is•ter

pre-reg-is-ter•ing
pre-reg-is-tra-tion
pre-req-ui-site
pre-roga-tive
pre-school

pre-schooler
pre-scribe
pre-scrib•ing
pre-scrip-tion
pre-sea•son

pres-ence
pres-ent *(n., adj.)*
pre-sent *(v.)*
pre-sent-able
pre-sen-ta-tion

pre-senter
pre-sent•ing
pres-ently
pres-ents *(n.)*
pre-sents *(v.)*

pres-er-va-tion
pre-ser-va-tive
pre-serve
pre-server
pre-ser-vice

pre-serv•ing
pre•set
pre-shrunk
pre-side
presi-den-cies

presi-dency
presi-dent
president--elect
presi-den-tial
pre-sid•ing

pre-soak
press-board
pressed
presses
press-ing

pres-sure
pres-sur-ized
pres-sur-iz•ing
pres-tige
pres-ti-gious

pre-stress
pre-sum-able
pre-sum-ably
pre-sume
pre-sum•ing

pre-sump-tion
pre-sump-tive
pre-sump-tu•ous
pre-sump-tu-ously
pre-sup-pose

pre-sup-poses
pre-sup-pos•ing
pre-teen
pre-tend
pre-tender

pre-tend•ing
pre-tense
pre-ten-sion
pre-ten-tious
pre-test

pre-test•ing
pre-text
pre-trial
pret-tied
pretty

pret-ty•ing
pret-zel
pre-vail
pre-vail•ing
preva-lence

preva-lent
pre-vari-cate
pre-vari-cat•ing
pre-vari-ca-tion
pre-vari-ca•tor

pre-vent
pre-vent-able
pre-ven-ta-tive
pre-vent•ing
pre-ven-tion

pre-ven-tive
pre-view
pre-view•ing
pre-vi•ous
pre-vi-ously

preyed
prey-ing
priced
price-less
prices

pric-ing
pricked
prick-ing
prickly
prided

pride-ful
pried
pries
priest-hood
priestly

prig-gish
pri-macy
pri-ma-ries
pri-mar•ily
pri-mary

pri-mate
primed
primer
pri-me•val
prim-ing

primi-tive
primped
prim-rose
princely
prin-cess

prin-ci•pal
prin-ci-pali-ties
prin-ci-pal•ity
prin-ci-pally
prin-ci•ple

prin-ci-ples
print-able
printed
printer
print-ers

print-head
print-ing
print-out *(n.)*
prior
pri-ori-ties

pri-ori-tize
pri-or•ity
prism
prison
pris-oner

p

pris-on•ers
pris-ons
pris-tine
pri-vacy
pri-vate

pri-vately
pri-vat•ize
privi-lege
privi-leged
privi-leges

priv-ily
privy
prize
prized
prize-fighter

prizes
proba-bili-ties
proba-bil•ity
prob-able
prob-ably

pro-bate
pro-ba-tion
pro-ba-tional
pro-ba-tion•ary
pro-ba-tioner

probed
prob-ing
prob-lem
prob-lem-atic
pro-ce-dural

pro-ce-dur-ally
pro-ce-dure
pro-ceed
pro-ceed•ing
pro-ceed-ings

pro-ceeds
pro-cess
pro-cesses
pro-cess•ing
pro-ces-sion

pro-ces-sional
pro-ces•sor
pro-ces-sors
pro-claim
pro-claim•ing

proc-la-ma-tion
pro-clivi-ties
pro-cliv•ity
pro-cras-ti-nate
pro-cras-ti-nates

pro-cras-ti-nat•ing
pro-cras-ti-na-tion
pro-cras-ti-na•tor
pro-cre•ate
pro-cre-ates

pro-cre-at•ing
pro-cre-ation
pro-cre-ative
proc-tor
pro-cur-able

pro-cure
pro-cure-ment
pro-curer
pro-cur•ing
prod-ded

prod-ding
prodi-gal
pro-di-gious
prod-igy
pro-duce

pro-ducer
pro-duc•ers
pro-duces
pro-duc•ing
prod-uct

pro-duc-tion
pro-duc-tive
pro-duc-tively
pro-duc-tive-ness
pro-duc-tiv•ity

prod-ucts
pro-fane
pro-fan•ing
pro-fani-ties
pro-fan•ity

pro-femi-nist
pro-fess
pro-fesses
pre-fess•ing
pro-fes-sion

pro-fes-sional
pro-fes-sion-al•ism
pro-fes-sion-al•ize
pro-fes-sion-ally
pro-fes-sion•als

pro-fes•sor
pro-fes-so-rial
prof-fer
prof-fer•ing
pro-fi-ciency

pro-fi-cient
pro-fi-ciently
pro-file
pro-fil•ing
profit

prof-it-able
prof-it-ably
prof-ited
prof-it•ing
prof-it-less

prof-its
pro-found
pro-foundly
pro-fuse
pro-fusely

pro-fu-sion
proge-nies
pro-geni•tor
prog-eny
prog-no•ses

prog-no•sis
prog-nos•tic
prog-nos-ti-cate
prog-nos-ti-cat•ing
prog-nos-ti-ca-tion

prog-nos-ti-ca•tor
pro-gram
pro-gram-ma•ble
pro-gram-matic
pro-gram•mer

pro-gram-mers
pro-gram-ming
prog-ress (n.)
pro-gress (v.)
pro-gresses

pro-gress•ing
pro-gres-sion
pro-gres-sive
pro-gres-sively
pro-hibit

pro-hib-ited
pro-hib-it•ing
pro-hi-bi-tion
pro-hi-bi-tion•ist
pro-hibi-tive

pro-hib•its
pro-ject (v.)
proj-ect (n.)
pro-jected
pro-jec-tile

pro-ject•ing
pro-jec-tion
pro-jec-tion•ist
pro-jec-tive
pro-jec•tor

pro-le-tar•ian
pro-le-tar•iat
pro--life
pro-lif-er•ate
pro-lif-er-at•ing

pro-lif-era-tion
pro-lific
pro-logue
pro-long
pro-lon-gate

pro-lon-ga-tion
pro-long•ing
prome-nade
prome-nad•ing
promi-nence

promi-nent
promi-nently
pro-mis-cu•ity
pro-mis-cu•ous
pro-mis-cu-ously

prom-ise
prom-ises
prom-is•ing
prom-is-sory
prom-on-tory

pro-mot-able
pro-mote
pro-moter
pro-mot•ing
pro-mo-tion

pro-mo-tional
prompt
prompted
prompt-ing
promptly

prompt-ness
pro-mul-gate
pro-mul-gat•ing
pro-mul-ga-tion
pro-noun

pro-nounce
pro-nounce-ment
pro-nounces
pro-nounc•ing
pronto

pro-nun-cia-tion
proofer
proof-ing
proof-read
proof-reader

proof-reading
proofs
pro-pa-ganda
pro-pa-gan-dist
pro-pa-gan-dize

p

propa-gate
propa-gated
propa-gat•ing
propa-ga-tion
propa-ga•tor

pro-pane
pro•pel
pro-pel-lant
pro-pel•ler
pro-pel-ling

pro-pels
pro-pen-sity
proper
prop-erly
prop-er-ties

prop-erty
prophe-cies
proph-ecy
prophe-sied
prophe-sies

proph-esy
proph-esy•ing
prophet
pro-phetic
proph-ets

pro-phy-lac•tic
pro-pi-ti•ate
pro-pi-ti-at•ing
pro-pi-tia-tion
pro-pi-tia-tory

pro-po-nent
pro-por-tion
pro-por-tional
pro-por-tion•ate
pro-por-tion-ately

pro-por-tion•ing
pro-posal
pro-pos•als
pro-pose
pro-poses

pro-pos•ing
propo-si-tion
pro-pound
pro-pounder
pro-pound•ing

propped
prop-ping
pro-pri-etary
pro-pri-etor
pro-pri-etor-ship

pro-pri•ety
pro-pul-sion
pro-pyl•ene
pro-rate
pro-rat•ing

pro-ra-tion
pro-sce-nium
pro-scribe
pro-scrib•ing
pro-scrip-tion

pro-scrip-tive
prose-cute
prose-cut•ing
prose-cu-tion
prose-cu•tor

prose-lyte
prose-lytes
prose-lyt•ing
prose-ly-tize
prose-ly-tiz•ing

pros-pect
pros-pect•ing
pros-pec-tive
pros-pec-tively
pros-pec•tor

pro-spec•tus
pro-spec-tuses
pros-per
pros-per•ing
pros-per•ity

pros-per•ous
pros-tate
pros-ta-tec-tomy
pros-the•ses
pros-the•sis

pros-thetic
pros-thet•ics
prosth-odon-tics
pros-ti-tute
pros-ti-tut•ing

pros-ti-tu-tion
pros-trate
pros-trat•ing
pros-tra-tion
pro-tago-nist

pro-tect
pro-tect•ing
pro-tec-tion
pro-tec-tion•ism
pro-tec-tion•ist

pro-tec-tive
pro-tec-tive-ness
pro-tec•tor
pro-tegé
pro-tein

pro-test	pro-vin-cial•ism	psy-che-delic
prot-es-tant	pro-vin-cially	psy-chi-at•ric
Prot-es-tant•ism	prov-ing	psy-chia-trist
pro-tester	pro-vi-sion	psy-chia•try
pro-test•ing	pro-vi-sional	psy-chic
pro-to•col	pro-vi-sion-ally	psy-chi•cal
pro•ton	provo-ca-tion	psy-chi-cally
pro-to-plasm	pro-voca-tive	psy•cho
pro-to-type	pro-voke	psy•cho-analy•sis
pro-to-typ•ing	pro-vok•ing	psy•cho-ana-lyst
pro-tract	pro-vost	psy•cho-ana-lyze
pro-tract•ing	prow-ess	psy•cho-log-ical
pro-trac-tion	prowler	psy•cho-logi-cally
pro-trac•tor	prowl-ers	psy•cholo-gies
pro-trude	prowl-ing	psy•cholo-gist
pro-trud•ing	prox-ies	psy•cholo-giz•ing
pro-tru-sion	prox-im•ity	psy-chol•ogy
pro-tru-sive	proxy	psy•cho-met-rics
proudly	pru-dence	psy•cho-mo•tor
pro-union	pru-dent	psy•cho-path
prov-able	pru-dently	psy•cho-pathic
proved	prud-ish	psy-cho•sis
proven	pruned	psy•cho-so-matic
prov-erb	pruner	psy•cho-ther•apy
pro-ver-bial	prun-ing	psy-chotic
pro-vide	pry•ing	pu•berty
provi-dence	psalm	pu•bes-cent
provi-dent	psalm-ist	pubic
provi-den-tial	pseu•do-clas•sic	pub•lic
provi-dently	pseu•do-code	pub-li-ca-tion
pro-vider	pseu•do-lan-guage	pub-li-cist
pro-vid•ers	pseud-onym	pub-lic•ity
pro-vid•ing	psych	pub-li-cize
prov-ince	Psy•che	pub-li-ciz•ing
pro-vin-cial	psyched	pub-licly

pub-lish
pub-lisher
pub-lish•ers
pub-lishes
pub-lish•ing

pud-ding
pud•dle
pueblo
puffi-ness
pu•gi-lism

pu•gi-list
pu•gi-lis•tic
pug-na-cious
pug-nac•ity
Pu•lit-zer

pulled
pul•let
pul•ley
pull-ing
pull-out (n.)

pull-over (n.)
pul-mo-nary
pul•pit
pul•sar
pul-sate

pul-sat•ing
pul-sa-tion
pul-sa•tor
pulses
puls-ing

pul-ver•ize
pul-ver-izes
pul-ver-iz•ing
pum•ice
pum•mel

pum-mel•ing
pumped
pum-per-nickel
pump-ing
pump-kin

punched
punches
punch-ing
punchy
punc-tili•ous

punc-tual
punc-tu-al•ity
punc-tu•ate
punc-tu-at•ing
punc-tua-tion

punc-ture
punc-tur•ing
pun•dit
pun-gent
pun•ish

pun-ish-able
pun-ishes
pun-ish•ing
pun-ish-ment
pu•ni-tive

pun-ster
punted
punter
punt-ing
puny

pupil
pu•pils
pup•pet
pup-pe-teer
pup-petry

pup-pets
pup-pies
puppy
pur-chase
pur-chaser

pur-chas•ers
pur-chases
pur-chas•ing
pure-bred
purely

pur-ga-tory
purged
purges
purg-ing
pu•ri-fi-ca-tion

pu•ri-fied
pu•ri-fier
pu•ri-fies
pu•rify
pu•ri-fy•ing

pur•ist
pu•ri-tan
pu•ri-tan•ism
pu•rity
pur-loin

pur-loin•ing
pur•ple
pur-plish
pur-port
pur-port-edly

pur-port•ing
pur-pose
pur-pose•ful
pur-pose-fully
pur-posely

purr-ing
purser
pur-sual
pur-su-ance
pur-su•ant

pur•sue
pur-su•ing
pur-suit
pur-veyor
pur-view

push
push--button *(adj.)*
pushes
push-ing
push-over

push--up
pushy
put--down *(n.)*
pu•trid
putter *(n.)*

put•ter *(v.)*
put-tered
put-ter•ing
put-ters
put-ting

putty
puz•zle
puz-zle-ment
puz-zles
puz-zling

pgy-mies
pgymy
pylon
py•lons
pyra-mid

py•ro-ma•nia
py•ro-ma-niac
py•ro-tech-nics
py•thon

quack-ery
quad-ran•gle
quad-rant
quad-ra-phonic
qua-drille

qua-dril-lion
quad-ri-ple•gia
quad-ri-ple•gic
qua-dru•ple
qua-dru-pli-cate

qua-dru-pling
quag-mire
quak-ing
quali-fi-ca-tion
quali-fied

quali-fier
quali-fi•ers
quali-fies
qual-ify
quali-fy•ing

quali-ta-tive
quali-ties
qual-ity
qualm
quan-da-ries

quan-dary
quan-ti-fied
quan-ti-fier
quan-ti-fies
quan-tify

quan-ti-fy•ing
quan-ti-ta-tive
quan-ti-ties
quan-tity
quar-an-tine

quar-an-tin•ing
quar-rel
quar-rel•ing
quar-rel-some
quar-ried

quar-ries
quarry
quar-ry•ing
quar-ter
quarter-back

quarter-final
quarter-finalist
quar-ter-lies
quar-terly
quarter-master

quar-tet
quar-tile
quarto
qua•sar
qua•ver

qua-ver•ing
quea-sily
quea-si-ness
queasy
Que•bec

q

quelled
quell-ing
quenched
quenches
quench-ing

quench-less
que-ried
que-ries
queru-lous
query

que-ry•ing
ques-tion
ques-tion-able
ques-tion•ing
ques-tion-naire

queue
queued
queue-ing
queues
quib-ble

quib-bler
quib-bles
quib-bling
quicken
quick-ened

quick-en•ing
quick-ens
quicker
quick-est
quickie

quickly
quick-ness
quick-sand
quick-silver
qui-es-cence

qui-es-cent
quiet
qui-eted
qui-etly
qui•et-ness

quilted
quilt-ing
quince
qui-nine
quin-quen-nial

quin-tet
quin-til-lion
quin-tu•ple
quin-tu-plet
quipped

quip-ping
quirky
quit-claim
quit-ter
quit-ting

quiver
quiv-ered
quiv-er•ing
quizzed
quiz-zes

quiz-zi•cal
quiz-zing
quo•rum
quota
quot-able

quo•tas
quo-ta-tion
quoted
quo-tient
quot-ing

R

rabbi
rab•bis
rab•bit
rab•ble
rabid

ra•bies
rac-coon
race-course
race-horse
racer

race-track
race-way
ra•cial
ra•cially
rac•ing

rac•ism
rac•ist
rac-ists
racket
racke-teer

racke-teer•ing
rack-ets
rack-ing
racquet-ball
racy

radar
ra•dar-scope
ra•dial
ra•di-ance
ra•di-ant

ra•di-antly	raider	ram-bling
ra•di-ate	raid-ers	ram-bunc-tious
ra•di-ates	raid-ing	rami-fi-ca-tion
ra•di-at•ing	railed	ram•jet
ra•dia-tion	rail-ing	rammed
ra•dia-tor	rail-road	ram-ming
rad-ical	rail-roading	ram-page
radi-cally	rail-way	ram-pa-geous
radii	rai-ment	ram-pag•ing
radio	rain-bow	ram-pant
ra•dio-ac•tive	rain-coat	ram•rod
ra•di-oed	rain-drop	ram-rods
ra•di-oing	rained	ram-shackle
ra•di-olo-gist	rain-fall	ranched
ra•di-ol•ogy	rain-ing	rancher
ra•dios	rain-maker	ran-chero
ra•dio-sco•pic	rain-making	ranch-ers
ra•dio-sonde	rain-storm	ranches
ra•dio-tele-graph	rain-water	ranch-ing
ra•dio-ther•apy	rainy	ran•cid
rad•ish	raised	ran-cid-ness
ra•dium	raises	ran•cor
ra•dius	rai•sin	ran-cor•ous
radon	rais-ing	ran•dom
raf•fle	rai-sins	ran-dom-iza-tion
rafted	raked	ran-dom•ize
raf•ter	rak•ing	ran-dom-iz•ing
raf-ters	rak•ish	ran-domly
raged	ral-lied	ran-dom-ness
rages	ral-lies	ranged
rag•ged	rally	range-land
rag•ing	ral-ly•ing	ranger
rag-time	RAM	rang-ers
rag-weed	ram•ble	ranges
raided	ram-bler	rangi-ness

r

rang-ing	rasp-berry	rat-trap
rangy	rasp-ing	rau-cous
ranked	raspy	rau-cous-ness
rank-ing	ras•ter	raun-chy
ran•kle	ratchet	rav•age
rank-ness	ratch-ets	rav-ag•ing
ran-sack	rated	ravel
ran-sack•ing	rater	rav-eled
ran•som	rather	rav-el•ing
ran-som•ing	raths-kel•ler	rav•els
ran-soms	rati-fi-ca-tion	raven
ranted	rati-fied	rav-en•ous
rant-ing	rat•ify	ra•vine
rapid	rat-ify•ing	rav•ing
ra•pid-ity	rat•ing	ravi-oli
rap-idly	rat-ings	rav•ish
rap•ids	ratio	rav-ishes
rap•ing	ra•tion	rav-ish•ing
rapped	ra•tio-nal	rav-ish-ingly
rap-ping	ra•tio-nale	raw-hide
rap-port	ra•tio-nal•ist	rayon
rap-ture	ra•tio-nal-is•tic	razed
rap-tur•ous	ra•tio-nal-iza-tion	razes
rap-tur-ously	ra•tio-nal•ize	raz•ing
rar-efied	ra•tio-nal-iz•ing	razor
rar•efy	ra•tio-nally	ra•zors
rar-efy•ing	ra•tion-ing	re•ac-credit
rarely	ra•tios	re•ac-credi-ta-tion
rari-ties	rat•tan	re•ac-cred-ited
rar•ity	rat•tle	re•ac-cred-it•ing
ras•cal	rattle-brained	reached
ras-cal•ity	rat-tler	reaches
rashes	rat-tles	reach-ing
rash-ness	rattle-snake	re•ac-quaint
rasp-ber-ries	rat-tling	re•ac-quainted

re•ac-quire
react
re•acted
re•act-ing
re•ac-tion

re•ac-tion•ary
re•ac-ti-vate
re•ac-ti-vat•ing
re•ac-ti-va-tion
re•ac-tor

read-abil•ity
read-able
reader
read-ers
read-ied

readily
readi-ness
read-ing
re•ad-just
re•ad-just-ment

re•ad-mis-sion
re•ad-mit
re•ad-mit-tance
re•ad-mit•ted
re•ad-mit-ting

read-out
ready
ready-ing
re•af-firm
re•af-fir-ma-tion

re•af-firm•ing
re•align
re•align-ing
re•align-ment
re•al-ism

re•al-ist
re•al-is•tic
re•al-is-ti-cally
re•ali-ties
re•al-ity

re•al-iza-tion
re•al-ize
re•al-izes
re•al-iz•ing
re•al-lo-cate

re•al-lo-ca-tion
re•ally
re•al-ties
re•al-tor
re•alty

re•ana-lyze
re•ana-lyz•ing
reaped
reap-ing
re•ap-pear

re•ap-pear-ance
re•ap-pear•ing
re•ap-plied
re•ap-plies
re•ap-ply

re•ap-ply•ing
re•ap-point
re•ap-point•ing
re•ap-point-ment
re•ap-praisal

re•ap-praise
re•ap-praise-ment
re•ap-prais•ing
reared
rear-ing

rearm
re•ar-ma-ment
re•armed
re•arm-ing
re•ar-range

re•ar-range-ment
re•ar-ranges
re•ar-rang•ing
rea•son
rea-son-able

rea-son-ably
rea-son•ing
re•as-sem•ble
re•as-sem-bling
re•as-sem•bly

re•as-sess
re•as-sess-ment
re•as-sign
re•as-sign•ing
re•as-sign-ment

re•as-sur-ance
re•as-sure
re•as-sur•ing
re•bate
rebel

re•belled
re•bel-ling
re•bel-lion
re•bel-lious
reb•els *(n.)*

re•bels *(v.)*
re•birth
re•boot
re•born
re•bound

r

re•bound-ing
re•broad-cast
re•broad-cast•ing
re•buff
re•buff-ing

re•build
re•build-ing
re•built
re•buke
re•buk-ing

re•but-ment
re•but-tal
re•but-ting
re•cal-cu-late
re•cal-cu-lat•ing

re•cal-cu-la-tion
re•call
re•call-ing
re•cant
re•can-ta-tion

re•cant-ing
recap
re•ca-pitu-late
re•ca-pitu-lat•ing
re•ca-pitu-la-tion

re•ca-pitu-la-tive
re•capped
re•cap-ping
re•cap-ture
re•car-pet

re•car-pet•ing
re•cede
re•ced-ing
re•ceipt
re•ceipt-ing

re•ceiv-able
re•ceive
re•ceiver
re•ceiv-ers
re•ceiv-ing

re•cency
re•cent
re•cently
re•cep-ta•cle
re•cep-tion

re•cep-tion•ist
re•cep-tive
re•cep-tive-ness
re•cep-tor
re•cer-ti-fi-ca-tion

re•cer-ti-fied
re•cer-tify
re•cer-ti-fy•ing
re•cess
re•cesses

re•cess-ing
re•ces-sion
re•ces-sional
re•ces-sion•ary
re•ces-sive

re•ces-sively
re•charge
re•charge-able
re•charg-ing
re•char-ter

re•char-ter•ing
re•check
re•check-ing
rec•ipe
reci-pes

re•cipi-ent
re•cip-ro•cal
re•cip-ro-cate
re•cip-ro-cat•ing
re•cip-ro-ca-tion

reci-proc•ity
re•cir-cu-late
re•cir-cu-lat•ing
re•cir-cu-la-tion
re•cital

reci-ta-tion
re•cite
re•cit-ing
reck-less
reck-lessly

reck-less-ness
reckon
reck-oned
reck-on•ing
reck-ons

re•claim
re•claim-ing
rec-la-ma-tion
re•class
re•clas-si-fied

re•clas-si-fies
re•clas-sify
re•clas-sify•ing
re•cline
re•cliner

re•clin-ers
re•clin-ing
re•cluse
re•clu-sive
rec-og-ni-tion

rec-og-niz-able
re•cog-ni-zance
rec-og-nize
rec-og-nizes
rec-og-niz•ing

re•coil
re•coil-ing
rec-ol-lect *(v.)*
rec-ol-lect•ing
rec-ol-lec-tion

re•colo-ni-za-tion
re•colo-nize
re•colo-niz•ing
rec-om-mend
rec-om-mended

rec-om-mend•ing
re•com-mis-sion
re•com-mis-sioned
re•com-mit
re•com-mit-ment

re•com-mit•tal
re•com-mit•ted
re•com-mit-ting
rec-om-pense
rec-om-pens•ing

re•com-pose
re•com-pres-sion
re•com-pute
rec-on-cile
rec-on-ciled

rec-on-cili-ation
rec-on-cil•ing
re•con-di-tion
re•con-di-tion•ing
re•con-figu-ra-tion

re•con-fig•ure
re•con-firm
re•con-fir-ma-tion
re•con-nais-sance
re•con-nect

re•con-nect•ing
re•con-nec-tion
re•con-noi•ter
re•con-se-crate
re•con-se-crat•ing

re•con-se-cra-tion
re•con-sider
re•con-sid-ered
re•con-sid-er•ing
re•con-sign-ment

re•con-sti-tute
re•con-sti-tut•ing
re•con-sti-tu-tion
re•con-struct
re•con-struc-tion

re•con-struc-tive
re•con-vene
re•con-ven•ing
rec•ord *(n.)*
re•cord *(v.)*

re•corder
re•cord-ing
rec-ords *(n.)*
re•count
re•coup

re•coup-ing
re•coup-ment
re•course
re•cover
re•cov-er-able

re•cov-ered
re•cov-er•ies
re•cov-er•ing
re•cov-ery
re--cre•ate

rec-re-ation
rec-re-ational
re•crimi-na-tion
re•cruit
re•cruiter

re•cruit-ers
re•cruit-ing
re•cruit-ment
rec•tal
rec-tally

rect-an•gle
rect-an-gu•lar
rec-ti-fi-able
rec-ti-fi-ca-tion
rec-ti-fied

rec-ti-fies
rec-tify
rec-ti-fy•ing
rec-tory
rec•tum

re•cu-per•ate
re•cu-per-at•ing
re•cu-pera-tion
re•cu-pera-tive
recur

re•curred
re•cur-rence
re•cur-rent
re•cur-ring
re•curs

r

re•cur-sion
re•cur-sive
re•cur-sively
re•cy-cla•ble
re•cy-cle

re•cy-cles
re•cy-cling
red•den
red-dened
red-den•ing

re•deco-rate
re•deco-rat•ing
re•deco-ra-tion
re•dedi-cate
re•dedi-cat•ing

re•dedi-ca-tion
re•deem
re•deem-able
re•deemer
re•deem-ing

re•de-fine
re•de-fin•ing
re•demp-tion
re•demp-tive
re•de-ploy

re•de-sign
re•des-ig-nated
re•des-ig-nat•ing
re•des-ig-na-tion
re•de-sign•ing

re•de-velop
re•de-vel-op•ing
re•de-vel-op-ment
re•di-rect
re•di-rector

re•dis-cover
re•dis-covery
re•dis-trict
re•dis-trict•ing
red-line

red-lin•ing
redo
re•do-ing
redo-lence
re•done

re•draft
re•draft-ing
re•dress
re•dresses
re•dress-ing

re•duce
re•duces
re•duc-ible
re•duc-ing
re•duc-tion

re•dun-dan-cies
re•dun-dancy
re•dun-dant
re•dun-dantly
red-wood

re•edu-cate
reek-ing
re•elect
re•elect-ing
re•elec-tion

reeled
reel-ing
re•em-pha•sis
re•em-pha-size
re•em-pha-siz•ing

re•em-ploy
re•em-ploy•ing
re•en-act
re•en-act•ing
re•en-act-ment

re•en-force
re•en-forc•ing
re•en-list
re•en-list•ing
re•en-list-ment

re•en-ter
re•en-ter•ing
re•en-trance
re•en-tries
re•en-try

re•es-tab-lish
re•es-tab-lishes
re•es-tab-lish•ing
re•evalu-ate
re•evalu-at•ing

re•evalu-ation
re•ex-ami-na-tion
re•ex-am•ine
re•ex-am-in•ing
refer

ref-eree
ref-er•eed
ref-er-ee•ing
ref-er-ence
ref-er-ences

ref-er-enc•ing
ref-er-enda
ref-er-en•dum
ref-er-en-tial
re•fer-ral

re•ferred
re•fer-ring
re•fers
re•fig-ure
re•fig-ur•ing

re•file
re•fill
re•fill-able
re•fill-ing
re•fi-nance

re•fi-nances
re•fi-nanc•ing
re•fine
re•fine-ment
re•finer

re•fin-er•ies
re•fin-ery
re•fin-ing
re•fin-ish
re•fin-ishes

re•fin-ish•ing
re•flect
re•flect-ing
re•flec-tion
re•flec-tive

re•flec-tor
re•flex
re•flexes
re•fo-cus
re•fo-cus•ing

re•for-es-ta-tion
re•form
re•form-able
re•for-mat
ref-or-ma-tion

re•for-ma-tive
re•for-ma-to-ries
re•for-ma-tory
re•for-mat•ted
re•for-mat-ting

re•form-ing
re•for-mu-late
re•for-mu-lat•ing
re•for-ti-fied
re•for-tify

re•for-ti-fy•ing
re•fract
re•fract-ing
re•frac-tion
re•frac-tive

re•frac-tor
re•frac-tory
re•frain
re•frain-ing
re•fresh

re•fresher
re•freshes
re•fresh-ing
re•fresh-ingly
re•fresh-ment

re•fried
re•frig-er•ate
re•frig-er-at•ing
re•frig-era-tion
re•frig-era•tor

re•frig-era-tors
re•fuel
re•fuel-ing
ref•uge
refu-gee

re•ful-gence
re•ful-gent
re•fund
re•fund-able
re•fund-ing

re•fur-bish
re•fur-bishes
re•fur-bish•ing
re•fur-bish-ment
re•fur-nish•ing

re•fusal
re•fuse (v.)
ref•use (n.)
re•fuses
re•fus-ing

re•fut-able
re•fute
re•fut-ing
re•gain
re•gain-ing

regal
re•ga-lia
re•gal-ing
re•gard
re•gard-ing

re•gard-less
re•gatta
re•gat-tas
re•gency
re•gen-er•ate

re•gen-er-ates
re•gen-er-at•ing
re•gen-era-tion
re•gen-era-tive
re•gen-era•tor

r

re•gents
re•gime
regi-ment
regi-men•tal
regi-men-ta-tion

regi-ment•ing
re•gion
re•gional
re•gion-ally
reg-is•ter

reg-is-ter•ing
reg-is-ters
reg-is-trant
reg-is-trar
reg-is-tra-tion

reg-is•try
re•gress
re•gresses
re•gress-ing
re•gres-sion

re•gres-sive
re•gret
re•gret-ful
re•gret-fully
re•gret-ta•ble

re•gret-ta•bly
re•gret-ted
re•gret-ting
re•group
re•group-ing

regu-lar
regu-larly
regu-late
regu-lates
regu-lat•ing

regu-la-tion
regu-la-tive
regu-la•tor
regu-la-tory
re•gur-gi-tate

re•gur-gi-tat•ing
re•gur-gi-ta-tion
rehab
re•ha-bili-tate
re•ha-bili-tates

re•ha-bili-tat•ing
re•ha-bili-ta-tion
re•ha-bili-ta-tive
re•hash
re•hash-ing

re•hear-ing
re•hearsal
re•hears-als
re•hearse
re•hears-ing

re•heat
re•heat-ing
re•hire
re•hir-ing
reign

reign-ing
re•ig-nite
re•ig-nit•ing
re•im-burs-able
re•im-burse

re•im-burse-ment
re•im-burses
re•im-burs•ing
rein
re•in-car-nate

re•in-car-nat•ing
re•in-car-na-tion
rein-deer
re•in-force
re•in-force-ment

re•in-forces
re•in-forc•ing
rein-ing
re•in-state
re•in-state-ment

re•in-stat•ing
re•in-sti-tute
re•in-sur-ance
re•in-sure
re•in-surer

re•in-sur•ing
re•in-tro-duced
re•in-vest
re•in-vest•ing
re•in-vest-ment

re•is-sue
re•is-su•ing
re•it-er•ate
re•it-er-at•ing
re•it-era-tion

re•it-era-tive
re•ject
re•ject-ing
re•jec-tion
re•joice

re•joic-ing
re•join
re•join-ing
re•ju-ve-nate
re•ju-ve-nat•ing

re•ju•ve•na•tion
re•kin•dle
re•kin•dling
re•la•bel
re•la•bel•ing

re•lapse
re•lapses
re•laps•ing
re•late
re•lat•ing

re•la•tion
re•la•tional
re•la•tion-ship
rela-tive
rela-tively

rela-tiv•ity
relax
re•lax-ant
re•lax-ation
re•laxed

re•laxer
re•lax-ing
relay
re•layed
re•lay-ing

re•lays
re•lease
re•leases
re•leas-ing
rele-gate

rele-gates
rele-gat•ing
rele-ga-tion
re•lent
re•lent-ing

re•lent-less
re•lent-lessly
rele-vance
rele-vant
re•li-abil•ity

re•li-able
re•li-ably
re•li-ance
re•li-ant
relic

rel•ics
re•lied
re•lief
re•lies
re•lieve

re•liev-ing
re•li-gion
re•li-gious
re•li-giously
re•lin-quish

re•lin-quish•ing
re•lin-quish-ment
rel•ish
rel-ishes
rel-ish•ing

re•live
re•liv-ing
re•lo-cate
re•lo-cates
re•lo-cat•ing

re•lo-ca-tion
re•luc-tance
re•luc-tant
re•luc-tantly
rely

re•ly-ing
re•main
re•main-der
re•main-ing
re•make

re•mak-ing
re•mand
re•mand-ing
remap
re•mark

re•mark-able
re•mar-ried
re•marry
re•mar-ry•ing
re•me-dial

reme-died
reme-dies
rem•edy
re•mem-ber
re•mem-ber-able

re•mem-ber•ing
re•mem-brance
re•mind
re•minder
re•mind-ers

re•mind-ing
remi-nisce
remi-nis-cence
remi-nis-cent
remi-nisces

remi-nisc•ing
re•miss
re•mis-sion
remit
re•mits

r

175

re•mit-tal
re•mit-tance
re•mit-tances
re•mit-ted
re•mit-ting

rem-nant
re•model
re•mod-eled
re•mod-el•ing
re•mon-strate

re•mon-stra-tion
re•mon-stra-tive
re•morse
re•morse-ful
re•morse-ful-ness

re•morse-less
re•mote
re•motely
re•mov-able
re•moval

re•move
re•mov-ing
re•mu-ner•ate
re•mu-ner-at•ing
re•mu-nera-tion

re•mu-nera-tive
re•mu-nera•tor
re•nais-sance
renal
re•name

ren•der
ren-der•ing
ren-dez-vous
ren-dez-vous•ing
ren-di-tion

rene-gade
rene-gad•ing
re•nege
re•neg-ing
re•ne-go-tia•ble

re•ne-go-ti•ate
re•ne-go-ti•ates
re•ne-go-ti•at•ing
re•ne-go-tia-tion
renew

re•new-able
re•newal
re•new-ing
re•news
re•nounce

re•nounce-ment
re•nounces
re•nounc-ing
reno-vate
reno-vat•ing

reno-va-tion
reno-va•tor
re•nown
rental
rent-als

rented
renter
rent-ers
rent-ing
re•num-ber

re•num-ber•ing
re•nun-cia-tion
re•nun-cia-tory
re•oc-cur
re•oc-cur-rence

re•oc-cur-ring
re•open
re•open-ing
re•or-der
re•or-der•ing

re•or-ga-ni-za-tion
re•or-ga-nize
re•or-ga-nizes
re•or-ga-niz•ing
re•ori-ent

re•ori-en-ta-tion
re•ori-ent•ing
re•pack
re•pack-ing
re•pagi-na-tion

re•paid
re•paint
re•paint-ing
re•pair
re•pair-able

re•pair-ing
repa-ra•ble
repa-ra-tion
rep-ar•tee
re•past

re•pa-tri•ate
re•pa-tri-at•ing
re•pa-tria-tion
re•pave
re•pav-ing

repay
re•pay-able
re•pay-ing
re•pay-ment
re•pays

re•peal
re•peal-ing
re•peat
re•peat-able
re•peat-edly

re•peater
re•peat-ing
repel
re•pelled
re•pel-lent

re•pel-ling
re•pels
re•pent
re•pen-tance
re•pen-tant

re•pent-ing
re•per-cus-sion
rep-er-toire
rep-er-tory
repe-ti-tion

repe-ti-tious
repe-ti-tiously
re•peti-tive
re•peti-tively
re•phrase

re•phrases
re•phras-ing
re•place
re•place-ment
re•places

re•plac-ing
re•plant
re•plant-ing
re•play
re•play-ing

re•plen-ish
re•plen-ish•ing
re•plen-ish-ment
re•plete
re•ple-tion

rep-lica
rep-li•cas
rep-li-cate
rep-li-cat•ing
rep-li-ca-tion

rep-li-ca-tive
re•plied
re•plies
reply
re•ply-ing

re•port
re•port-edly
re•porter
re•port-ers
re•port-ing

re•pose
re•poses
re•pos-ing
re•po-si-tion
re•po-si-tion•ing

re•posi-to-ries
re•posi-tory
re•pos-sess
re•pos-sess•ing
re•pos-ses-sion

rep-re-hend
rep-re-hend•ing
rep-re-hen-si•ble
rep-re-hen-sion
rep-re-hen-sive

rep-re-sent
rep-re-sen-ta-tion
rep-re-sen-ta-tive
rep-re-sent•ing
re•press

re•presses
re•press-ible
re•press-ing
re•pres-sion
re•pres-sive

re•prieval
re•prieve
re•priev-ing
rep-ri-mand
rep-ri-mand•ing

re•print
re•print-ing
re•pri-sal
re•prise
re•prises

re•pris-ing
re•proach
re•proach-able
re•proach-ing
rep-ro-bate

rep-ro-bat•ing
rep-ro-ba-tion
rep-ro-ba-tive
re•pro-cess
re•pro-cesses

re•pro-cess•ing
re•pro-duce
re•pro-duces
re•pro-duc-ible
re•pro-duc•ing

r

re•pro-duc-tion
re•pro-duc-tive
re•pro-gram
re•pro-gram-ming
re•pro-graph•ics

re•prog-ra•phy
re•proof
re•proval
re•prove
re•prov-ing

rep-tile
rep-til•ian
re•pub-lic
re•pub-li•can
re•pu-di•ate

re•pu-di-at•ing
re•pu-dia-tion
re•pug-nance
re•pug-nancy
re•pug-nant

re•pulse
re•pul-sion
re•pul-sive
re•pul-sive-ness
repu-ta•ble

repu-ta•bly
repu-ta-tion
re•pute
re•put-edly
re•put-ing

re•quest
re•quester
re•quest-ing
re•quiem
re•quire

re•quire-ment
re•quir-ing
req-ui-site
req-ui-si-tion
req-ui-si-tion•ing

re•quital
re•route
re•rout-ing
rerun
re•run-ning

re•runs
re•sal-able
re•sale
re•sched-ule
re•sched-ul•ing

re•scind
re•scind-ing
re•scis-sion
res•cue
res-cuer

res-cu•ing
re•search
re•searcher
re•search-ers
re•searches

re•search-ing
re•sell
re•sell-ing
re•sem-blance
re•sem-ble

re•sem-bling
re•sent
re•sent-ful
re•sent-ing
re•sent-ment

res-er-va-tion
re•serve
re•serv-edly
re•serv-ing
re•serv-ist

res-er-voir
reset
re•sets
re•set-ting
re•ship

re•ship-ment
re•ship-ping
re•shuf-fle
re•shuf-fling
re•side

resi-dence
resi-dences
resi-den-cies
resi-dency
resi-dent

resi-den-tial
re•sid-ing
re•sid-ual
re•sid-uals
re•sidu-ary

resi-due
re•sign
res-ig-na-tion
re•sign-ing
re•sil-ience

re•sil-ient
re•sil-iently
resin
res-in•ous
res•ins

re•sist
re•sis-tance
re•sis-tant
re•sist-ible
re•sist-ing

re•sist-less
reso-lute
reso-lutely
reso-lu-tion
re•solv-able

re•solve
re•solv-ing
reso-nance
reso-nant
reso-nate

reso-nat•ing
re•sort
re•sort-ing
re•sound
re•sound-ing

re•sound-ingly
re•source
re•source-ful
re•source-ful-ness
re•sources

re•spect
re•spect-abil•ity
re•spect-able
re•spect-ably
re•spect-ful

re•spect-fully
re•spect-ing
re•spec-tive
re•spec-tively
res-pi-rat•ing

res-pi-ra-tion
res-pi-ra•tor
re•spi-ra-tory
re•splen-dence
re•splen-dent

re•spond
re•spon-dent
re•sponder
re•spond-ing
re•sponse

re•sponses
re•spon-si-bili-ties
re•spon-si-bil•ity
re•spon-si•ble
re•spon-si•bly

re•spon-sive
re•spon-sive-ness
re•start
re•start-ing
re•state

re•state-ment
re•stat-ing
res-tau-rant
res-tau-ra-teur
rested

rest-ful
rest-ful-ness
rest-ing
res-ti-tut•ing
res-ti-tu-tion

res-ti-tu-tive
res-tive
res-tively
rest-less
rest-lessly

rest-less-ness
re•stock
re•stock-ing
res-to-ra-tion
re•stor-ative

re•store
re•stor-ing
re•strain
re•strainer
re•strain-ing

re•straint
re•strict
re•strict-ing
re•stric-tion
re•stric-tive

re•stric-tively
re•struc-ture
re•struc-tur•ing
re•sub-mis-sion
re•sub-mit

re•sub-mit•ted
re•sub-mit-ting
re•sult
re•sul-tant
re•sult-ing

re•sumé *(n.)*
re•sume *(v.)*
re•sumes
re•sum-ing
re•sump-tion

re•sur-face
re•sur-faces
re•sur-fac•ing
re•sur-gence
re•sur-gent

res-ur-rect
res-ur-rect•ing
res-ur-rec-tion
re•sus-ci-tate
re•sus-ci-tat•ing

re•sus-ci-ta-tion
re•sus-ci-ta•tor
re•tail
re•tailer
re•tail-ers

re•tail-ing
re•tain
re•tainer
re•tain-ers
re•tain-ing

re•take
re•taken
re•tak-ing
re•tali-ate
re•tali-ates

re•tali-ation
re•tal-ia-tory
re•tard
re•tar-dant
re•tar-da-tion

re•tard-ing
re•ten-tion
re•ten-tive
reti-cence
reti-cent

ret•ina
reti-nal
reti-nue
re•tire
re•tiree

re•tire-ment
re•tir-ing
re•tir-ingly
re•told
re•tool

re•tort
re•tort-ing
re•touch
re•trace
re•trac-ing

re•tract
re•trac-tile
re•tract-ing
re•trac-tion
re•trac-tor

re•train
re•train-ing
re•tread
re•tread-ing
re•treat

re•treat-ing
re•trench
re•trenches
re•trench-ing
re•trench-ment

re•trial
ret-ri-bu-tion
ret-ri-bu-tive
re•tried
re•tries

re•triev-able
re•trieval
re•trieve
re•triever
re•triev-ing

ret•ro-ac-tive
ret•ro-ac-tively
ret•ro-cede
ret•ro-ced•ing
ret•ro-ces-sion

ret•ro-ces-sive
ret•ro-fire
ret•ro-fir•ing
ret•ro-fit
ret•ro-flex

ret•ro-grade
ret•ro-gress
ret•ro-gresses
ret•ro-gress•ing
ret•ro-gres-sion

ret•ro-gres-sive
ret•ro-pul-sion
retro--rocket
ret•ro-spect
ret•ro-spec-tion

ret•ro-spec-tive
retry
re•try-ing
re•turn
re•turn-able

re•turn-ing
re•type
re•typ-ing
re•union
re•unite

re•unit-ing
re•up-hol-ster
re•up-hol-ster•ing
re•us-able
reuse

re•used	re•vers-ing	revo-lu-tion•ize
re•uses	re•ver-sion	revo-lu-tion-iz•ing
re•us-ing	re•vert	re•volv-able
re•value	re•vert-ing	re•volve
re•vamp	re•view	re•volver
re•vamp-ing	re•viewer	re•volv-ers
re•veal	re•view-ers	re•volv-ing
re•veal-ing	re•view-ing	revue
rev-eille	re•vile	re•vues
reve-la-tion	re•vil-ing	re•vul-sion
reve-la•tor	re•vise	revved
reve-la-tory	re•vises	rev-ving
rev-eled	re•vis-ing	re•ward
rev-el•ing	re•vi-sion	re•ward-ing
re•venge	re•visit	re•wind
re•venge-ful	re•vi-tal-iza-tion	re•wind-ing
reve-nue	re•vi-tal•ize	re•wire
re•ver-ber•ant	re•vi-tal-izes	re•wir-ing
re•ver-ber•ate	re•vi-tal-iz•ing	re•word
re•ver-ber-ates	re•vival	re•word-ing
re•ver-ber-at•ing	re•viv-als	re•words
re•ver-bera-tion	re•vive	re•work
re•ver-bera-tory	re•viv-ing	re•work-ing
re•vere	re•viv-ify	re•wound
rev-er-ence	re•vo-ca•ble	re•wove
rev-er-enc•ing	re•vo-ca-tion	re•write
rev-er•end	re•vok-able	re•writ-ing
rev-er•ent	re•voke	re•writ-ten
rev-er-en-tial	re•vok-ing	re•wrote
rev-er-ently	re•volt	re•zone
rev-erie	re•volt-ing	re•zon-ing
re•ver-sal	revo-lu-tion	rhap-sody
re•verse	revo-lu-tion-aries	rheo-stat
re•verses	revo-lu-tion•ary	rheo-static
re•vers-ible	revo-lu-tion•ist	rheto-ric

r

rhe-tor-ical
rheto-ri-cian
rheu-matic
rheu-ma-tism
rheu-ma-toid

rheu-ma-tolo-gist
rheu-ma-tol•ogy
rhine-stone
rhi-noc-eros
Rhode Is•land

Rhode Is•lander
Rho-de•sia
Rho-de-sian
rho-dium
rho-do-den-dron

rhu-barb
rhyme
rhym-ing
rhythm
rhyth-mic

rhyth-mi•cal
rhythms
rib•bon
rib-bons
ri•bo-fla•vin

riches
richly
rich-ness
rick-ets
rick-ety

rick-shaw
rico-chet
rico-chet•ing
rid-dance
rid-ding

rid•dle
rider
rid•ers
rid-er-ship
ridi-cule

ridi-cul•ing
ri•dicu-lous
rid•ing
rifle
ri•fled

ri•fles
ri•fling
rigged
rig•ger
rig-ging

righ-teous
righ-teously
righ-teous-ness
right-ful
right-fully

rightly
rigid
ri•gid-ity
rig-idly
rig-ma-role

rigor
rig-or•ous
rig-or-ously
rig•ors
rimmed

rim-ming
ringed
ringer
ring-ing
ring-leader

ring-master
ring-side
ring-worm
rinsed
rinses

rins-ing
riot
ri•oted
ri•oter
ri•ot-ing

ri•ot-ous
ripen
rip-ened
rip-en•ing
rip•ens

rip-ping
rip•ple
rip-ples
rip-pling
risen

riser
rises
risi-bil•ity
ris-ible
ris•ing

riski-ness
risk-ing
risky
ris•qué
rites

rit•ual
ritu-al•ism
ritu-al-is•tic
ritu-al-is-ti-cally
ritu-als

rival
ri•valed
ri•val-ing
ri•val-ries
ri•valry

ri•vals
river
river-bank
river-bed
river-boat

river-front
riv•ers
river-side
rivet
riv-eted

riv-et•ing
riv•ets
Ri•vi-era
roaches
road-block

road-ster
road-way
roamed
roam-ing
roared

roar-ing
roasted
roast-ing
robbed
rob•ber

rob-ber•ies
rob-bers
rob-bery
rob-bing
robin

rob•ins
robot
ro•bot-ics
ro•bot-iza-tion
ro•bot-ize

ro•bots
ro•bust
ro•bustly
ro•bust-ness
rocked

rocker
rock-ers
rocket
rock-eted
rock-et•ing

rock-etry
rock-ets
rock-ing
rocky
ro•dent

rodeo
ro•deos
rogu-ish
roll-back (n.)
rolled

roller
roll-ers
rol-lick
rol-lick•ing
roll-ing

roll-out
ro•mance
ro•mances
ro•manc-ing
Ro•ma-nia

Ro•ma-nian
ro•man-tic
ro•man-ti-cally
ro•man-ti-cist
ro•man-ti-cize

ro•man-ti-cizes
ro•man-ti-ciz•ing
roofed
roofer
roof-ers

roof-ing
roof-top
rook-ery
rookie
roomed

roomer
room-ful
room-ier
roomi-ness
room-ing

room-mate
roomy
roosted
rooster
roost-ers

roost-ing
rooted
root-ing
roped
ropes

rop•ing
ro•sary
rose-bud
rose-bush
rose-bushes

ro•se-ola
roses
rose-water
rosin
ros•ter

ros-ters
ros-trum
rosy
ro•tary
ro•tate

ro•tat-ing
ro•ta-tion
ro•ta-tional
ro•tis-serie
ro•to-gra-vure

rotor
ro•to-till
Roto-tiller
rot•ted
rot•ten

rot-ting
ro•tund
ro•tunda
ro•tun-dity
ro-tundly

rouges
rough-age
roughed
roughen
rough-ened

rough-en•ing
rough-ens
rougher
rough-est
rough-house

rough-housing
rough-ing
roughly
rough-neck
rough-shod

roug-ing
rou-lette
round-about
rounded
round-ing

roundly
roundup *(n.)*
round-ups
roused
rouses

rous-ing
roust-about
rouster
routed
router

rou-tine
rou-tinely
rout-ing
rov•ing
row-boat

row-dies
row-di-ness
rowdy
rowed
row•ing

royal
roy-ally
roy-al-ties
roy-alty
rubbed

rub•ber
rub-ber•ize
rub-ber-izes
rubber-neck
rub-bery

rub-bing
rub-bish
rub•ble
ru•bella
ru•be-ola

ru•bies
ruby
ruckus
rud•der
rud-di-ness

ruddy
rudely
rude-ness
ru•di-ment
ru•di-men-tary

ruf-fian
rugby
rug•ged
rug-gedly
rug-ged-ness

ruin
ru•ined
ru•in-ing
ru•in-ous
ruled

rule-less
ruler
rul•ers
rul•ing
rul-ings

Ru•ma•nian
rumba
rum•bas
rum•ble
rum-bles

rum-bling
rum-mage
rum-mages
rum-mag•ing
rummy

rumor
ru•mored
ru•mor-ing
rumor-monger
ru•mors

rum•ple
rum-ples
rum-pling
rum•pus
run-about

run-away
run-down *(n.)*
run--in *(n.)*
run•ner
run-ners

runner--up *(n.)*
runners--up *(n. pl.)*
run-ning
runny
run•off *(n.)*

run-offs *(n. pl.)*
run•way
run-ways
rup-ture
rup-tur•ing

rural
ru•rally
rushed
rushes
rush-ing

rus•set
Rus•sia
Rus-sian
rusted
rus•tic

rus•tle
rus-tler
rus-tling
rust-proof *(adj.)*
rust-proofing *(adj.)*

rusty
ruth-less
ruth-lessly
rut-ted
rut-ting

Sab-bath
sab-bat-ical
saber
sa•bers
sable

sabo-tage
sabo-tag•ing
sabo-teur
sac-cha•rin
sa•chet

sack-ful
sack-ing
sac-ra-ment
sac-ra-men•tal
sa•cred

sa•credly
sac-ri-fice
sac-ri-fi-cial
sac-ri-fic•ing
sac-ri-lege

sac-ri-le-gious
sa•cro-il•iac
sac-ro-sanct
sa•crum
sad•den

sad-den•ing
sad•der
sad-dest
sad•dle
saddle-bag

sad-dled
sad-dles
sad-dling
sa•dism
sa•dist

sa•dis-tic
sa•dis-ti-cally
sadly
sad-ness
sa•do-mas-och•ist

sa•fari
sa•fa-ris
safe-guard
safe-guarding
safe-keeping

S

185

safely	sa•lient	samu-rai
safer	sa•line	sana-to-rium
safety	sa•liva	sanc-ti-fied
saf-flower	sali-vate	sanc-ti-fies
sa•ga-cious	sali-vat•ing	sanc-tify
sa•ga-ciously	sali-va-tion	sanc-ti-fy•ing
sa•gac-ity	salmon	sanc-ti-mo-nious
sagas	sal-mo-nella	sanc-ti-mony
sage-brush	salon	sanc-tion
sagged	sa•lons	sanc-tion•ing
sag-ging	sa•loon	sanc-tity
sail-boat	salsa	sanc-tu-ar•ies
sailed	salted	sanc-tu•ary
sail-ing	sal-tine	sanc-tum
sailor	salt-ing	san•dal
sail-ors	salt-shaker	sand-bag
sainted	salty	sand-bagging
saint-hood	salu-ta-tion	sand-blast
saint-li-ness	sa•lu-ta-to-rian	sand-blasting
saintly	sa•lu-ta-tory	sand-box
sal-abil•ity	sa•lute	sand-boxes
sal-able	sa•lut-ing	sanded
sa•la-cious	salv-able	sander
salad	sal-vage	sand-hog
sal•ads	sal-vage-able	sand-ing
sa•lami	sal-vages	sand-paper
sala-ried	sal-vag•ing	sand-pile
sala-ries	sal-va-tion	sand-piper
sal•ary	Sa•mari-tan	sand-stone
sales	same-ness	sand-storm
sales-clerk	Samoa	sand-wich
sales-people	Sa•moan	sand-wiches
sales-person	sam•ple	sandy
sali-cylic	sam-pler	sanely
sa•lience	sam-pling	sane-ness

san-gui-nary	sa•ti-ate *(v.)*	sau•téd
san-guine	sa•ti-at•ing	sau-té•ing
san-guinely	sa•ti-ety	sav•age
sani-tar•ian	satin	sav-agely
sani-tar•ium	sat•ire	sav-ages
sani-tary	sa•tiric	sa•vant
sani-tate	sa•tir-ical	saved
sani-tat•ing	sati-rist	saver
sani-ta-tion	sati-rize	sav•ers
sani-tize	sati-rizes	sav•ing
sani-tiz•ing	sati-riz•ing	sav-ings
san•ity	sat-is-fac-tion	sav•ior
San-skrit	sat-is-fac-to-rily	savor
Santa	sat-is-fac-tory	sa•vored
sap-ling	sat-is-fied	sa•vor-ing
sapped	sat-is-fier	sa•vory
sap-phire	sat-is-fies	sav-vies
sar-casm	sat-isfy	savvy
sar-cas•tic	sat-is-fy•ing	saw-dust
sar-cas-ti-cally	satu-rate	sawed
sar-coph•agi	satu-rat•ing	saw-horse
sar-copha•gus	satu-ra-tion	saw•ing
sar-dine	Sat-ur•day	saw-mill
sa•rong	Sat•urn	saxo-phone
sa•shay	sau•ced	say•ing
sa•shay-ing	sauce-pan	say-ings
Satan	sau•cer	scabbed
sa•tanic	sauces	scab-bing
sa•tan-ical	saucy	scaf-fold
sa•tan-ism	sau-er-kraut	scaf-fold•ing
satchel	sauna	scalded
satch-els	saun-ter	scald-ing
sat-el-lite	saun-ter•ing	scaled
sat-el-loid	sau-sage	scal-ing
sa•tia-ble	sauté	scal-lion

scal-lop
scalped
scal-pel
scalp-ing
scam-per

scam-per•ing
scampi
scan-dal
scan-dal•ize
scan-dal-izes

scan-dal-iz•ing
scan-dal•ous
Scan-di-na•via
Scan-di-na-vian
scanned

scan-ner
scan-ning
scant-ily
scanty
scape-goat

scap-ula
scapu-lar
scarcely
scar-ci-ties
scar-city

scare-crow
scared
scarf
scar-ing
scar-la-tina

scar-let
scarred
scar-ring
scarves
scary

scathe
scath-ing
scat-ter
scat-ter•ing
scav-enge

scav-en•ger
scav-eng•ing
sce-nario
sce-nar•ios
scen-er•ies

scen-ery
sce•nic
scented
scep-ter
sched-ule

sched-uler
sched-ul•ing
schema
sche-matic
sche-mat•ics

schemed
schemer
schem-ing
schism
schis-matic

schisms
schizo-phre•nia
schizo-phrenic
schizo-phren•ics
schizos

scholar
schol-arly
schol-ars
schol-ar-ship
scho-las•tic

scho-las-ti-cally
scho-las-tics
schooled
school-ing
school-teacher

school-work
schoo-ner
sci-atic
sci-at•ica
sci-ence

sci-ences
sci-en-tific
sci-en-tifi-cally
sci-en-tist
scin-til-late

scin-til-lat•ing
scis-sors
scoffed
scoff-ing
scolded

scold-ing
scooped
scoop-ful
scoop-ing
scooted

scooter
scoot-ers
scoot-ing
scop-ing
scorched

scorcher
scorch-ing
score-board
score-card
scored

score-keeper	scratchi-ness	scrounger
score-less	scratch-ing	scroung-ing
scorer	scratchy	scrubbed
scor-ers	scrawled	scrub-bing
scor-ing	scrawl-ing	scrubby
scorned	scrawny	scruffy
scorn-ful	screamed	scrump-tious
scorn-ing	scream-ing	scrunches
scor-pion	screeched	scrunch-ing
Scotch	screech-ing	scru-ple
Scot-land	screened	scru-pu-lous
scoun-drel	screen-ing	scru-pu-lously
scoured	screen-play	scru-ta•ble
scourged	screen-writer	scru-ti-nies
scourges	screw-ball	scru-ti-nize
scourg-ing	screw-driver	scru-ti-nizes
scouted	screwy	scru-ti-niz•ing
scouter	scrib-ble	scru-tiny
scout-ers	scrib-bler	scuba
scout-ing	scrib-bles	scu•bas
scout-master	scrib-bling	scuffed
scowled	scrim-mage	scuff-ing
scowl-ing	scrim-mages	scuf-fle
scrab-ble	scrim-mag•ing	scuf-fling
scrag-gly	scrimped	scul-lery
scram-ble	scrimpy	sculpted
scram-bler	scripted	sculpt-ing
scram-bling	script-ing	sculp-tor
scrap-book	scrip-tural	sculp-ture
scraped	scrip-tur-ally	sculp-tur•ing
scraper	scrip-ture	scur-ried
scrapped	script-writer	scur-ries
scrap-ping	scrolled	scur-ry•ing
scratched	scroll-ing	scurry
scratches	scrounged	scurvy

scut-tle	sea-son•ing	sec-tar•ian
scuttle-butt	sea-sons	sec-tion
scut-tled	seat-belt	sec-tional
scut-tling	seated	sec-tion-al•ize
scythe	seat-ing	sec-tion-al-iz•ing
sea-board	sea-wall	sec-tion•ing
sea-coast	sea-ward	sec•tor
sea-farer	sea-water	sec-tor•ing
sea-faring	sea-weed	sec-tors
sea-food	sea-worthy	secu-lar
sea-going	se•cede	secu-lar•ity
seal-ant	se•ced-ing	secu-lar-iza-tion
sealer	se•ces-sion	secu-lar•ize
seal-ing	se•ces-sion•ist	secu-lar-iz•ing
seam-less	se•clude	se•cure
seam-ster	se•clud-ing	se•curely
sé•ance	se•clu-sion	se•cur-ing
sea-plane	sec•ond	se•cu-ri-ties
sea-port	sec-ond-arily	se•cu-rity
searched	sec-ond•ary	sedan
searcher	sec-onded	se•dans
search-ers	second-hand	se•date
search-ing	sec-ond•ing	se•dat-ing
search-light	sec-ondly	se•da-tion
seared	sec-onds	se•da-tive
sear-ing	se•crecy	sed-en-tary
sea-shell	se•cret	sedi-ment
sea-shore	sec-re-tarial	sedi-men-tary
sea-sick	sec-re-tar•iat	sedi-men-ta-tion
sea-sickness	sec-re-tar•ies	se•di-tion
sea-side	sec-re-tary	se•di-tion•ary
sea•son	se•crete	se•di-tion•ist
sea-son-able	se•cret-ing	se•di-tious
sea-sonal	se•cre-tion	se•duce
sea-soner	se•cretly	se•duc-ing

se•duc-tion
se•duc-tive
see-able
seeded
seed-ing

seed-ling
seedy
see•ing
seeker
seek-ers

seemed
seem-ing
seem-ingly
seemly
seep-age

seeped
seep-ing
seer-sucker
see•saw
see-saw•ing

seethed
seeth-ing
seg-ment
seg-men-ta-tion
seg-ment•ing

seg-re-gate
seg-re-gat•ing
seg-re-ga-tion
seg-re-ga-tion•ist
seg-re-ga-tive

seis-mic
seis-mo-graph
seis-mo-gra-pher
seis-mo-graphic
seis-mog-ra•phy

seis-mo-log-ical
seis-molo-gist
seis-mol•ogy
seis-mome•ter
seized

seiz-ing
sei-zure
sel•dom
se•lect
se•lect-ing

se•lec-tion
se•lec-tive
se•lec-tiv•ity
se•lects
self--abhorrence

self--abuse
self--abusive
self--addressed
self--assurance
self--assured

self--centered
self--cleaning
self--composed
self--conceit
self--concious

self--confidence
self--confident
self--contained
self--control
self--defense

self--destruction
self--discipline
self--educated
self--employed
self--esteem

self--evaluation
self--explanatory
self--governed
self--help
self--image

self--important
self--imposed
self--indulgence
self--inflicted
self--insured

self-ish
self-ishly
self--made
self--motivated
self--organized

self--paced
self--pity
self--praise
self--protection
self--regard

self--reliance
self--respect
self--restraint
self--righteous
self--satisfaction

self--starter
self--sufficient
self--supporting
self--sustaining
self--taught

self--winding
self--worth
sell-able
seller
sell-ers

S

sell-ing
sell-out
se•man-ti•cal
se•man-ti•cist
se•man-tics

sema-phore
sem-blance
semen
se•mes-ter
semi-ac-tive

semi-an-nual
semi-arid
semi-au-to-matic
semi-cir•cle
semi-civi-lized

semi-clas-si•cal
semi-co•lon
semi-co•ma-tose
semi-con-duc•tor
semi-con-scious

semi-fi•nal
semi-fi-nal•ist
semi-for•mal
semi-gloss
semi--invalid

semi-monthly
semi-nar
semi-nar•ian
semi-nar•ies
semi-nary

semi-pre-cious
semi-pri-vate
semi-pro
semi-pro-fes-sional
semi-re-tired

semi-skilled
semi-sweet
Semi-tism
semi-trailer
semi-trop-ical

semi-trop•ics
semi-weekly
sen•ate
sena-tor
sena-to-rial

sender
send-ers
send-ing
send--off *(n.)*
se•nile

se•nil-ity
se•nior
se•nior-ity
sen-sa-tion
sen-sa-tional

sen-sa-tion-al•ism
sen-sa-tion-al•ize
sen-sa-tion-ally
sensed
sense-less

sense-lessly
senses
sen-si-bil•ity
sen-si•ble
sen-si•bly

sens-ing
sen-si-tive
sen-si-tivi-ties
sen-si-tiv•ity
sen-si-tize

sen-si-tiz•ing
sen•sor
sen-so-rial
sen-so-ri-mo•tor
sen-sory

sen-sual
sen-su•ous
sen-su-ously
sen-tence
sen-tences

sen-tenc•ing
sen-ti-ment
sen-ti-men•tal
sen-ti-men-tal•ist
sen-ti-men-tal•ity

sen-ti-men-tally
sen-ti•nel
sen-ti-nels
sen-tries
sen•try

sepa-ra•ble
sepa-rate
sepa-rately
sepa-rat•ing
sepa-ra-tion

sepa-ra•tor
Sep-tem•ber
sep•tet
sep•tic
sep•tum

sep-ul-cher
se•pul-chral
se•quel
se•quence
se•quencer

se•quences
se•quenc-ing
se•quen-tial
se•quen-tially
se•ques-ter

se•ques-ter•ing
se•quin
se•quoia
se•rape
se•ra-pes

sere-nade
sere-nader
sere-nad•ing
ser-en-dipi-tous
ser-en-dip•ity

se•rene
se•renely
se•ren-ity
ser-geant
se•rial

se•ri-al-iza-tion
se•ri-al•ize
se•ri-al-izes
se•ri-al-iz•ing
se•ri-ally

se•ries
serif
se•ri-ous
se•ri-ously
ser•mon

ser-mon•ize
ser-mons
se•ro-log-ical
se•rol-ogy
ser-pent

ser-pen-tine
ser-rated
ser-ra-tion
serum
se•rums

ser-vant
served
server
serv-ers
ser-vice

ser-vice-able
ser-vices
ser-vic•ing
serv-ing
ser-vi-tude

ses•ame
ses-sion
set-back (n.)
set•tee
set-ting

set•tle
set-tle-ment
set-tler
set-tling
setup (n.)

set•ups (n.)
seven
sev-en-teen
sev-enth
sev-en-ties

sev-enty
sever
sev-eral
sev-er-ally
sev-er-ance

se•vere
sev-ered
se•verely
se•ver-ity
sew•age

sewed
sewer
sew-er•age
sew•ers
sew•ing

sewn
sexa-ge-narian
sex•ist
sex-tant
sex•tet

sex-tets
sex•ton
sex-tu-plet
sex•ual
sexu-al•ity

sexu-al•ize
sexu-al-iz•ing
sexu-ally
sexy
shab-bi-ness

shabby
shackle
shack-led
shack-les
shaded

shadi-ness
shad-ing
shadow
shad-owed
shad-ow•ing

S

shad-ows
shad-owy
shady
shafted
shaft-ing

shaggy
shake-down *(n.)*
shaken
shaker
shak-ers

shake--up *(n.)*
shak-ily
shaki-ness
shak-ing
shaky

shal-low
shal-lower
shal-low-ness
sham-bles
shamed

shame-ful
shame-fully
shame-less
shame-lessly
sham-ing

sham-poo
sham-pooed
sham-poo•ing
sham-rock
shang-hai

shang-haied
shan-ties
shanty
shaped
shape-less

shape-li-ness
shapely
shap-ing
share-able
share-cropper

share-cropping
shared
share-holder
share-owner
share-ware

shar-ing
sharpen
sharp-ened
sharp-ener
sharp-en•ing

sharp-ens
sharper
sharp-est
sharply
sharp-ness

sharp-shooter
sharp-shooting
shat-ter
shat-ter•ing
shatter-proof

shaven
shaver
shav-ers
shav-ing
sheared

shear-ing
sheathe
sheathed
sheath-ing
shed-ding

sheep-herder
sheep-herding
sheep-ish
sheep-ishly
sheep-ish-ness

sheep-skin
sheered
sheer-ing
sheer-ness
sheet-ing

Sheet-rock
shel-lac
shel-lacked
shel-lack•ing
shelled

shell-fish
shell-ing
shel-ter
shel-ter•ing
shelve *(v.)*

shelves
shelv-ing
she-nani•gan
shep-herd
shep-herd•ing

sher-bet
sher-iff
Shet-land
shied
shield

shielded
shield-ing
shifted
shift-ing
shift-less

shift-lessly
shift-less-ness
shifty
shim-mer
shim-mer•ing

shim-mies
shimmy
shim-my•ing
shin-dig
shined

shin-gle
shin-gler
shin-gling
shin-ing
shiny

ship-load
ship-ment
shipped
ship-per
ship-ping

ship-shape
ship-yard
shirked
shirk-ing
shirt-ing

shirt-sleeves
shirt-tail
shiver
shiv-ered
shiv-er•ing

shiv-ers
shocked
shocker
shock-ing
shock-ingly

shock-proof
shock--wave
shod-dily
shod-di-ness
shoddy

shoed
shoe-horn
shoe-ing
shoe-lace
shoe-maker

shoe-string
shooed
shoo-ing
shooter
shoot-ers

shoot-ing
shoot--out (n.)
shop-keeper
shop-lift
shop-lifter

shop-lifting
shopped
shop-per
shop-ping
shop-talk

shop-worn
shore-line
shor-ing
short-age
short-cake

short-change
short-changing
short-coming
short-cut
shorted

shorten
short-ened
short-en•ing
short-ens
shorter

short-est
short-fall
short-hand
short-handed
short-ing

shortly
short-ness
short-sighted
short-sighted-ness
short-stop

short-wave
shot-gun
shoul-der
shoul-der•ing
shouldn't

shouted
shout-ing
shoved
shovel
shov-eled

shov-el•ful
shov-el•ing
shov-els
shov-els•ful
shov-ing

show-boat
show-case
show-casing
show-down
showed

S

shower	shud-der•ing	sick-ened
show-ered	shuf-fle	sick-en•ing
show-er•ing	shuffle-board	sick-ens
show-ers	shuf-fled	sicker
show-ery	shuf-fling	sick-est
show-ing	shunned	sick-ish
show--off (n.)	shun-ning	sickle
show-piece	shunt	sick-li-ness
show-room	shunted	sick-ling
show-stopper (n.)	shunt-ing	sickly
showy	shushed	sick-ness
shrap-nel	shushes	sick--out
shred-ded	shush-ing	sick-room
shred-der	shut-down (n.)	side-arm (adj.)
shred-ding	shut--eye	side-band
shrewder	shut--in (n.)	side-board
shrewdly	shut-off (n.)	side-burns
shrewd-ness	shut-out (n.)	side-car
shrieked	shut-ter	sided
shriek-ing	shutter-bug	side-kick
shrill-ness	shut-ter•ing	side-light
shrink-age	shut-ting	side-line
shrink-ing	shut-tle	side-saddle
shrivel	shuttle-cock	side-show
shriv-eled	shut-tled	side-splitting
shriv-el•ing	shut-tling	side-step (v.)
shriv-els	shyly	side-swipe
shrouded	shy-ness	side-swiping
shroud-ing	shy-ster	side-track
shrub-ber•ies	Sia-mese	side-walk
shrub-bery	sib-ling	side-wall
shrugged	Si•cil-ian	side-ways
shrug-ging	Sic•ily	side-winder
shrunken	sick-bed	sid•ing
shud-der	sicken	sieges

si•esta
siev-ing
sifted
sifter
sift-ers

sift-ing
sighed
sigh-ing
sighted
sight-ing

sight-less
sightly
sight-see *(v.)*
sight--seeing
sight-seer

sig•nal
sig-nal•ing
sig-nals
sig-na-tory
sig-na-ture

sign-board
signed
signer
sign-ers
sig•net

sig-nifi-cance
sig-nifi-cant
sig-nifi-cantly
sig-ni-fied
sig-ni-fies

sig-nify
sig-ni-fy•ing
sign-ing
sign-post
si•lence

si•lenc-ing
si•lent
si•lently
sil-hou-ette
sil•ica

sili-con
sili-cone
sili-co•sis
silken
silk-worm

silky
sil-li-ness
silly
sil•ver
silver-smith

sil-ver-ware
sil-very
simi-lar
simi-lari-ties
simi-lar•ity

simi-larly
sim•ile
si•mili-tude
sim•mer
sim-mer•ing

sim•ple
sim-pler
sim-plest
sim-plex
sim-plic•ity

sim-pli-fi-ca-tion
sim-pli-fied
sim-pli-fies
sim-plify
sim-pli-fy•ing

sim-plis•tic
sim-plis-ti-cally
sim•ply
simu-late
simu-lat•ing

simu-la-tion
simu-la-tive
simu-la•tor
si•mul-cast
si•mul-cast•ing

si•mul-ta-neous
si•mul-ta-neously
sin-cere
sin-cerely
sin-cer•est

sin-cer•ity
sinew
sin•ews
sin•ewy
sin•ful

sin-fully
sin-ful-ness
singe
singed
singe-ing

singer
sing-ers
sing-ing
sin•gle
sin-gles

sin-gu•lar
sin-gu-lar•ity
sin-gu-larly
sin-is•ter
sink-able

S

sinker	six-teen	skier
sink-hole	sixth	ski•ers
sink-ing	six-ties	ski•ing
sin-less	sixty	skilled
sin-lessly	siz-able	skil-let
sin-less-ness	sized	skill-ful
sinned	sizes	skill-fully
sin•ner	siz•ing	skimmed
sin-ners	siz•zle	skim-ming
sin-ning	siz-zles	skimped
sinus	siz-zling	skimpi-ness
si•nuses	skate-board	skimp-ing
si•nus-itis	skate-boarding	skimpy
si•phon	skated	skin-flint
si•phon-ing	skater	skin-less
sipped	skat-ers	skinned
sip-ping	skat-ing	skin-ning
sired	skein	skinny
siren	skele-tal	skin-tight
si•rens	skele-ton	skipped
sir-loin	skep-tic	skip-per
sis•ter	skep-ti•cal	skip-ping
sis-terly	skep-ti-cism	skir-mish
sis-ters	sketch-book	skir-mish•ing
sit•com	sketched	skirted
sit-coms	sketches	skirt-ing
sit•ter	sketch-ing	skit-ter
sit-ting	sketchy	skit-tish
situ-ate	skewed	skiv-vies
situ-ates	skewer	skivvy
situ-at•ing	skew-ered	skul-dug-gery
situ-ation	skew-ers	skull-cap
situ-ational	skew-ing	sky•cap
sit--up *(n.)*	skid-ded	sky-caps
six--pack	skid-ding	sky diver *(n.)*

198

sky-diving	slated	slen-der
sky-jack	slat-ing	slen-der•ize
sky-jacker	slaugh-ter	slen-der-iz•ing
sky-jacking	slaughter-house	sleuth
sky•lab	slaugh-ter•ing	sleuth-hound
sky-lark	slaved	sliced
sky-light	slav-ery	slic-ing
sky-line	slav-ing	slicked
sky-rocket	slay-ing	slicker
sky-rocketing	slea-zily	slick-ness
sky-scraper	slea-zi-ness	slider
sky-walk	sleazy	slid-ers
sky-ward	sled-ded	slid-ing
sky-writer	sled-ding	slighted
sky-writing	sledge-hammer	slighter
slacken	sledg-ing	slight-est
slack-ened	sleek-ness	slight-ing
slack-en•ing	sleeper	slightly
slack-ens	sleep-ers	slight-ness
sla•lom	sleep-ily	slim-mer
slammed	sleepi-ness	sling-ing
slam-ming	sleep-ing	sling-shot
slan-der	sleep-less	slink-ing
slan-der•ing	sleep-less-ness	slinky
slan-der•ous	sleep-walk	slip-cover
slan-der-ously	sleep-walker	slip-page
slanted	sleep-walking	slipped
slant-ing	sleep-wear	slip-per
slap-happy	sleepy	slip-pery
slapped	sleet-ing	slip-ping
slap-ping	sleeved	slip-shod
slap-stick	sleeve-less	slither
slashed	sleigh	slith-ered
slashes	sleigh-ing	slith-er•ing
slash-ing	sleight	slith-ery

S

slit-ting
sliver
slob-ber
slob-bered
slob-ber•ing

slo•gan
slo-gans
sloped
slop-ing
slop-pily

slop-pi-ness
sloppy
slosh-ing
sloshy
sloth-ful

sloth-ful-ness
slot-ted
slouchi-ness
slouch-ing
slouchy

sloven
slo-ven-li-ness
slov-enly
slow-down
slowed

slower
slow-est
slow-ing
slowly
slow-ness

slow-poke
slugged
slug-ging
slug-gish
slug-gishly

slug-gish-ness
sluic-ing
slum-ber
slum-ber•ing
slummed

slum-ming
slump-ing
slurped
slurp-ing
slurred

slur-ring
slushy
slyly
sly-ness
smacked

smack-ing
smaller
small-est
small-ish
small-ness

small-pox
smarted
smarter
smart-ing
smartly

smart-ness
smashed
smash-ingly
smat-ter
smat-ter•ing

smeared
smear-ing
smelled
smell-ing
smelly

smelted
smelter
smiled
smil-ing
smirked

smirk-ing
smith-er-eens
smit-ing
smit-ten
smoggy

smoked
smoke-house
smoke-less
smoker
smok-ers

smoke-stack
smok-ing
smoky
smol-der
smol-der•ing

smoothed
smoother
smooth-est
smooth-ing
smoothly

smooth-ness
smor-gas-bord
smother
smoth-ered
smoth-er•ing

smudg-ing
smudgy
smug-gling
smutty
snacked

snack-ing
snafu
snagged
snag-ging
snak-ing

snap-dragon
snap-ping
snappy
snap-shot
snared

snar-ing
snarled
snarl-ing
snatched
snatch-ing

snazzy
sneak
sneaker
sneak-ers
sneak-ing

sneaky
sneered
sneer-ing
sneer-ingly
sneezed

sneez-ing
sneezy
snicker
snick-ered
snick-er•ing

snide-ness
sniffed
sniff-ing
snif-fle
sniper

snip-pety
snitched
snitches
snitch-ing
snob-bery

snob-bish
snob-bish-ness
snobby
snooper
snoop-ers

snoop-ing
snoopy
snoozed
snoozes
snooz-ing

snored
snorer
snor-ing
snor-kel
snor-kel•ing

snort-ing
snow-ball
snow-bank
snow-bird
snow-blower

snow-bound
snow-drift
snow-drop
snowed
snow-fall

snow-flake
snow-ing
snow-mobile
snow-mobiling
snow-pack

snow-plow
snow-shoe
snow-shoeing
snow-slide
snow-storm

snow-suit
snowy
snubbed
snub-bing
snug-gle

snug-gles
snug-gling
snugly
snug-ness
soaked

soak-ing
soap-box
soaped
soap-ing
soapy

soared
soar-ing
sobbed
sob-bing
sober

so•bered
so•ber-ing
so•bri-ety
so--called
soc•cer

so•cia-bil•ity
so•cia-ble
so•cial
so•cial-ism
so•cial-ist

S

so•cial-is•tic
so•cial-ite
so•ci-al•ity
so•cial-iza-tion
so•cial-ize

so•cial-izes
so•cial-iz•ing
so•cially
so•ci-etal
so•ci-et•ies

so•ci-ety
so•cio-eco-nomic
so•cio-log-ical
so•cio-logi-cally
so•ci-olo-gies

so•ci-olo-gist
so•ci-ol•ogy
socked
socket
sock-ets

sock-ing
So•cratic
soda
sod•ded
sod•den

sod-ding
so•dium
sod•omy
sofa
sofas

soft-ball
soft-cover
soften
soft-ened
soft-ener

soft-ens
soft-hearted
softly
soft-ness
soft-ware

soggy
soiled
so•journ
so•journer
so•journ-ing

so•lace
so•lac-ing
solar
so•lar-ium
sol•der

sol-der•ing
sol-ders
sol-dier
sol-diered
sol-dier•ing

solely
sol•emn
so•lem-nity
sol-em-nize
sol-em-niz•ing

sol-emnly
so•le-noid
so•licit
so•lici-ta-tion
so•lic-ited

so•lic-it•ing
so•lici-tor
so•lici-tous
so•lici-tude
solid

soli-dar•ity
so•lidi-fied
so•lid-ify
so•lidi-fy•ing
so•lid-ity

sol-idly
so•lilo-quies
so•lilo-quist
so•lilo-quize
so•lilo-quiz•ing

so•lilo-quy
soli-taire
soli-tary
soli-tude
so•loed

so•lo-ist
solos
sol-stice
solu-bil•ity
solu-bi-lize

solu-bi-liz•ing
sol-uble
sol-ubly
so•lu-tion
solv-able

solved
sol-vency
sol-vent
solv-ing
som•ber

som-berly
som-ber-ness
som-brero
some-body
some-day

some-how
some-one
some-place
som-er-sault
some-thing

some-time
some-way
some-what
some-where
som-no-lence

som-no-lent
sonar
so•nata
song-bird
song-book

song-fest
sonic
son•net
soothed
sooth-ing

sooth-ingly
sooth-sayer
so•phis-tic
so•phis-ti•cal
so•phis-ti-cated

so•phis-ti-ca-tion
soph-istry
sopho-more
sopho-moric
sopped

sop-ping
soppy
so•prano
sor-cerer
sor-cery

sor•did
sor-didly
sorely
sore-ness
sor-ghum

so•rori-ties
so•ror-ity
sor•row
sor-row•ful
sor-row•ing

sor-rows
sorry
sorted
sorter
sor•tie

sort-ing
sort-key
sounded
sounder
sound-est

sound-ing
sound-ness
sound-proof
sound-proofed
sound-proofing

souped
soupy
sources
sour-dough
soured

sour-ing
sour-ness
sour-puss
South Caro-lina
South Da•kota

South Da•ko-tan
south-east
south-eastern
south-erly
south-ern

South-erner
south-ward
south-wardly
south-west
south-western

sou-ve•nir
sou-ve-nirs
sov-er-eign
sowed
sow•ing

soy-bean
space-craft
space-flight
space-port
spaces

space-ship
space-walker
space-walking
spac-ing
spa-cious

spa-ciously
spackle
spaded
spad-ing
spa-ghetti

Spain
span-gle
Span-iard
Span-ish
spanked

S

spank-ing
spanned
span-ning
spared
spare-ribs

spar-ing
spar-ingly
sparked
spar-kle
spar-kler

spar-kling
sparred
spar-ring
spar-row
sparsely

spar-sity
spasm
spas-modic
spas-modi-cally
spasms

spas-tic
spa-tial
spat-ter
spat-ter•ing
spat-ula

spawned
spawn-ing
spay-ing
speak-able
speak-easy

speaker
speaker-phone
speak-ers
speak-ing
speared

spear-fish
spear-head
spear-headed
spear-head•ing
spear-ing

spear-mint
spe-cial
spe-cial•ist
spe-cial-iza-tion
spe-cial•ize

spe-cial-izes
spe-cial-iz•ing
spe-cially
spe-cial-ties
spe-cialty

spe•cie
spe-cies
spe-cific
spe-cifi-cally
speci-fi-ca-tion

speci-fic•ity
speci-fied
speci-fies
spec-ify
speci-fy•ing

speci-men
speckle
speck-led
speck-ling
spec-ta•cle

spec-tacu•lar
spec-tacu-larly
spec-ta•tor
spec-ta-tors
spec-ter

spec-trum
specu-late
specu-lat•ing
specu-la-tion
specu-la-tive

specu-la•tor
speeches
speech-less
speed-boat
speeded

speeder
speed-ers
speed-ily
speed-ing
speed-ome•ter

speed-way
speedy
spell-binder
spell-binding
spell-bound

spelled
speller
spell-ing
spe-lunker
spe-lunk•ing

spender
spend-ers
spend-ing
spewed
spew-ing

spher-ical
spheri-cally
spher-oid
sphinx
sphinxes

spiced
spices
spicy
spi•der
spi-dery

spied
spiel
spies
spiked
spik-ing

spill-age
spilled
spill-ing
spill-way
spin-ach

spi•nal
spi-nally
spin-dle
spine-less
spinet

spin-ner
spin-ning
spin--off
spin-ster
spi•ral

spi-ral•ing
spirit
spir-ited
spir-it•ing
spir-its

spiri-tual
spiri-tu-al•ism
spiri-tu-al•ist
spiri-tu-al•ity
spiri-tu-al•ize

spiri-tu-ally
spiri-tu•ous
spit-ball
spite-ful
spite-fully

spite-ful-ness
spit-ting
spit-toon
splash-down *(n.)*
splashed

splashes
splash-ing
splashy
splat-ter
spleen

splen-did
splen-didly
splen-dor
spliced
splicer

splices
splic-ing
splin-ter
splin-ter•ing
splin-ting

split-ting
splotch
splotchy
splurged
splurges

splurg-ing
spoil-able
spoil-age
spoiled
spoiler

spoil-ing
spoil-sport
spo•ken
spokes-person
sponged

spong-ing
spongy
spon-sor
spon-so-rial
spon-sor•ing

spon-sor-ship
spon-ta-ne•ity
spon-ta-ne•ous
spon-ta-ne-ously
spoofed

spoof-ing
spooked
spooki-ness
spook-ing
spooky

spooler
spool-ing
spooned
spoo-ner•ism
spoon-ful

spoons-ful
spo-radic
spo-radi-cally
sported
sport-ing

sports-cast
sports-caster
sports-wear
sports-writer
sporty

S

spot-less
spot-lessly
spot-less-ness
spot-light
spot-ted

spot-ter
spot-ting
spotty
spouses
spouted

spout-ing
sprained
sprain-ing
sprawled
sprawler

sprawl-ing
sprayed
sprayer
spray-ing
spreader

spread-ing
spread-sheet
spright-li-ness
sprightly
spring-board

spring-ing
spring-time
springy
sprin-kle
sprin-kler

sprin-kling
sprinted
sprinter
sprint-ing
sprocket

sprouted
sprout-ing
spruced
spruc-ing
spry-ness

spunki-ness
spunky
spu-ri•ous
spu-ri-ously
spurred

spur-ring
spurted
spurt-ing
sput-ter
sput-ter•ing

spu•tum
spy-glass
spy•ing
squab-ble
squab-bling

squad-ron
squalid
squal-idly
squan-der
squan-der•ing

squared
squarely
squar-ing
squashed
squashes

squash-ing
squat-ted
squat-ter
squat-ting
squawked

squawk-ing
squeaked
squeak-ing
squealed
squealer

squeal-ing
squea-mish
squea-mishly
squee-gee
squeezed

squeezes
squeez-ing
squelched
squelches
squelch-ing

squinted
squint-ing
squirm-ing
squir-rel
squirted

squirt-ing
stabbed
stab-ber
stab-bing
sta-bile

sta-bil•ity
sta-bi-li-za-tion
sta-bi-lize
sta-bi-lizer
sta-bi-lizes

sta-bi-liz•ing
sta•ble
sta-bles
stac-cato
stacked

stack-ing	stalk-ing	starches
sta•dia	stalled	starch-ing
sta-dium	stall-ing	starchy
staffed	stal-lion	star-dom
staff-ing	stal-wart	stared
stage-coach	stam-ina	star-fish
staged	stam-mer	star-gazer
stage-hand	stam-merer	star-gazing
stages	stam-mer•ing	star-ing
stage-struck	stamped	starkly
stag-ger	stam-pede	stark-ness
stag-ger•ing	stam-ped•ing	star-less
stag-ing	stamper	star-light
stag-nancy	stamp-ing	star-ling
stag-nant	stand--alone *(adj.)*	starred
stag-nantly	stan-dard	star-ring
stag-nate	stan-dard-iza-tion	starry
stag-nat•ing	stan-dard•ize	started
stag-na-tion	stan-dard-izes	starter
stained	stan-dard-iz•ing	start-ers
stain-ing	standby *(n.)*	start-ing
stain-less	stand-ing	star-tle
stair-case	stand-off *(n.,adj.)*	star-tling
stair-way	stand-off•ish	start--up *(n.)*
stair-well	stand-out *(n.)*	star-va-tion
staked	stand-point	starved
stake-out *(n.)*	stand-still	starv-ing
stak-ing	stanza	stashed
sta-lac-tite	stan-zas	stashes
sta-lag-mite	sta•ple	stash-ing
stale-mate	sta-pler	stated
stale-mat•ing	sta-ples	state-hood
stale-ness	sta-pling	state-li-ness
stalked	star-board	stately
stalker	starched	state-ment

S

state-room	steady	ste-nog-ra•phy
state-side	steady-ing	step-child
state-wide	steal-ing	step-children
static	stealth	step-ladder
stat-ing	stealthy	stepped
sta-tion	steam-boat	step-ping
sta-tion•ary	steamed	stepping-stone
sta-tio•ner	steamer	step-wise
sta-tio-nery	steam-ers	ste•reo
sta-tion•ing	steam-ing	ste-reo-phonic
sta-tis•tic	steam-roller	ste-reo-type
sta-tis-ti•cal	steam-rolling	ste-reo-typ•ing
sta-tis-ti-cally	steam-ship	ster-ile
stat-is-ti-cian	steel-worker	ste-ril•ity
sta-tis-tics	steeped	ster-il-iza-tion
statu-ary	steepen	ster-il•ize
statue	steep-ened	ster-il-izes
stat-ues	steep-en•ing	ster-il-iz•ing
statu-esque	steeper	ster-ling
statu-ette	stee-ple	sternly
stat-ure	steeple-chase	ster-num
sta•tus	steeple-jack	stetho-scope
stat-ute	steeply	ste-ve-dore
statu-tory	steep-ness	ste-ve-dor•ing
staunchly	steer-age	stew-ard
staunch-ness	steered	stew-ard-ship
stayed	steer-ing	sticker
stay-ing	stel-lar	stick-ers
stead-fast	stemmed	stick-ing
stead-fastly	stem-ming	stick-ler
stead-fast-ness	stenches	stickup *(n.)*
stead-ied	sten-cil	stick-ups *(n.)*
steadier	sten-cil•ing	sticky
steadily	ste-nog-ra-pher	stiffen
steadi-ness	steno-graphic	stiff-ener

stiff-en•ing	stitched	ston-ing
stiff-ens	stitch-ery	stooped
sti•fle	stitches	stoop-ing
sti-fling	stitch-ing	stop-gap
stigma	stock-ade	stop-light
stig-ma-tize	stock-ad•ing	stop-over *(n.)*
stig-ma-tizes	stock-broker	stop-page
stig-ma-tiz•ing	stocked	stopped
still-birth	stock-holder	stop-per
still-born	stock-holding	stop-ping
stilled	stock-ing	stop-watch
still-ness	stock-pile	stor-able
stilted	stock-piling	stor-age
stimu-lant	stock-room	stored
stimu-late	stocky	store-front
stimu-lat•ing	stock-yard	store-house
stimu-la-tion	stodg-ily	store-keeper
stimu-la-tive	stodgy	store-room
stimu-la•tor	stoic	store-wide
stim-uli	sto-ical	sto-ries
stimu-lus	stoi-cally	stor-ing
stinger	stok-ing	stormed
sting-ing	stolen	stormi-ness
stingy	stom-ach	storm-ing
stinker	stomach-ache	stormy
stink-ing	stom-ach•ing	story
stint-ing	stomped	story-book
sti-pend	stomp-ing	story-board
stipu-late	stone-cutter	story-boarding
stipu-lates	stone-cutting	story-teller
stipu-lat•ing	stoned	story-telling
stipu-la-tion	stone-wall *(v.)*	stout-hearted
stirred	stone-walling *(v.)*	stoutly
stir-ring	stone-ware	stout-ness
stir-rup	stone-work	stow-age

S

stow-away (n.)
stowed
stow-ing
strad-dle
strad-dler

strad-dling
strag-gle
strag-gler
strag-gling
strag-gly

straight-edge
straighten
straight-ened
straight-ener
straight-en•ing

straight-ens
strained
strainer
strain-ing
strait

strait-jacket
strait-laced
stranded
strangely
strange-ness

stranger
strang-ers
strang-est
stran-gle
stran-gler

stran-gles
stran-gling
stran-gu-late
stran-gu-lat•ing
stran-gu-la-tion

strap-less
strapped
strap-ping
strata
strata-gem

stra-te•gic
stra-te-gi-cally
strate-gies
strate-gist
strat-egy

strati-fi-ca-tion
strati-fied
strati-fies
strat-ify
strati-fy•ing

strato-sphere
stra-tum
stra-tus
straw-ber-ries
straw-berry

strayed
stray-ing
streaked
streaker
streak-ing

streaky
streamed
streamer
stream-ing
stream-line

street-walker
street-wise
strengthen
strength-ened
strength-en•ing

strenth-ens
strenu-ous
strenu-ously
strenu-ous-ness
strep-to-cocci

strep-to-coc•cus
strep-to-my•cin
stressed
stresses
stress-ful

stress-ing
stretch-able
stretched
stretcher
stretch-ers

stretches
stretch-ing
strew-ing
strewn
stricken

stricter
strict-est
strictly
stri-dent
stri-dently

strid-ing
strike-breaker
strike-breaking
strike-out (n.)
strike-over

striker
strik-ers
strik-ing
strik-ingly
strin-gent

strin-gently	stub-bing	stu•por
stringer	stub-ble	stur-dily
string-ing	stub-born	stur-di-ness
strip-ing	stub-born-ness	sturdy
strip-ling	stucco	stur-geon
stripped	stuc-coed	stut-ter
strip-per	stu-dent	stut-terer
strip-ping	stu-dent body	stut-ter•ing
strip-tease	stud-ied	style-book
strip-teaser	stud-ies	styled
strived	stu•dio	styl-ing
striven	stu-dios	styl-ish
striv-ing	stu-di•ous	styl-ist
stroked	stu-di-ously	sty-lis•tic
strok-ing	study	sty-lis-ti-cally
strolled	study-ing	styl-ized
stroller	stuffed	styl-iz•ing
stroll-ing	stuffer	sty•lus
strong-box	stuffi-ness	sty-luses
stron-ger	stuff-ing	sty•mie
stron-gest	stuffy	sty-mie•ing
strong-hold	stum-ble	sty-mies
strongly	stum-bling	sty-rene
struc-tural	stump-ing	suavely
struc-tur-ally	stunned	suave-ness
struc-ture	stun-ning	sub-agent
struc-tur•ing	stunt-ing	sub-as-sem•bly
strug-gle	stu-pe-fied	sub-av-er•age
strug-gling	stu-pefy	sub-base-ment
strummed	stu-pe-fy•ing	subbed
strum-ming	stu-pen-dous	sub-bing
strut-ted	stu-pen-dously	sub-classes
strut-ting	stu•pid	sub-clas-sify
strych-nine	stu-pid•ity	sub-clause
stubbed	stu-pidly	sub-com-mit•tee

S

sub-com-pact
sub-con-scious
sub-con-sciously
sub-con-ti-nent
sub-con-ti-nental

sub-con-tract
sub-con-tract•ing
sub-con-trac•tor
sub-cul-ture
sub-di-rec-to-ries

sub-di-rec-tory
sub-di-vide
sub-di-vid•ing
sub-di-vi-sion
sub•due

sub-du•ing
sub-freez•ing
sub-grav•ity
sub-group
sub-head

sub-head•ing
sub-ject
sub-ject•ing
sub-jec-tive
sub-jec-tively

sub-ju-gate
sub-ju-gat•ing
sub-ju-ga-tion
sub-junc-tive
sub-lan-guage

sub-lease
sub-leas•ing
sub•let
sub-let-ting
sub-li-mate

sub-li-mat•ing
sub-li-ma-tion
sub-lime
sub-limi•nal
sub-ma-chine

sub-ma-rine
sub-merge
sub-merg•ing
sub-merse
sub-mers-ible

sub-mer-sion
sub-mis-sion
sub-mis-sive
sub-mis-sive-ness
sub•mit

sub-mits
sub-mit•tal
sub-mit•ted
sub-mit-ting
sub-or-bital

sub-or-di-nate
sub-or-di-nat•ing
sub-or-di-na-tion
sub-para-graph
sub-plot

sub-poena
sub-poe-na•ing
sub-poe•nas
sub-ro-gate
sub-ro-gat•ing

sub-ro-ga-tion
sub-rou-tine
sub-sat-el-lite
sub-schema
sub-scribe

sub-scriber
sub-scrib•ers
sub-scrib•ing
sub-script
sub-script•ing

sub-scrip-tion
sub-sec-tion
sub-se-quent
sub-se-quently
sub-ser-vi-ence

sub-ser-vi•ent
sub•set
sub-side
sub-si-dence
sub-sid-iar•ies

sub-sid-iary
sub-si-dies
sub-sid•ing
sub-si-dize
sub-si-dizes

sub-si-diz•ing
sub-sidy
sub-sist
sub-sis-tence
sub-sist•ing

sub-soil
sub-sonic
sub-stance
sub-stan-dard
sub-stan-tial

sub-stan-tially
sub-stan-ti•ate
sub-stan-ti-ates
sub-stan-ti-at•ing
sub-stan-tia-tion

sub-stan-tive
sub-sta-tion
sub-sti-tute
sub-sti-tut•ing
sub-sti-tu-tion

sub-strate
sub-stra•tum
sub-string
sub-sur-face
sub-sys•tem

sub-ter-fuge
sub-ter-ra-nean
sub-ti•tle
sub-ti-tling
sub•tle

sub-tlety
sub-topic
sub-to•tal
sub-to-taled
sub-to-tal•ing

sub-tract
sub-tract•ing
sub-trac-tion
sub-type
sub•urb

sub-ur•ban
sub-ur-ban•ite
sub-ur•bia
sub-urbs
sub-ver-sion

sub-ver-sive
sub-vert
sub-vert•ing
sub•way
sub-zero

suc-ceed
suc-ceed•ing
suc-cess
suc-cesses
suc-cess•ful

suc-cess-fully
suc-ces-sion
suc-ces-sive
suc-ces•sor
suc-cinct

suc-cinct-ness
suc•cor
suc-cor•ing
suc-cors
suc-cu-lence

suc-cu-lent
suc-cu-lently
suc-cumb
suc-cumb•ing
sucker

suck-ers
suck-ing
su•crose
suc-tion
Sudan

Su•dan-ese
sud•den
sud-denly
sud-den-ness
sued

suf•fer
suf-ferer
suf-fer•ing
suf-fice
suf-fi-cient

suf-fi-ciently
suf-fic•ing
suf•fix
suf-fixes
suf-fix•ing

suf-fo-cate
suf-fo-cates
suf-fo-cat•ing
suf-fo-ca-tion
suf-frage

suf-frag•ist
suf-fuse
suf-fus•ing
suf-fu-sion
sugar

sugar-coated
sugar-coating
sug-ared
sug-ar-less
sug•ary

sug-gest
sug-gest-ible
sug-gest•ing
sug-ges-tion
sug-ges-tive

sug-ges-tive-ness
sui-cidal
sui-cide
suing
suit-abil•ity

suit-able
suit-case
suited
suit-ing
suitor

S

suit-ors	sun•dae	su•per-ego
sul-fide	Sun•day	su•per-fi-cial
sul•fur	Sun-days	su•per-fi-cially
sul-fu-rous	sun•der	su•per-flu•ity
sulked	sun-dial	su•per-flu•ous
sulki-ness	sun-down	su•per-hu•man
sulk-ing	sun-dries	su•per-im-pose
sulky	sun•dry	su•per-im•poses
sul•len	sun-fast	su•per-im-pos•ing
sul-len-ness	sun-flower	su•per-in-tend
sul•try	sun-glasses	su•per-in-ten-dent
sum-ma-ries	sunken	su•pe-rior
sum-ma-ri-za-tion	sun-lamp	su•pe-ri-ori-ties
sum-ma-rize	sun-light	su•pe-ri-or•ity
sum-ma-rizes	sunned	su•per-la-tive
sum-ma-riz•ing	sun-nier	su•per-mar•ket
sum-mary	sun-ning	su•per-nal
sum-ma-tion	sunny	su•per-nally
summed	sun-rise	su•per-natu•ral
sum•mer	sun-roof	su•per-natu-rally
sum-mer•ing	sun-screen	su•per-power
sum-mers	sun•set	su•per-pow•ers
summer-time	sun-shade	su•per-scribe
sum-mery	sun-shine	su•per-scrib•ing
sum-ming	sun-spot	su•per-script
sum•mit	sun-stroke	su•per-scrip-tion
sum•mon	sun•tan	su•per-sede
sum-mon•ing	sunup	su•per-seded
sum-mons	super	su•per-sed•ing
sump-tu•ous	su•perb	su•per-sonic
sump-tu-ously	su•per-charged	su•per-sti-tion
sun-beam	su•per-charger	su•per-sti-tious
sun-belt	su•per-cil-ious	su•per-struc-ture
sun-bonnet	su•per-com-puter	su•per-vise
sun-burn	su•per-crit-ical	su•per-vises

su•per-vis•ing
su•per-vi-sion
su•per-vi•sor
su•per-vi-sory
sup•per

sup-plant
sup-plant•ing
sup-ple-ment
sup-ple-men•tal
sup-ple-men-tary

sup-ple-ment•ing
sup-pli-cate
sup-pli-cat•ing
sup-pli-ca-tion
sup-plied

sup-plier
sup-pli•ers
sup-plies
sup•ply
sup-ply•ing

sup-port
sup-porter
sup-port•ers
sup-port•ing
sup-por-tive

sup-pose
sup-pos-edly
sup-poses
sup-pos•ing
sup-po-si-tion

sup-po-si-tional
sup-posi-tory
sup-press
sup-presses
sup-press•ing

sup-pres-sion
sup-pres-sive
su•prema-cist
su•prem-acy
su•preme

sur-charge
sure-fire
sure-footed
surely
sur•est

surety
sur-face
sur-faces
sur-fac•ing
surf-board

surfed
sur-feit
sur-feit•ing
surfer
surf-ers

surf-ing
surged
sur-geon
sur-ger•ies
sur-gery

surges
sur-gi•cal
sur-gi-cally
surg-ing
sur-li-ness

surly
sur-mise
sur-mises
sur-mis•ing
sur-mount

sur-mount-able
sur-mount•ing
sur-name
sur-pass
sur-passes

sur-pass•ing
sur-plus
sur-pluses
sur-prise
sur-prises

sur-pris•ing
sur-pris-ingly
sur-re-al•ism
sur-re-al•ist
sur-ren•der

sur-ren-der•ing
sur-ro-gate
sur-round
sur-round•ing
sur-round-ings

sur•tax
sur-veil-lance
sur•vey
sur-vey•ing
sur-veyor

sur-veys
sur-vival
sur-vive
sur-viv•ing
sur-vi•vor

sus-cep-ti•ble
sus-pect
sus-pect•ing
sus-pend
sus-pend•ers

S

215

sus-pend•ing	Swa-zi-land	swin-dler
sus-pense	swear-ing	swin-dling
sus-pense-ful	sweat-band	swing-ing
sus-pen-sion	sweated	swiped
sus-pi-cion	sweater	swip-ing
sus-pi-cious	sweat-ers	swish-ing
sus-pi-ciously	sweat-ing	Swiss
sus-tain	sweat-pants	switch-back
sus-tain-able	sweats	switch-board
sus-tain•ing	sweat-shirt	switched
sus-te-nance	sweat-shop	switches
su•ture	sweaty	switch-ing
su•tur-ing	Swe•den	Swit-zer-land
swabbed	Swed-ish	swivel
swab-bing	sweeper	swiv-eled
swad-dling	sweep-ers	swiv-el•ing
swag-ger	sweep-ing	swol-len
swag-ger•ing	sweep-stakes	sword-fish
swal-low	sweeten	syl-labi
swal-low•ing	sweet-ened	syl-labic
swamped	sweet-ener	syl-labi-cate
swamp-ing	sweet-en•ing	syl-labi-ca-tion
swamp-land	sweet-ens	syl-la•ble
swanky	sweet-heart	syl-la•bus
swapped	swell-ing	syl-lo-gism
swap-ping	swel-ter	sym-bi-otic
swarmed	swel-ter•ing	sym•bol
swarm-ing	swerved	sym-bolic
swash-buckler	swerv-ing	sym-bol-ical
swash-buckling	swiftly	sym-boli-cally
swat-ted	swift-ness	sym-bol•ism
swat-ter	swim-mer	sym-bol•ize
swat-ting	swim-ming	sym-bol-izes
sway-backed	swim-suit	sym-bol-iz•ing
sway-ing	swin-dle	sym-bol•ogy

sym-bols
sym-met•ric
sym-met-ri•cal
sym-me•try
sym-pa-thetic

sym-pa-thize
sym-pa-thiz•ing
sym-pa•thy
sym-phonic
sym-pho-nies

sym-phony
sym-po•sia
sym-po-sium
symp-tom
symp-tom-atic

syna-gogue
sync
syn-chro-ni-za-tion
syn-chro-nize
syn-chro-nizer

syn-chro-nizes
syn-chro-niz•ing
syn-chro-nous
syn-di-cate
syn-di-cat•ing

syn-di-ca-tion
syn-di-ca•tor
syn-drome
syn-er•gic
syn-er-gism

syn-er-gist
syn-er-gis•tic
syn-ergy
syn-fuels
syn-onym

syn-ony-mous
syn-ony-mously
syn-op•ses
syn-op•sis
syn-op•tic

syn•tax
syn-the•sis
syn-the-size
syn-the-sizer
syn-the-sizes

syn-the-siz•ing
syn-thetic
Syria
Syr•ian
sy•ringe

syrup
syr•upy
sys•tem
sys-tem-atic
sys-tem-at-ical

sys-tem-atize
sys-tem-atiz•ing
sys-tolic

tabbed
tab-bing
tab-er-na•cle
table
tab-leau

tab-leaux
table-cloth
ta•bled
ta•bles
table-spoon

tab•let
table-top
table-ware
ta•bling
tab-loid

taboo
ta•boos
tabu-lar
tabu-late
tabu-lat•ing

tabu-la-tion
tabu-la•tor
ta•chome-ter
tacit
taci-turn

tacked
tacki-ness
tack-ing
tackle
tack-led

tack-ling
tacky
tact-ful
tact-fully
tact-ful-ness

taf-feta
taffy
tag-board
tagged
tag-ging

Ta•hiti	tan-gent	tar-iffs
Ta•hi-tian	tan-ger•ine	tar•mac
tail-back	tan-gi•ble	tar-nish
tail-bone	tan•gle	tar-nishes
tailed	tan-gling	tar-nish•ing
tail-gate	tango	tar-papered
tail-gating	tangy	tar-pau•lin
tail-ing	tanker	tarred
tail-light	tank-ers	tar-ried
tai•lor	tanned	tarry
tai-lor•ing	tan•ner	tar-ry•ing
tainted	tan-nery	tar•tar
taint-ing	tan-ning	tartly
Tai•wan	tan-ta-lize	tart-ness
Tai-wan•ese	tan-ta-lizes	task-ing
take-down *(n.)*	tan-ta-liz•ing	task-master
taken	tan-ta-mount	Tas-ma•nia
take-off *(n.)*	tan-trum	Tas-ma-nian
take-over *(n.)*	taped	tas•sel
taker	taper	tasted
take--up *(n.)*	ta•pered	taste-ful
tak•ing	ta•per-ing	taste-fully
tale-bearer	tap-es-tries	taste-less
tal•ent	tap-es•try	taste-lessly
tal-ents	tap•ing	taster
talk-ative	tapi-oca	tast-ing
talked	tapped	tasty
talk-ing	tap-ping	tat•ter
tal-lied	tar-dies	tat-ter•ing
tal•low	tar-di-ness	tat•tle
tam•per	tardy	tat-tler
tamp-er•ing	tar•get	tat-tles
tam-pers	tar-get•ing	tat-tling
tam•pon	tar-gets	tat•too
tan•dem	tar•iff	tat-too•ing

taunted	tear-gassing	tele-cast•ers
taunter	tear-ing	tele-cast•ing
taunt-ing	tear-jerker	tele-com-mut•ing
taunt-ingly	teased	tele-con-fer-ence
tautly	teas-ing	tele-copy•ing
tav•ern	teas-ingly	tele-gram
tawny	tea-spoon	tele-graph
tax-able	tech-nic	tele-graphed
taxa-tion	tech-ni•cal	te•leg-ra-pher
taxed	tech-ni-cali-ties	tele-graphic
taxes	tech-ni-cal•ity	tele-graph•ing
taxi	tech-ni-cally	te•leg-ra•phy
taxi-cab	tech-ni-cian	tele-ki-ne•sis
taxi-der•mic	Tech-ni-color	tele-lec-ture
taxi-der-mist	tech-nique	tele-mar-ket•ing
taxi-dermy	tech-no-log-ical	te•leme-try
tax•ied	tech-no-logi-cally	tele-pathic
taxi-ing	tech-nolo-gies	te•lepa-thy
tax•ing	tech-nolo-gist	tele-phone
tax-on•omy	tech-nol•ogy	tele-phonic
tax-payer	te•dious	tele-phon•ing
tax-paying	te•dium	te•le-phony
teach-able	tee•ing	tele-photo
teacher	teen-age	tele-play
teach-ers	teen-ager	tele-printer
teaches	teeny-bopper	tele-pro-cess•ing
teach-ing	tee-tered	tele-scope
teamed	tee-ter•ing	tele-scopic
team-ing	teethed	tele-scop•ing
team-mate	teeth-ing	tele-text
team-ster	tee-to-taler	tele-thon
team-work	Tef•lon	Tele-type
tea•pot	tele-cast	tele-vise
tear-drop	tele-casted	tele-vises
tear-ful	tele-caster	tele-vis•ing

t

tele-vi-sion
tele-writ•ing
telex
tel-exed
teller

tell-ers
tell-ing
tell-tale
tem•per
tem-pera-ment

tem-pera-men•tal
tem-per-ance
tem-per•ate
tem-pera-ture
tem-per•ing

tem-pest
tem-pes-tu•ous
tem-plate
tem•ple
tempo

tem-po•ral
tem-po-rally
tem-po-rar•ies
tem-po-rar•ily
tem-po-rary

temp-ta-tion
tempted
tempt-ing
tempt-ingly
te•na-cious

te•na-ciously
te•nac-ity
ten-ancy
ten•ant
ten-ants

tended
ten-den-cies
ten-dency
ten•der
ten-der•ing

ten-der•ize
ten-der-izer
ten-der-izes
ten-der-iz•ing
ten-der-loin

ten-derly
ten-der-ness
tend-ing
ten•don
tene-ment

tenet
te•nets
Ten-nes-sean
Ten-nes•see
ten•nis

tensed
tens-ing
ten-sion
ten-ta•cle
ten-ta-tive

ten-ta-tively
tenu-ous
tenu-ously
ten•ure
tepid

tera-bit
termed
ter-mi•nal
ter-mi-nally
ter-mi-nate

ter-mi-nat•ing
ter-mi-na-tion
ter-mi-na•tor
ter-mi-nol•ogy
ter-mi•nus

ter-mite
ter-race
ter-races
ter-rac•ing
ter-rain

ter-ra•pin
ter-rar•ium
ter-res-trial
ter-ri•ble
ter-rific

ter-ri-fied
ter-ri-fies
ter-rify
ter-rify•ing
ter-ri-to-rial

ter-ri-to-ries
ter-ri-tory
ter•ror
ter-ror•ism
ter-ror•ist

ter-ror•ize
ter-ror-izes
ter-ror-iz•ing
tersely
terse-ness

ter-tiary
tes-ta-ment
tes-ta-men-tary
tes-tate
tes-ta•tor

tested	theo-lo-gian	thick-ener
tes-ticu•lar	theo-log-ical	thick-en•ing
tes-ti-fied	theo-logi-cally	thick-ens
tes-ti-fier	the-ol•ogy	thicker
tes-ti-fies	theo-rem	thick-est
tes-tify	theo-ret-ical	thick-ness
tes-ti-fy•ing	theo-reti-cally	thief
tes-ti-mo-nial	theo-ries	thiev-ery
tes-ti-mo-nies	theo-rist	thieves
tes-ti-mony	theo-rize	thiev-ing
test-ing	theo-riz•ing	thim-ble
testy	the•ory	think-able
teta-nus	thera-peu•tic	thinker
Texan	thera-pist	think-ers
Texas	ther-apy	think-ing
text-book	there-abouts	thin-ner
tex-tile	there-after	thin-ness
tex-tual	thereby	thin-ning
tex-ture	there-fore	thirsted
Thai-land	therein	thirsti-ness
Thai-lander	there-in-after	thirsty
thanked	there-with	thir-teen
thank-ful	ther-mal	thir-ties
thank-ful-ness	ther-mo-dy-namic	thir-ti•eth
thank-ing	ther-mo-fluid	thirty
thank-less	ther-mo-nu-clear	this-tle
thanks-giv•ing	ther-mo-stat	tho•rax
thawed	ther-mo-static	thorny
thaw-ing	the-sauri	thor-ough
the-ater	the-sau•rus	thorough-bred
the-at-ri•cal	the•ses	thorough-fare
the-at-ri-cally	the•sis	thor-oughly
the-at-rics	thia-mine	thor-ough-ness
them-selves	thicken	thought-ful
thence-forth	thick-ened	thought-fully

t

thought-ful-ness	throt-tling	tick-et•ing
thought-less	through-out	tick-ets
thought-lessly	through-put	tick-ing
thought-less-ness	through-way	tickle
thou-sand	throw-back *(n.)*	tick-ler
thrashed	thrower	tick-les
thrashes	throw-ing	tick-ling
thrash-ing	thrust-ing	tick-lish
thread-bare	thug-gery	tidal
threaded	thumbed	tid•bit
thread-ing	thumb-ing	tide-land
threaten	thumb-print	tide-water
threat-ened	thumb-tack	ti•died
threat-en•ing	thumped	ti•dily
threat-ens	thun-der	ti•di-ness
three-some	thunder-bird	tied
thresh-old	thunder-clap	tier
thrift-ily	thunder-cloud	tiger
thrift-less	thunder-head	tighten
thrift-less-ness	thun-der•ing	tight-ened
thrifty	thun-der•ous	tight-ener
thrilled	thunder-shower	tight-en•ing
thriller	thunder-storm	tight-ens
thrill-ers	Thurs-day	tighter
thrill-ing	thwarted	tight-est
thrill-ingly	thwart-ing	tight-fisted
thrived	thyme	tightly
thriv-ing	thy-roid	tight-ness
throaty	Tibet	tight-rope
throbbed	Ti•betan	tight-wad
throb-bing	tibia	tilde
throm-bo•sis	tib•iae	tiled
thronged	ticker	til•ing
throng-ing	ticket	tilled
throt-tle	tick-eted	till-ing

tilted	tin-kerer	ti•tlist
tilt-ing	tin-ker•ing	toad-stool
tim•ber	tin•kle	toasted
timber-land	tin-ni•tus	toaster
timber-line	tinny	toast-ers
tim•bre	tin•sel	toast-ing
timed	tin-smith	to•bacco
time-keeper	tinted	to•bog-gan
time-keeping	tint-ing	today
time-less	tiny	tod-dler
time-lessly	tipped	tod-dles
time-li-ness	tip-ping	tod-dling
timely	tip-si-ness	toe-hold
time--out	tip-ster	toe-nail
timer	tipsy	tof•fee
tim•ers	tip•toe	tofu
time-saver	tip-toe•ing	toga
time-saving	ti•rade	to•gether
time-table	tired	to•gether-ness
time-wise	tired-ness	tog-gery
timid	tire-less	tog•gle
ti•mid-ity	tire-lessly	tog-gling
tim-idly	tire-some	toiled
tim-id-ness	tir•ing	toi•let
tim•ing	tis•sue	toi-let-ries
tinc-ture	tis-sues	toi-letry
tinc-tur•ing	ti•tanic	toil-ing
tin•der	tithed	toil-some
tin-foil	tit-il-late	token
tinged	tit-il-lat•ing	to•ken-ism
tin•gle	tit-il-la-tion	to•kens
tin-gles	title	tol-er-able
tin-gling	ti•tled	tol-er-ance
tin•gly	title-holder	tol-er•ant
tin•ker	ti•tles	tol-er•ate

tol-er-at•ing
tol-era-tion
toll-booth
tolled
toll-gate

toll-house
toll-way
toma-hawk
to•mato
to•ma-toes

tomb-stone
to•mor-row
tonal
to•nal-ity
tone-less

toner
tongs
tongue
tonic
to•night

ton•ing
ton-nage
ton•sil
ton-sil-lec-tomy
ton-sil-li•tis

ton-sils
ton-so-rial
tool-box
tooled
tool-ing

tool-kit
tool-maker
tool-shed
tooth-ache
tooth-brush

tooth-less
tooth-paste
tooth-pick
toothy
toot-ing

topaz
top-coat
topic
top-ical
topi-cally

top•ics
top-less
top--notch
to•po-graphic
to•po-graph-ical

to•pog-ra-phies
to•pog-ra•phy
to•po-log-ical
to•pol-ogy
topped

top-ping
top•ple
top-pling
top-soil
torch-bearer

torches
to•re-ador
tor-ment
tor-ment•ing
tor-men•tor

tor-nado
tor-na-does
tor-pedo
tor-pe-doed
tor-pe-does

tor-pe-do•ing
torque
tor-rent
tor-ren-tial
tor•rid

torso
tor-ti•lla
tor-toise
tor-tu•ous
tor-ture

tor-tur•ing
tor-tur•ous
tossed
tosses
toss-ing

total
to•taled
to•tal-ing
to•tali-tar•ian
to•tal-ity

to•tally
to•tals
tot•ing
touch-back
touch-down

tou•ché
touched
touches
touch-ing
touch-pad

touchy
toughen
tough-ened
tough-en•ing
tough-ens

tougher
tough-ness
tou•pee
toured
tour-ing

tour-ism
tour-ist
tour-na-ment
tour-ney
tour-ni-quet

touted
tout-ing
to•ward
towed
towel

tow•els
tower
tow-ered
tow-er•ing
tow•ers

tow•ing
town-ship
tox-emia
toxic
tox-ic•ity

toxi-co-log-ical
toxi-colo-gist
toxi-col•ogy
toxin
tox•ins

toyed
toy-ing
trace-able
traced
tracer

tra-chea
trac-ing
tracked
track-ing
trac-tion

trac-tor
traded
trade--in (n.)
trade-mark
trader

trad-ing
tra-di-tion
tra-di-tional
traf-fic
traf-ficked

traf-fick•ing
trage-dies
trag-edy
tragic
trag-ical

trailed
trailer
trail-ing
trained
trainee

trainer
train-ers
train-ing
traipse
traipsed

trai-tor
trai-tor•ous
tra-jec-to-ries
tra-jec-tory
tramped

tramp-ing
tram-ple
tram-pling
tram-po-line
tram-way

tran-quil
tran-quil•ize
tran-quil-izer
tran-quil-izes
tran-quil-iz•ing

tran-quil-lity
trans-act
trans-act•ing
trans-ac-tion
trans-ac•tor

trans-at-lan•tic
trans-ceiver
tran-scend
tran-scended
tran-scen-dence

tran-scen-dency
tran-scen-dent
tran-scend•ing
tran-scribe
tran-scriber

tran-scrib•ing
tran-script
tran-scrip-tion
trans-ducer
tran-sect

trans-sec-tion
trans-fer
trans-fer-able
trans-feral
trans-fer-ence

trans-fer-ring
trans-fig•ure
trans-fig-ur•ing
trans-fix
trans-fix•ing

trans-fix•ion
trans-form
trans-for-ma-tion
trans-former
trans-form•ing

trans-fuse
trans-fus•ing
trans-fu-sion
trans-gress
trans-gress•ing

trans-gres-sion
trans-gres•sor
tran-sient
tran-sis•tor
tran-sis-tor•ize

tran-sis-tor-iz•ing
tran-sit
tran-si-tion
tran-si-tional
tran-si-tive

tran-si-tory
trans-late
trans-lat•ing
trans-la-tion
trans-la•tor

trans-lu-cence
trans-lu-cent
trans-lu•nar
trans-mi-grate
trans-mi-gra-tion

trans-mis-sion
trans-mit
trans-mit•tal
trans-mit-tance
trans-mit•ted

trans-mit•ter
trans-mit-ting
trans-mit•ting
trans-mu-ta-tion
trans-oce-anic
trans-or-bital

trans-par-en-cies
trans-par-ency
trans-par•ent
trans-par-ently
tran-spire

tran-spir•ing
trans-plant
trans-plant•ing
tran-spon•der
trans-port

trans-por-ta-tion
trans-port•ing
trans-pose
trans-poses
trans-pos•ing

trans-po-si-tion
trans-verse
tra-peze
trapped
trap-per

trap-ping
trashed
trashes
trash-ing
trashy

trauma
trau-matic
trau-ma-tism
trau-ma-tize
trau-ma-tiz•ing

tra-vail
tra-vail•ing
travel
trav-eled
trav-eler

trav-el•ers
trav-el•ing
trav-el-ogue
trav-els
tra-verse

tra-vers•ing
trav-es-ties
trav-esty
trawl-ers
trawl-ing

treach-er•ies
treach-er•ous
treach-ery
tread-ing
trea-dle

tread-mill
trea-son
trea-son•ous
trea-sure
trea-surer

trea-sur•ers
trea-sur•ies
trea-sur•ing
trea-sury
treat-able

reated   tri-bu•nal   tri-par-tite

reated	tri-bu•nal	tri-par-tite
rea-ties	tri-bune	tri•ple
reat-ing	tribu-tar•ies	trip-let
rea-tise	tribu-tary	trip-li-cate
reat-ment	trib-ute	trip-li-ca-tion
reaty	tri-ceps	trip-ling
re•ble	tricked	tri•pod
reed	trick-ery	tripped
ree-ing	trick-ing	trip-ping
rekked	trickle	trite-ness
rek-king	trick-led	tri-umph
rel-lis	trick-les	tri-um-phant
rem-ble	trick-ling	tri-um-phantly
rem-bling	trick-ster	tri-umph•ing
re-men-dous	tricky	trivia
re-men-dously	tri-cy•cle	triv-ial
remor	tri-dent	trivi-ally
rem-ors	tried	trol-ley
rench	tries	trom-bone
rench-ing	tri•fle	tromped
rend-ing	tri-fo-cals	tromp-ing
rendy	trig-ger	trooped
repi-da-tion	trig-ger•ing	trooper
res-pass	tri-glyc-er-ides	troop-ers
res-passer	trigo-no-met•ric	troop-ing
res-passes	trigo-no-met-ri•cal	tro•phies
res-pass•ing	trigo-nome•try	tro•phy
res-tle	tril-lion	tro•pic
rial	tril-ogy	trop-ical
ri•als	trimmed	tro-pics
ri-an•gle	trim-mer	tro-po-pause
ri-an-gu•lar	trim-ming	tro-po-sphere
ri-an-gu-la-tion	Trin-ity	trot-ted
ribal	trin-ket	trot-ter
ribu-la-tion	trios	trot-ting

t

trou-ba-dour
trou-ble
trouble-maker
trouble-shoot
trouble-shooting

trou-ble-some
trou-bling
trounced
trounces
trounc-ing

troupe
trou-sers
trowel
trow-els
tru-ancy

tru•ant
trucker
truck-ers
truck-ing
truck-load

true-ness
truf-fle
truly
trumped
trum-pet

trum-peted
trum-peter
trum-pet•ing
trump-ing
trun-cate

trun-cat•ing
trun-ca-tion
trun-dle
trusses
trusted

trustee
trust-ees
trust-ful
trust-ing
trust-wor-thi-ness

trust-worthy
trusty
truth-ful
truth-fully
truth-ful-ness

try•ing
try•out (n.)
tubal
tube-less
tu•ber-cu•lar

tu•ber-cu-lo•sis
tub•ing
tu•bu-lar
tucked
tuck-ing

Tues-day
tugged
tug-ging
tu•ition
tulip

tu•lips
tum•ble
tum-bler
tum-bling
tumor

tu•mor-ous
tu•mors
tu•mult
tu•mul-tu•ous
tuned

tune-ful
tuner
tune--up (n.)
tung-sten
tunic

tun•ing
tun•nel
tun-nel•ing
tur•ban
tur-bine

tur-bo-charged
tur-bo-charger
tur-bo-jet
tur-bo-prop
tur-bo-pump

tur-bu-lence
tur-bu-lent
tur•gid
tur•key
tur-keys

tur-moil
turn-about
turn-coat
turn-down (n.)
turned

turn-ing
tur•nip
turn-key
turn-off (n.)
turn-out (n.)

turn-over (n.)
turn-pike
turn-stile
turn-table
tur-pen-tine

ur-quoise
ur•tle
urtle-dove
urtle-neck
us•sle

us-sling
u•te-lage
utor
u•tored
u•to-rial

u•tor-ing
u•tors
ux•edo
welfth
wen-ties

wen-ti•eth
wenty
wi-light
win-ax•ial
wing-ing

win-kle
win-kling
wirled
wirl-ing
wisted

wister
wist-ing
wo-fold
wo-some
wo--thirds

y•coon
ying
ype-bar
ype-cast
ype-casting

typed
type-face
type-set
type-setter
type-setting

type-write
type-writer
type-writing
type-written
ty•phoid

ty•phoon
ty•phus
typ-ical
typi-fied
typi-fies

typ•ify
typ-ify•ing
typ•ing
typ•ist
ty•po-graphic

ty•po-graph-ical
ty•po-graphi-cally
ty•pog-ra•phy
ty•ran-ni•cal
tyr-anny

ty-rant

ubiq-ui-tous
ubiq-uity
Uganda
Ugan-dan
ug•li-ness

ugly
Ukraine
Ukrai-nian
uku-lele
ulcer

ul•cer-ate
ul•cer-ous
ul•cers
ul•te-rior
ul•ti-mate

ul•ti-mately
ul•ti-ma•tum
ul•tra-mod•ern
ul•tra-sonic
ul•tra-sound

ul•tra-vio•let
um•bil-ical
um•brella
um•pire
un•abashed

un•abash-edly
un•able
un•abridged
un•ac-cept•able
un•ac-claimed

un•ac-count-able
un•ac-cred•ited
un•ac-cus-tomed
un•ac-quainted
un•ad-vertised

un•ad-vis-able
un•af-fected
un•af-fili-ated
un•af-ford-able
un•afraid

un•aided	un•be-com•ing	un•combed
un•al-ter-able	un•be-known	un•com-fort-abl
un•al-tered	un•be-liev-able	un•com-mit•ted
una-nim•ity	un•be-liev•ing	un•com-mon
unani-mous	un•bend-ing	un•com-pen-sate
unani-mously	un•bi-ased	un•com-plain•in
un•an-nounced	un•born	un•com-pleted
un•an-swered	un•break-able	un•com-pli-cate
un•an-tici-pated	un•bri-dled	un•con-cern
un•ap-pe-tiz•ing	un•bro-ken	un•con-cerned
un•ap-pointed	un•buck-led	un•con-di-tiona
un•ap-pre-ci-ated	un•bund-ling	un•con-nected
un•ap-proach-able	un•bur-dened	un•con-scious
un•ap-proved	un•busi-ness-like	un•con-sciously
un•ar-gu-able	un•but-ton	un•con-soled
un•armed	un•called	un•con-sumed
un•ashamed	un•canny	un•con-test-abl
un•as-sem-bled	un•car-ing	un•con-tested
un•as-signed	un•ceas-ingly	un•con-trol-la•bl
un•as-sisted	un•cen-sored	un•con-trolled
un•as-sorted	un•cer-tain	un•con-ven-tiona
un•as-sum•ing	un•cer-tainty	un•con-vinced
un•at-tached	un•change-able	un•cooked
un•at-tain-able	un•changed	un•co-op-era-tive
un•at-tended	un•chang-ing	un•co-or-di-nated
un•at-trac-tive	un•chari-ta•ble	un•cor-rected
un•au-tho-rized	un•chaste	un•cou-ple
un•avail-able	un•checked	un•cou-pling
un•avoid-able	un•civi-lized	un•couth
un•avoid-ably	un•claimed	un•covered
un•aware	un•clas-si-fied	un•crate
un•bal-anced	uncle	un•crowded
un•bear-able	un•clean	unc-tion
un•beat-able	un•clear	unc-tu•ous
un•beaten	un•clut-tered	uncut

un•dam-aged
un•daunted
un•de-cided
un•de-ci-pher-able
un•de-clared

un•deco-rated
un•defeated
un•de-fined
un•de-liv-er-able
un•de-liv-ered

un•de-mand•ing
un•demo-cratic
un•de-ni-able
un•de-pend-able
under

un•der-achiever
un•der-age
un•der-arm
un•der-bid
un•der-bid-ding

un•der-brush
un•der-car-riage
un•der-charge
un•der-clothes
un•der-cloth•ing

un•der-coat
un•der-coat•ing
un•der-cover
un•der-cur-rent
un•der-cut

un•der-cut-ting
un•der-dog
un•der-draw•ers
un•der-dress
un•der-em•ployed

un•der-es-ti-mate
un•der-ex-po-sure
un•der-foot
un•der-gar-ment
un•dergo

un•der-go•ing
un•der-gradu•ate
un•der-ground
un•der-growth
un•der-hand

un•der-handed
un•der-line
un•der-lin•ing
un•der-ly•ing
un•der-mine

un•der-neath
un•der-paid
un•der-pass
un•der-priced
un•der-privi-leged

un•der-score
un•der-scor•ing
un•der-sell
un•der-sell•ing
un•der-shirt

un•der-signed
un•der-sold
un•der-staffed
un•der-stand
un•der-stand-able

un•der-stand•ing
un•der-stated
un•der-stood
un•der-study
un•der-take

un•der-taken
un•der-taker
un•der-tak•ing
un•der-tow
un•der-wa•ter

un•der-way *(adj.)*
un•der-wear
un•der-weight
un•der-went
un•der-world

un•der-write
un•der-writer
un•der-writ•ing
un•de-serv•ing
un•de-sir-able

un•de-tected
un•de-vel-oped
un•de-vi-at•ing
un•di-gested
un•di-gest-ible

un•dig-ni-fied
un•di-min-ished
un•dis-ci-plined
un•dis-closed
un•dis-cov-ered

un•dis-puted
un•dis-turbed
un•di-vided
undo
un•do-ing

un•done
un•doubt-edly
un•dress
un•dress-ing
un•drink-able

undue	un•ex-plored	un•hal-lowed
un•du-late	un•fail-ing	un•hap-pi-ness
un•du-la-tion	un•fail-ingly	un•happy
un•duly	un•fair	un•harmed
un•dy-ing	un•faith-ful	un•har-ness
un•earned	un•fa-mil•iar	un•healthy
un•earthly	un•fash-ion-able	un•heard
un•easy	un•fas-tened	un•her-alded
un•eco-nom-ical	un•fath-om-able	un•hesi-tat•ing
un•ed-ited	un•fa-vor-able	un•hinged
un•edu-ca•ble	un•felt	un•hur-ried
un•edu-cated	un•fin-ished	uni-cam-eral
un•emo-tional	unfit	uni-cel-lu•lar
un•em-ploy-able	un•flap-pa•ble	uni-corn
un•em-ployed	un•flat-ter•ing	uni-cy•cle
un•em-ploy-ment	un•flinch-ing	un•iden-ti-fied
un•en-cum-bered	un•fold	uni-fi-ca-tion
un•end-ing	un•fold-ing	uni-fied
un•en-force-able	un•fore-see-able	uni-form
un•en-joy-able	un•fore-seen	uni-for-mity
un•equaled	un•for-get-ta•ble	uni-formly
un•equipped	un•for-giv-able	unify
un•equivo-cal	un•for-giv•ing	uni-fy•ing
un•equivo-cally	un•for-got•ten	uni-lat-eral
un•err-ing	un•for-tu-nate	un•imag-in-able
un•eth-ical	un•for-tu-nately	un•imagi-na-tive
un•even	un•founded	un•im-por-tant
un•event-ful	un•friendly	un•in-cor-po-rated
un•ex-celled	un•furl	un•in-formed
un•ex-cit•ing	un•furl-ing	un•in-hab-it-able
un•ex-cus-able	un•fur-nished	un•in-hib-ited
un•ex-cused	un•god-li-ness	un•in-sured
un•ex-pected	un•godly	un•in-tel-li-gi•ble
un•ex-pect-edly	un•grate-ful	un•in-ten-tional
un•ex-plained	un•guarded	un•in-ter-ested

un•in-ter-est•ing
un•in-ter-rupted
un•in-vited
union
union-ize

union-iz•ing
uni-po•lar
unique
uniquely
unique-ness

uni•sex
uni•son
unite
united
unit-ing

unit-ize
unity
uni-ver•sal
uni-verse
uni-ver-si-ties

uni-ver-sity
un•just
un•jus-ti-fied
un•justly
un•kempt

un•kind
un•know-ing
un•know-ingly
un•known
un•law-ful

un•leaded
un•less
un•li-censed
un•like
un•like-li-hood

un•likely
un•lim-ited
un•listed
un•load
un•load-ing

un•lock
un•lock-ing
un•loved
un•lucky
un•man-age-able

un•mar-ket-able
un•mar-ried
un•men-tion-able
un•men-tioned
un•mer-ci-fully

un•mind-ful
un•mis-tak-able
un•miti-gated
un•mo-ti-vated
un•named

un•natu-ral
un•nec-es-sar•ily
un•nec-es-sary
un•needed
un•neigh-borly

un•no-tice-able
un•no-ticed
un•num-bered
un•ob-tain-able
un•oc-cu-pied

un•of-fi-cial
un•of-fi-cially
un•opened
un•op-posed
un•or-ga-nized

un•or-tho•dox
un•pack
un•pack-ing
un•paid
un•par-al-leled

un•par-don-able
un•planned
un•play-able
un•pleas-ant
un•pleas-santly

un•plugged
un•popu-lar
un•prece-dented
un•pre-dict-able
un•pre-pared

un•pre-ten-tious
un•prin-ci-pled
un•pro-duc-tive
un•pro-fes-sional
un•prof-it-able

un•prom-is•ing
un•pro-tected
un•proved
un•pun-ished
un•quali-fied

un•quench-able
un•ques-tion-able
un•ques-tioned
un•ranked
un•ravel

un•re-al-is•tic
un•rea-son-able
un•rec-og-niz-able
un•re-fined
un•re-hearsed

u

un•re-lent•ing
un•re-li-able
un•re-peat-able
un•re-pen-tant
un•re-ported

un•re-solved
un•rest
un•re-strained
un•re-stricted
un•righ-teous

un•righ-teously
un•rip-ened
un•ri-valed
un•roll
un•roll-ing

un•ruly
un•safe
un•said
un•sala-ried
un•salted

un•sanc-tioned
un•sani-tary
un•sat-is-fac-tory
un•sat-is-fied
un•satu-rated

un•sa-vory
un•scathed
un•scented
un•schooled
un•scram-bled

un•screw
un•scru-pu-lous
un•sea-son-able
un•sea-soned
un•seemly

un•seen
un•self-ish
un•self-ish-ness
un•ser-vice-able
un•set-tled

un•shaken
un•sightly
un•signed
un•skilled
un•so-cia•ble

un•soiled
un•sold
un•so-lic-ited
un•solved
un•soothed

un•speak-able
un•speci-fied
un•spoiled
un•spo-ken
un•sport-ing

un•spot-ted
un•steady
un•stop-pa•ble
un•struc-tured
un•strung

un•suc-cess•ful
un•suc-cess-fully
un•suit-able
un•suited
un•sung

un•su-per-vised
un•sup-ported
un•sure
un•sur-passed
un•sus-pected

un•sweet-ened
un•tal-ented
un•tamed
un•tan-gled
un•tapped

un•ten-able
un•thank-ful
un•think-able
un•thought-ful
un•tidy

untie
un•tied
until
un•timely
un•tir-ingly

unto
un•told
un•touch-able
un•to-ward
un•trained

un•treated
un•tried
un•trod-den
un•trou-bled
un•true

un•ty-ing
un•us-able
un•used
un•usual
un•usu-ally

un•veiled
un•wanted
un•war-ranted
un•wa-ver•ing
unwed

un•wel-come
un•wieldy
un•will-ing
un•will-ing-ness
un•wind

un•wind-ing
un•wise
un•wisely
un•wit-ting
un•wit-tingly

un•work-able
un•worldly
un•wor-ried
un•wor-thily
un•wor-thy

un•wound
un•wrap
un•wrap-ping
un•writ-ten
un•yield-ing

un•zipped
un•zip-ping
up•beat
up•braid
up•bring-ing

up•com-ing
up•date
up•dat-ing
upend
up•grade

up•grad-ing
up•heaval
up•held
up•hold
up•hold-ing

up•hol-ster
up•hol-ster•ing
up•hol-stery
up•keep
up•lift

up•lift-ing
up•load
up•load-ing
upon
upper

up•per-case
up•per-cut
up•per-most
up•pity
up•right

up•right-ness
up•ris-ing
up•roar
up•roari-ous
up•root

up•root-ing
upset
up•set-ting
up•shot
up•side

up•stage
up•stag-ing
up•stairs
up•start
up•stream

up•tight
up•time
up•town
up•turn
up•ward

up•wardly
ura-nium
urban
ur•bane
ur•ban-ite

ur•ban-ize
ur•ban-iz•ing
ur•chin
urged
ur•gency

ur•gent
ur•gently
urges
urg•ing
uri•nal

uri-naly•sis
uri-nary
uro-log-ical
urolo-gist
urol-ogy

us•able
usage
us•ages
used
use•ful

use-ful-ness
use-less
use-less-ness
user
users

uses
usher
ush-ered
ush-er•ing
ush•ers

using
usual
usu-ally
usurp
usurped

usurp-ing
usury
Utah
Utahan
uten-sil

utili-ties
util-ity
uti-li-za-tion
uti-lize
uti-lizes

uti-liz•ing
ut•most
uto•pia
utter
ut•ter-ance

ut•tered
ut•ter-ing
ut•terly

va•can-cies
va•cancy
va•cant
va•cate
va•cat-ing

va•ca-tion
va•ca-tion•ing
vac-cil-late
vac-cil-lat•ing
vac-cil-la-tion

vac-ci-nate
vac-ci-nat•ing
vac-ci-na-tion
vac-cine
vac•uum

vacu-um•ing
va•grant
vague
vaguely
vague-ness

vale-dic-to-rian
vale-dic-tory
val-en-tine
valet
val-iant

val-iantly
valid
vali-date
vali-dat•ing
vali-da-tion

va•lid-ity
va•lise
val•ley
val-leys
valor

valu-able
value
val•ued
val•ues
valu-ing

valve
vam-pire
van•dal
van-dal•ism
van-dal•ize

van-dal-iz•ing
van-dals
va•nilla
van•ish
van-ishes

van-ish•ing
van•ity
van-quish
van-quish•ing
van-tage

vapid
vapor
va•por-ize
va•por-izer
va•por-iz•ing

vari-able
vari-ance
vari-ant
vari-ation
vari-cose

var•ied
var•ies
va•ri-et•ies
va•ri-ety
vari-ous

var-nish
var-nishes
var-nish•ing
var-sity
vary

vary-ing
vas-cu•lar
va•sec-tomy
vas•sal
vastly

vast-ness
vaude-ville
vault
vaulted
vault-ing

vec•tor
veered
veer-ing
vege-ta•ble
vege-tar•ian

vege-tate
vege-tat•ing
vege-ta-tion
ve•he-mence
ve•he-ment

ve•he-mently
ve•hi-cle
ve•hicu-lar
veiled
veil-ing

Vel•cro
vel-croed
ve•loc-ity
ve•lour
vel•vet

vended
ven-detta
vend-ing
ven•dor
ven-dors

ve•neer
ven-er-able
ven-er•ate
ven-era-tion
ve•ne-real

Ve•ne-tian
Vene-zu•ela
Vene-zue•lan
ven-geance
venge-ful

veni-son
venom
ven-om•ous
vented
ven-ti-late

ven-ti-lat•ing
ven-ti-la-tion
ven-ti-la•tor
vent-ing
ven-tri•cle

ven-trilo-quism
ven-trilo-quist
ven-ture
ven-ture-some
ven-tur•ing

ven-tur•ous
venue
ve•rac-ity
ve•randa
ver•bal

ver-bal•ize
ver-bal-izes
ver-bal-iz•ing
ver-bally
ver-ba•tim

ver-biage
ver-bose
ver-bos•ity
ver-bo•ten
ver-dant

ver-dict
veri-fi-ca-tion
veri-fied
veri-fier
veri-fies

ver•ify
veri-fy•ing
veri-ta•ble
Ver-mont
Ver-monter

ver-nacu•lar
ver-sa-tile
ver-sa-til•ity
versed
verses

ver-sion
ver•sus
ver-te•bra
ver-te-brae
ver-te-brate

ver-ti•cal
ver-tigo
ves-pers
ves•sel
vested

ves-ti-bule
vest-ing
vest-ment
ves•try
vet-eran

vet-er•ans
vet-eri-nar•ian
vet-eri-nary
veto
ve•toed

ve•toes
ve•to-ing
vexa-tion
vexed
vex•ing

via
vi•able
via-duct
vi•brant
vi•brantly

vi•brate
vi•brat-ing
vi•bra-tion
vi•bra-tor
vicar

vic-ar•age
vi•cari-ous
vi•cari-ously
vices
vice versa

vi•cin-ity
vi•cious
vi•ciously
vi•cis-si-tude
vic•tim

vic-tim•ize
vic-tim-izes
vic-tim-iz•ing
vic-tim-less
vic-tims

vic•tor
vic-to-ries
vic-to-ri•ous
vic-to-ri-ously
vic-tory

video
vid-eo-cas-sette
vid-eo-disk
vid•eos
vid-eo-tape

vid-eo-tap•ing
vid-eo-tex
vied
Viet-nam
Viet-nam•ese

viewed
viewer
view-ers
view-ing
view-point

vigil
vigi-lance
vigi-lant
vigi-lante
vigor

vig-or•ous
vig-or-ously
vile-ness
vil•ify
vili-fy•ing

villa
vil-lage
vil-lager
vil-lages
vil-lain

vil-lain•ous
vin-di-cate
vin-di-cates
vin-di-cat•ing
vin-di-ca-tion

vin-dica-tive
vin-dic-tive
vine-gar
vine-yard
vin-tage

vinyl
vio-la•ble
vio-late
vio-lat•ing
vio-la-tion

vio-la•tor
vio-lence
vio-lent
vio-lently
vio•let

vio•lin
vio-lin•ist
viper
viral
vir•gin

vir-ginal
Vir-ginia
Vir-gin•ian
vir-gin•ity
vir•ile

vi•ril-ity
vir-tual
vir-tu-ally
vir•tue
vir-tu•oso

vir-tu•ous
vir-tu-ously
virus
vi•ruses
vises

visi-bil•ity
vis-ible
vis-ibly
vi•sion
vi•sion-ary

visit
visi-ta-tion
vis-ited
vis-it•ing
visi-tor

vis•its
visor
vi•sors
vista
vi•sual

vi•su-al•ize
vi•su-al-iz•ing
vi•su-ally
vita
vitae

vital
vi•tal-ity
vi•tal-ize
vi•tal-izer
vi•tal-izes

vi•tal-iz•ing
vi•tally
vi•tals
vi•ta-min
vit-re•ous

vi•va-cious
vi•va-ciously
vi•vac-ity
vivid
viv-idly

viv-id-ness
vivi-sec-tion
vo•cabu-lar•ies
vo•cabu-lary
vocal

vo•cal-ist
vo•cal-ize
vo•cal-izes
vo•cal-iz•ing
vo•cally

vo•ca-tion
vo•ca-tional
vo•ca-tion-ally
vo•cif-er•ous
vo•cif-er-ously

vogue
vogu-ish
voice-band
voiced
voice-less

voice-print
voices
voic-ing
void-ance
voided

void-ing
vola-tile
vola-til•ity
vola-til•ize
vola-til-iz•ing

vol-ca•nic
vol-cano
vol-ca-noes
vo•li-tion
vol•ley

volley-ball
vol-ley•ing
volt-age
vol•ume
volu-met•ric

vo•lu-mi-nous
vol-un-tarily
vol-un-tary
vol-un-teer
vol-un-teer•ing

vo•lup-tuous
vo•ra-cious
vo•ra-ciously
vo•ra-cious-ness
vo•rac-ity

voted
voter
vot•ers
vot•ing
vouched

voucher
vouch•ers
vowed
vowel
vow•els

vow-ing
voy•age
voy-ager
voy-ag•ing
voy•eur

V

239

voy-eur•ism
vul-ca-nize
vul-ca-niz•ing
vul•gar
vul-gar•ism

vul-gar•ity
vul-gar•ize
vul-gar-iz•ing
vul-ner-able
vul-ture

vying

wacki-ness
wacky
wad-ding
waded
wad•ing

wafer
wa•fers
waf•fle
waf-fling
waged

wager
wa•ger-ing
wa•gers
wages
wag-ging

wag•ing
wagon
wag-oner
wag•ons
wailed

wail-ing
wain-scot
wain-scot•ing
wain-wright
waist-band

waist-line
waited
waiter
wait-ers
wait-ing

waived
waiver
waiv-ers
waiv-ing
wake-ful-ness

waken
wak-ened
wak-en•ing
wak•ing
walka-thon

walked
walker
walk-ers
walk-ing
walk-out (n.)

walk-way
wall-board
wal•let
wall-flower
wal•lop

wal-loped
wal-lop•ing
wal-lowed
wal-low•ing
wall-paper

wall-papered
wall-papering
wal-nuts
wal•rus
waltzed

waltzes
waltz-ing
wan•der
wan-derer
wan-der•ing

wan-der-lust
wan-ders
wands
wan•ing
wanted

want-ing
wan•ton
war•ble
war-bler
war-bling

war•den
ward-robe
ware-house
ware-houses
ware-housing

war-fare
war-head
warily
wari-ness
war-like

war-lock
warmed
warmer
warm-est
warm-hearted

warm-ing	watches	wavy
warmly	watch-ful	waxed
war-monger	watch-ing	waxen
warmth	watch-maker	waxes
warm--up *(n.)*	water	wax•ing
warned	water-borne	wax-works
warn-ing	water-color	way-bill
war-rant	water-course	way-farer
war-ran•tee	water-craft	way-faring
war-ran-ties	wa•tered	way•lay
war-ranty	water-fall	way-side
war-rior	water-fowl	way-ward
war-ship	water-front	weaken
war-time	wa•ter-ing	weak-ened
wash-able	water-logged	weak-en•ing
wash-cloth	water-mark	weak-ens
washed	water-melon	weaker
washer	water-proof	weak-est
wash-ing	water-proofing	weak-hearted
Wash-ing•ton	wa•ters	weak-ling
Wash-ing-to-nian	water-shed	weak-ness
wash-out *(n.)*	water-side	weak-nesses
wash-rag	water-skiing	wealth
wash-room	water-tight	wealthi-ness
wash-tub	water-way	wealthy
waste-basket	water-works	weapon
wasted	wa•tery	weap-onry
waste-ful	watt-age	weap-ons
waste-ful-ness	waved	wear-able
waste-land	wave-length	wea-ried
waste-paper	waver	wea-rily
wast-ing	wa•vered	wea•ri-ness
watch-band	wa•ver-ing	wear-ing
watch-dog	wa•vers	wea-ri-some
watched	wav•ing	weary

W

wea-ry•ing
wea•sel
weather
weath-ered
weath-er•ing

weath-er-iz•ing
weather-proof
weaved
weaver
weav-ing

webbed
web-bing
web-foot
wed•ded
wed-ding

wedged
wedges
wedg-ing
wed-lock
Wednes-day

weeded
weeder
weed-ing
weedy
week-day

week-end
week-ender
week-lies
weekly
weep-ing

weepy
wee•vil
weighed
weigh-ing
weighted

weight-ily
weighti-ness
weight-ing
weight-less
weight-less-ness

weird-ness
weirdo
wel-come
wel-com•ing
welded

welder
weld-ing
wel-fare
well--being
welter-weight

west-erly
west-ern
West-erner
West-er-ners
west-ern•ize

west-ern-iz•ing
West Vir-ginia
West Vir-ginian
west-ward
wet-back

wet-land
wet-ness
wet-ting
whaler
whal-ing

wharf
wharf-age
wharves
what-ever
what-so-ever

wheel-barrow
wheel-chair
wheeled
wheel-ing
wheezes

wheez-ing
when-ever
where-abouts
whereas
whereby

where-fore
wherein
whereof
whereto
wher-ever

where-with
whether
whet-ted
whet-ting
which-ever

whiffed
whiff-ing
whim-per
whim-per•ing
whim-si•cal

whim-si-cally
whimsy
whined
whiner
whin-ing

whip-lash
whipped
whipper-snapper
whip-ping
whirled

whirl-ing	wicked	wil•low
whirl-pool	wick-edly	will-power
whirl-wind	wick-ed-ness	winced
whirly-bird	wicket	winc-ing
whisked	wide-band	wind-break
whis-ker	widely	wind-chill
whis-key	widen	winded
whisk-ing	wid-ened	wind-fall
whis-per	wid•ens	wind-ing
whis-per•ing	wid-en•ing	wind-mill
whis-tle	wider	win•dow
whis-tling	wide-spread	win-dow•ing
whiten	wid•est	window-pane
whit-ened	wid•get	win-dows
whit-ener	widow	wind-pipe
white-ness	wid-owed	wind-screen
whit-en•ing	wid-ower	wind-shield
whit-est	wid•ows	wind-storm
white-wall	width-wise	wind-swept
white-wash	wigged	wind-ward
whither	wig-ging	windy
whit-tle	wig•gle	wine-press
whit-tling	wig-gling	win-er•ies
who-dunit	wig•wam	win•ery
who-ever	wild-cat	winged
whole-hearted	wil-der-ness	wing-span
whole-heartedly	wild-est	winked
whole-sale	wild-flower	wink-ing
whole-saler	wild-life	win-less
whole-saling	willed	win•ner
whole-some	will-ful	win-ning
whole-some-ness	will-fully	win-some
wholly	will-ing	win•ter
whom-ever	will-ingly	win-ter•ing
whoop-ing	will-ing-ness	win-ter•ize

W

win-ter-izes
win-ter-iz•ing
winter-kill (n.)
win-ters
winter-time

win•try
wiped
wiper
wip•ers
wip•ing

wire-cutter
wired
wire-less
wire-tap
wire-tapping

wir•ing
wiry
Wis-con•sin
Wis-con-sin•ite
wis•dom

wise-acre
wise-crack
wise-cracking
wisely
wiser

wished
wishes
wish-ful
wish-ing
wist-ful

witch-craft
witches
witch-ing
with-draw
with-drawal

with-draw•als
with-draw•ing
with-drawn
wither
with-ered

with-er•ing
with-held
with-hold
with-hold•ing
within

with-out
with-stand
with-stood
wit-ness
wit-nesses

wit-ness•ing
wit-ti-cism
witty
wives
wiz•ard

wiz-ardry
woe-fully
woe-ful-ness
wolf
wol-ver•ine

wolves
woman
women
won•der
won-der•ful

won-der•ing
won-der-land
won-drous
won-drously
wood-cutter

wood-cutting
wooded
wood-land
wood-pile
wood-shed

wood-work
wood-working
woofer
woolen
worded

wordi-ness
word-ing
word-less
wordy
work-able

worka-holic
work-book
worked
worker
work-ers

work-flow
work-group
work-ing
work-out (n.)
work-place

work-room
work-sheet
work-shop
work-station
work-week

worldly
world-wide
wor-ried
wor-ries
wor-ri-some

worry
wor-ry•ing
worsen
wors-ened
wors-en•ing

wors-ens
wor-ship
wor-thily
wor-thi-ness
worth-less

worth-less-ness
worth-while
wor•thy
wounded
wound-ing

wran-gle
wran-gling
wrap-around
wrapped
wrap-per

wrap-ping
wreck-age
wrecked
wrecker
wreck-ing

wrenched
wrenches
wrench-ing
wres-tle
wres-tler

wres-tling
wretched
wring-ing
wrin-kle
wrist-watch

write--in *(n.)*
write--off *(n.)*
writer
writ-ers
writ-ing

writ-ten
wrong-doing
wrong-ful
wrongly
Wyo-ming

Wyo-ming•ite

xe•ro-graphic
xe•rog-ra•phy
xerox *(v.)*
xe•roxed
xe•rox-ing

X ray *(n.)*
x--ray *(v.)*
xy•lo-phone

yacht
yacht-ing
Yan•kee
yard-age
yard-stick

yawn-ing
year-book
yearly
yearn-ing
yell-ing

yel•low
yes-ter•day
yielded
yield-ing
yip•pie

yo•gurt
yon•der
young-ster
your-self
your-selves

youth-ful
Yu•go-slav
Yu•go-sla•via

Zaire
Zair-ian
Zam•bia
Zam-bian
zealot

zeal-ous
zeal-ously
ze•nith
ze•ro-ing
zest-ful

zig•zag
zip•per
zir-co-nium
zo•diac
zom•bie

zoo-log-ical
zoo-logi-cally
zo•olo-gist
zo•ol-ogy
zoom-ing

GUIDELINES FOR SPELLING

Although the English language contains many exceptions to established methods of spelling, the following guidelines will help the user of this manual be more consistent in spelling words correctly.

1. If a one-syllable word ends in a single consonant preceded by a single vowel, double the final consonant when adding a suffix beginning with a vowel: *run... running*.

2. If a word of two or more syllables is stressed on the last syllable and ends in a single consonant preceded by a single vowel, double the final consonant when adding a suffix beginning with a vowel, provided the stress does not change position: *recur... recurrence*.

3. If a word ends in a silent *e* preceded by a consonant, the *e* is usually retained when a suffix beginning with a consonant is added: *encourage... encouragement*.

4. If a word ends in a silent e preceded by a consonant, the *e* is usually dropped when a suffix beginning with a vowel is added: *encourage... encouraging*.

5. If a word ends in *ie*, drop the *e* and change the *i* to *y* when adding the suffix *-ing*: *lie... lying*. (This is done to prevent two *i*'s from coming together.)

6. If a word ends in *y* preceded by a consonant, the *y* generally changes to *i* when any suffix except *-ing* is added: *reply ... replied*.

7. If a word ends in *y*, retain the final *y* when adding the suffix *-ing*: *cry... crying*.

8. If a word ends in *y* preceded by a vowel, retain the *y* when adding a suffix: *relay ... relayed*.

9. If *e* and *i* occur together in a word, the *i* generally precedes the *e* in all but the following circumstances: (a) when the "long" sound of *e* follows *c*: *receive* (*ri sēv´*), (b) when the two vowels together are pronounced as "long" *a* (*a*): *neighbor* (*nā´b ǀ er*), (c) when the two vowels together are pronounced as "long" *i* (*ī*): *height* (*hīt*), and (d) when the two vowels together are pronounced as "short" *i* (*ĭ*), following the letter *f*: *counterfeit* (*koun´t ǀ er fĭt*).

10. Regular nouns are usually made plural by the addition of *-s: hand... hands*.

11. Nouns ending in *s*, *x*, *z*, *cb*, *sb*, and *ss* are made plural by the addition of *-es*: *atlas... atlases, bush... bushes*.

12. Nouns ending in *y* preceded by a vowel are made plural by the addition of *-s: toy... toys*. Nouns ending in *y* preceded by a consonant are made plural by changing the *y* to *i* and adding *-es: pony ... ponies*. Proper nouns ending in *y* are made plural by the addition of *-s: Terry ... Terrys*.

13. Hyphenated compound nouns and unhyphenated compound nouns spelled as more than one word are made plural by the addition of *-s* to the principal term: *runner-up ... runners-up*. Unhyphenated compound nouns spelled as one word are usually made plural by the addition of *-s* to the last term, unless the compound contains a noun with an irregular plural: *firehouse ... firehouses*, but *eyetooth... eyeteeth*.

14. Generally, nouns ending in *f* or *fe* are made plural by the addition of *-s: chief... chiefs*. In some cases, however, such nouns are made plural by changing the *f* to *v* and adding *-es: knife... knives*.

15. Nouns ending in *o* preceded by a vowel are made plural by the addition of *-s: folio ... folios*. However, some nouns ending in an *o* preceded by a consonant are made plural by the addition of *-es: embargo... embargoes*.

16. Irregular nouns are made plural by changes within the word: *goose... geese*.

17. Some nouns appear plural in form, but are singular in use: *linguistics*.

18. Some nouns are always plural in use: *cattle*.

19. Some nouns have the same spelling for both singular and plural forms: *headquarters*.

20. Foreign nouns generally retain their original plurals: datum ... data. However, as a result of frequent use, many foreign terms have come to be made plural by the simple addition of the standard English *-s* to the singular form: *bureau ... bureaus*. When foreign nouns have both English and foreign plurals, the English form is preferred.

21. Letters, numerals, and symbols are made plural by the addition of an apostrophe and *-s: +... +'s, A ... A's*.